I WOULD NOT B

The Life and Work of
Robert Stephen Hawker
1803-1875

'Yet am I fain some deeds of mine should live –
I would not be forgotten in this land . . .'

The Quest of the Sangraal

PATRICK HUTTON

TABB HOUSE

First published 2004
Tabb House, 7 Church Street, Padstow
Cornwall, PL28 8BG

Hardback ISBN 1873951442
Paperback ISBN 1873951485

British Library Cataloguing-in-Publication Date:
a catalogue record of this title is available from
the British Library

Printed and bound in Great Britain by TJ International Ltd, Padstow, Cornwall

Contents

Note on Poems

Most of Hawker's poems have been out of print for some time. It has therefore seemed sensible to provide the texts of those which are referred to within the book.

Some long poems have been relegated to an Appendix and the full texts of poems from *Tendrils*, published when he was seventeen, are not included. Others are inserted at relevant places for ease of reference, if sometimes at the expense of continuity, in the text. They are listed alphabetically in the Index as **Individual Poems** under **Hawker, the Rev. Robert Stephen**, with the page reference of the full text in bold.

The only poem not by Hawker that is considered in detail, Tennyson's 'The Holy Grail', is not reprinted here because readers who are sufficiently interested can easily come by a copy.

Acknowledgements

I should like to express my thanks to Dr Piers Brendon for allowing me to quote from his *Hawker of Morwenstow*, which I found altogether helpful when I was writing this book; also to Mr John Michell, who agreed that I could quote from his biography of John Blight, *A Short Life at the Land's End*. Many thanks also to Andy Carter for the use of his photographic material; and I am particularly grateful to Jill Wellby who, with her husband Richard, is the present owner of Morewenstow Vicarage. It is a wonderful place to stay, and she has let me range freely among her remarkable collection of 'Hawkeriana'.

Patrick Hutton, 2004

Introduction

The coast of North Cornwall runs from Land's End, by way of St Ives, Newquay, Padstow and Tintagel, to Bude and beyond. For much of the year most of this famous coast-line is crowded with holiday-makers, enjoying the sandy beaches, the spectacular cliffs and sea, and perhaps the sun. Thousands of people love it and return year after year.

The life of the subject of this book, Robert Stephen Hawker, Hawker of Morwenstow, is set on the same coast, but its least popular stretch, stark and unwelcoming, running due north from Bude to the boundary with Devon at Marsland Mouth. It is sometimes known as 'Hawker Country'.

Bays are not to be found in this part of Cornwall. The word is 'Mouth', and each of them has devoured a good many wrecks in its time. This coast is short on sandy beaches, and there are few paths to encourage the visitor down to sea level. The cliffs are for the most part massive and sheer, with sharp black reefs running out into the sea. Only the hardier variety of walkers on the Coastal Path are likely to experience the scene, scarcely disturbing the peace because they are part of it, as they marvel at the steep valleys and streams which fling themselves off the cliffs in spectacular waterfalls, with the sea sparkling away to the horizon, and the island of Lundy, flat-topped like an old aircraft carrier, standing clear a few miles to the north-east. The few cottages and farmhouses hardly intrude, with just the occasional hum of a tractor representing the twenty-first century. A visitor will instantly recognise one substantial intrusion, something called CSOS Morwenstow, a Composite Signals Organisation Station, an outpost of GCHQ Cheltenham, visible for miles and incongruously very secret, with huge white saucer-shapes pointing to the sky. Unlovely as they are, they do not succeed in detracting notably from the amazing quality of this stretch of coastline. In a way they add to it, solitary and unaccommodating, not inviting argument.

Hawker however would have been outraged, and delighting as he did in defying authority would have devoted himself to seeing them off.

As a foretaste of his life story, here is his own description of the Morwenstow coastline.

My seaward boundary was a stretch of bold and rocky shore, an inter-change of lofty headland and sudden gorge, the cliffs from three hun-dred to four hundred and fifty feet of perpendicular or gradual height, and the valleys gushing with torrents, which bounded rejoicingly to-wards the sea, and leaped at last, amid a cloud of spray, into the waters. So stern and pitiless is the iron-bound coast, that in the memory of one man upwards of eighty wrecks have been counted within a reach of fifteen miles, with only here and there the rescue of a living man.[1]

Robert Stephen Hawker, Vicar of Morwenstow from 1835 to 1875, was far and away the most significant person ever to have lived in this obscure corner of Cornwall. He is widely known for his eccentricity, but deserves to be further renowned as poet, mystic and priest. This book tries to restore the balance, and to demonstrate his almost physical love of God, his care for his parishioners, and his special concern for the shipwrecked sailors whose bodies were flung up on his parish's cruel shore. His mysticism keeps breaking through, in his letters as well as his poetry. But how does he rank as a poet? That is harder to assess.

He never won critical acclaim. Three separate collections of his poems were published during the twenty-five years following his death; but only selections, and occasional representations in anthologies, have appeared over the last hundred years. There are several reasons for this. The quality of his poetry varies sharply. Most of it that bears reprinting can be found within these pages. As we shall see, he would have benefited from the presence looking over his shoulder of a 'neighbourly authority' other than his gentle wife. Secondly, he tended to be out of sympathy with his time. He would indeed have regarded that as an understatement, writing as he did 'There seems to be no shadow of sympathy between the men of my generation and myself'. A century and a half later, that hardly matters, indeed it has acquired its own historical interest, but it would not have commended him to his contemporaries. Thirdly, he was far removed from the literary world of London coteries and salons and the colonies of enthusiasts in cities and towns throughout the country. He described himself, in his frequent gloomy moments, as living 'among these faraway rocks, unprofited, unpraised and unknown'. It is true in a sense that he never had a chance.

Now it is surely time to look again, for the balance of his reputation to be put right, and for him to be established, after years of neglect, as a highly original thinker and a fine and important poet.

1

Early Days, 1803-1829

Robert Stephen Hawker was born in Plymouth on December 3rd, 1803, and was christened by his uncle, the Rev. John Hawker, at Stoke Damerel church four weeks later. It is surprising that the service was not conducted by his grandfather, Dr Robert Hawker, vicar of Charles Church near the centre of the city and one of the foremost preachers of his day, who acted as the boy's guardian for much of his childhood. Robert Stephen's father, Jacob, is a relatively shadowy figure, a doctor by profession who was later to take orders and become vicar of Stratton in North Cornwall, near Morwenstow. Of his mother still less is known, apart from the fact, quirky even by Hawker's standards, that when he was planning the new vicarage at Morwenstow he had the kitchen chimney designed to resemble her tomb (other chimneys were modelled on the towers of churches with which he had been associated). Like the Grenville family in the sixteenth and seventeenth centuries which he admired so much, it seems that the Hawkers skipped a generation in terms of distinction. The son of Sir Richard of the Revenge, Bernard, quietly minded his estates, and in turn his sons, Beville and Richard, were prominent as leaders of the King's Army of the West in the Civil War. Grandfather and grandson Hawker, both called Robert, achieved some fame, while Jacob, son and father, made no impact on the world.

Charles Church was built in the seventeenth century as a rallying point for Plymouth's puritans, with a door in the east wall of the chancel so that the altar could not stand there. Dr Hawker 'in doctrine was a high Calvinist, and one of the most popular extemporaneous speakers in the kingdom. His voice was powerful, yet harmonious, and as a pulpit orator he was impressive and fascinating'.[1] He was much in demand in London, and preached to George III a number of times: the tradition is that the king would hand him a text as he mounted the pulpit. His *Collected Works* fill ten large volumes. In 1802 he founded the formidably named Great Western Society for

Dispersing Religious Tracts among the Poor in the Western Districts, and these publications are still to be found: small, compact, twenty pages long on average, making no concessions to the limited education of his intended readership. His most popular book was entitled *The Poor Man's Morning and Evening Portion*, and his concern for the welfare of the poor was as strong as his grandson's. That grandson inherited his personality, though not his brand of churchmanship.

Such evidence as exists suggests that the two Roberts, grandfather and grandson, each met his match in the other, and certainly the boy does not seem to have suffered from a repressed upbringing. Various stories are told about their dealings with one another, but they are too patently apocryphal to be worth repeating; and this is a good moment to introduce an important caveat with regard to the life history of Robert Stephen Hawker. He was a great story-teller himself, and his best-known biographer, Sabine Baring-Gould, was another, if anything even more inventive. Again and again it is impossible to separate truth from exaggeration or indeed falsehood. It is necessary from the start to bear in mind the warning of C. E. Byles, his son-in-law and most important biographer:

In telling a story the Vicar would preserve such a gravity of counte-nance, however amazing his assertions, that his hearers never quite knew whether or not he was serious. He said once to a friend who called, "Did you meet a wagonette full of people? I stuffed them up with all kinds of nonsense, and they believed every word!"
This habit of hoaxing became so ingrained in his nature that per-haps, as he grew older, he was hardly able to distinguish between jest and earnest, fact and fancy, belief and simulated belief.[2]

Hawker's own reminiscence of his ancestor – not his grandfather, but himself as a boy in Plymouth – can stand for the stories:

The child is father of the man. I look back and I discern my ancestor, a shrinking apprehensive boy: clad in clouted clothes, hurrying through the streets away from the scorn of other boys, crouching among the pledges in a pawnbroker's warehouse in a reeky Plymouth street, to devour *The Arabian Nights* and with an imagery of mind even then crea-tive, clothing that foul den with forms of fancy's mould until that Southside Street became the Palace of Aladdin's Lamp.[3]

When the boy was about ten he was sent to boarding school, probably to his grandfather's relief; and his father, now ordained and curate of Stratton, had him home for the holidays. His capacity for practical joking now becomes apparent. He seems to have caused havoc in that little country town. He painted the doctor's horse with black and white stripes and then organised an urgent call which required him to ride through the town. He sat out on a rock in Bude Bay dressed as a mermaid, combing his long locks and singing appropriate songs, until a farmer announced to the crowd which had gathered that he would shoot the mysterious creature. Other jokes were more cruel, involving for instance, when he was still in Plymouth, old spinster ladies receiving visits from undertakers to measure them up for their coffins.

Such stories are exultantly recorded, or invented, by Sabine Baring-Gould in his entertaining but profoundly unreliable and unsatisfactory biography,[4] published in 1876 within a year of Hawker's death. There will not be much reference henceforth to this version of his life, even though it is the best known one: not at least until the last chapter, when the principal motive for the travesty will become apparent.

Hawker's schooldays are not well recorded. After a short period as a boarder at Liskeard Grammar School, where presumably he did not settle, he was sent to work at a solicitor's office in Plymouth, but this again did not last. But now in 1819 a piece of relative good fortune intervened. He did not himself reckon that good fortune and hence happiness came his way very often. As will become increasingly apparent, he was something of a depressive. Many years later, at the end of his copy of a volume containing his Oxford Prize Poem, 'Pompeii', he wrote its date, 1827, and added:

> 1828. B.A.
> 1829. A Deacon
> 1831. A Priest
> 1834. The Vicar of Morwenstow
> The above dates specify the only satisfactory eras of my life

The cheering development of 1819 does not rate a mention. His aunt, Mrs Hodson, took his education in hand and paid the fees for him to go to Cheltenham Grammar School. This school, now Pate's Grammar School, does at least commemorate him a little. One of the houses was named after him, and a history of the school published in 1974 expresses pride in him. It cannot have been difficult to find him a place, because the school was actually going through 'perhaps the worst period of its history' at the time. The headmaster, the Rev. William Henry Hawkins, had a brisk way with pupils who troubled him, tying them to their seats with rope, 'using unbecoming language' as he did so. The governors expressed the view that 'a mode of coercion like this appears . . . to offend against every principle of propriety',[5] but Hawkins remained in post for a further thirteen years. Hawker was probably too large for such treatment, and he plainly flourished, not only moving straight on from the school to Oxford, but first, precociously enough, producing a book of poems entitled *Tendrils* in 1821 at the age of seventeen.

The book is dedicated 'To the Friends of My Early Boyhood', and his Preface suggests an attractive personality:

When a first attempt is submitted to public notice and judgment, its readers may very naturally desire to know somewhat concerning him who has the temerity to make it.

But the writer of the following rhymes has little in himself to excite interest, and less to afford gratification: he is content to wrap the veil of obscurity around his head until the voice of public opinion shall have passed by.

To apologise in some measure, however, for the abundant imperfections of the first effort of his pen, he would express a hope that the productions of one over whom eighteen summers have scarcely passed will carry some excuse with them; and as his motive for thrusting them on the world, he would plead that a measure of vanity has been meted to us all, and his portion has been in no wise withheld.

It is easy to be patronising about juvenilia, and so far as critics have noticed *Tendrils* at all, they have followed the pattern, for instance: 'The booklet was not remarkable in any way, and not even interesting save as another illustration of the fact that even in the work of unmistakably original poets imitativeness precedes individuality.'[6]

Actually there is plenty here not just of interest, but of merit. Inevitably one looks for indications of what is to come, and they can be found, for example in the most ambitious poem, 'The Fairy Vision', in which a 'Stranger' standing within a fairy ring is approached by a succession of 'Spirits' closely resembling the angels which enthralled him later. The first, with power to revive or take away life, cares for a man as he dies.

> I was sent to the bed of a dying man,
> And slow in his veins the life-blood ran, –
> I fanned with my wings the fever of death,
> And bare away gently his parting breath.

The fourth spirit, a bringer of beauty, again like his angels has the power to reach its destination with a thought: 'I glide o'er the waters with thought-speeding feet'; and these spirits also set forth his early delight in natural beauty, expressed by the second, who represents the inspiration of 'the minstrel'.

> O'er the curl of the fountain, the foam of the sea,
> The bloom of the field, and the leaf of the tree,
> O'er the cloud that rolls on with the storm in its breast,
> And the mist that comes down on the mountain to rest,
> O'er the raindrop of morn, and the evening tear,
> My magic I breathe, and to him they are dear!

The sea is the setting for the third spirit, who comforts the sorrowful, and brings a welcome dream to the young sailor longing for home.

> But the sea-bird sails past – and shrill is her scream,
> And in tears he awakens, but blesses the dream.

There is an echo of Caliban in *The Tempest*: 'that, when I waked, I cried to dream again'.

Hawker was close physically and spiritually to the sea throughout his life, and another poem in *Tendrils*, 'The Sea. A Fragment', was apparently written when he was thirteen.

> I love the ocean! from a very child
> It has been to me as a nursing breast,
> Cherishing wild fancies. –

>   . . . I was wont to rest
> Gazing upon it, when the breeze was wild,
> And think that every wave reared its white arms
> To grasp and chide the wind that rolled along
> In fitful buffetings, chanting its hoarse song
> As in stern mockery! Such a scene had charms
> For my young heart.

When he was a little older, and apparently feeling his age, he wrote 'A Night-Sketch, Written on Efford Down Cliff, in the Autumn of 1820'.

> 'Tis sweet to be alone on such a night:
> The vanisht joys of youth and youthful days,
> Borne upon memory's pinions, waken then
> The long hushed note of gladness – hope's fair dreams
> Whisper of joy . . .

Efford Manor was the home of Charlotte I'ans, twenty years older than he, soon to be his first wife, and he must be writing specifically about her in 'A Remembrance'.

> Smiles have been mine, and gentle hearts have yearned
> In love toward me in my pilgrimage!
> And there was one, whose smile was valued more
> By my young soul than all the common lurings,
> The snares of beauty for unpractised feeling.
> More suns had shone on her than had been mine
> By many a summer; but she still was fair,
> And every charm was mellowed into sweetness.

As he sets off on the next stage of his 'pilgrimage', presumably his return to Cheltenham, he calls to say goodbye to her.

> I found her in her bower, her place of life,
> A spot that overlooked the wrathless ocean:
> She bade me gaze upon a swelling wave,
> That rushed unbridled on – a frowning rock
> Reared in its path, and it was lost in foam!

Another came in gentleness, and soft
It glided by in silvery loveliness . . .

She bids him a tender farewell, and this was plainly a specially painful one. Here and elsewhere, especially in a poem called 'Night', Hawker records the peculiar poignancy of memories of home recalled from boarding school: he speaks for generations of children weeping under the bedclothes on the first night of term. Again here and elsewhere, indeed throughout *Tendrils*, the language is highly wrought, with the poetic diction of the time over-employed: pilgrim, bower, breast, a dozen more examples in passages not quoted; and the style is imitative of his established fellow-poets, Byron and Moore in particular. But the feeling is entirely personal.

I have been a young pilgrim from the place
Which holds my all of love: and though my staff
Of wandering is but green, I love to think
Upon the hour when my warm heart shall hail
Its vanished home once more . . .

. . . There is a spot
Where I have wandered in my lonely gladness,
And asked for no communion save the link
With memory cherisht. . . .
'Tis a lone rock, and sea-waves swell around
As soft and gently as the heaving bosom
Of matin-beauty at affection's tale! . . .
I do believe that I should weep, if aught
Had marr'd its beauty, if it did not smile
As when I last was there to sigh farewell.

Here is a boy, a young man, who loved his home and wanted it to be always there for him, 'the place Which holds my all of love'. In this respect at least, he did not change much.

So Hawker expresses in *Tendrils* his particular affection for the I'ans family of Efford Manor. Colonel I'ans, who had died in 1816, was the father of four unmarried daughters of whom Charlotte was the second eldest. He had been a notable local figure, commander of the Cornish Provincial Cavalry, a magistrate for Cornwall and Devon, and also a humanitarian, concerned on at least two occasions with caring for shipwrecked sailors. His son-in-law was to be even more dramatically involved with wrecks, their victims and survivors. In a poem called 'The Wreck', published in 1840, Hawker commemorates one of the Colonel's experiences, first quoting the inscription 'on a silver goblet in my possession':

This cup is presented to Wrey I'ans, Esquire, by Edward and Robert Were Fox, of Wadebridge, on behalf of the proprietors of the cargo of the St Anna St Joseph, Captain Antony de Fonseca Rosa, wrecked at Bude, the 7th of August, 1790, for his care in saving the same, and particular attention to the unfortunate crew.

Perhaps the most remarkable feature of this poem is that of its eighteen verses, only the last three were written by Hawker, and the rest by Charlotte, who was to become his wife in 1823. In that same year, Hawker matriculated at Pembroke College, Oxford.

She, it seems, could turn a good strong verse. Captain de Rosa's pilot disenchants him as he thinks he is approaching his native Spain:

> Thou seest dark Cornwall's rifted shore,
> Old Arthur's stern and rugged keep:
> There, where proud billows dash and roar,
> His haughty turret guards the deep.

She will at least have helped him with several of his poems, especially those which link with German legends: she knew the language well, and was plainly a cultivated person altogether. Sadly, no likeness of her exists, and we have to rely on written descriptions. To quote two, the first describing her in 1816, the year that her father died, four years before her marriage, 'She was tall, fair, and comely, with suave and winning manners, and very accomplished'.[7] The second comes from 'The Diary of an Oxford Lady' – Mrs Jeune, who will be met again – written thirty years later, '. . . a lady many years older than himself and with a sadly strong Cornish accent, but a woman of good common sense, well read and informed: in her youth she must have boasted of no small beauty'.[8]

They were married by his father, Vicar of Stratton, on November 6th, 1823. She was forty-one, he not quite twenty. It was an extraordinarily happy marriage, and when she died in 1863 Hawker was left completely shattered, 'nearly forty years and never 5 nights away from her'. It has to be added that there are hints in his poetry of the frustrations of a virile young man tied to such a much older woman.

Baring-Gould tells a story to account for the surprising match, to the effect that Hawker was told by his father that on his curate's salary he could no longer afford to pay university fees, so dashed off to Efford and proposed to Charlotte.[9] This was strenuously denied by family and friends. He did run through her money when they were at Morwenstow, mainly for the benefit of his exceptionally poor parishioners, providing a bridge and a school, and engaging in countless acts of generosity; also, undeniably, building a large and comfortable vicarage. Given her gentle nature we can assume her acceptance: a less dramatic picture than Baring-Gould's, much more likely to be an accurate one.

They spent their honeymoon at Tintagel, where Hawker's interest in the Arthur Legend was first aroused, as he recalls in a letter a few months after Charlotte's death.

... we went from Stratton, where my father was vicar, to Dundagel in lodgings for a month – close to the castle of King Arthur and amid the legends of his life and deeds. There we used to roam about and read all that could be found about those old-world histories, and often was this legend of the Sangraal talked of as a fine subject for verse.[10]

So, in those first weeks of their marriage, Charlotte helped to inspire his finest poem, 'The Quest of the Sangraal'.

Back at Oxford, Hawker was obliged to transfer from Pembroke College, which did not cater for married undergraduates, to Magdalen Hall. Baring-Gould tells another tale, that the newly-weds travelled from Cornwall to Oxford on horseback, she riding pillion behind him. It is certainly true that two of Charlotte's sisters came to live with them. Such an abundance of female company may actually have cramped Hawker's style, in only his second year at the university. He judged himself in retrospect not to have taken life too seriously, and this fits with both his established capacity for practical joking and his rather jaunty appearance, captured in a portrait in 1825. A desire to escape, even temporarily, from the shadow of his stern clerical forebears, might also have been a contributory factor, matching the state of mind of Matthew Arnold fifteen years later. In 'A Ride from Bude to Boss by Two Oxford Men', written in 1867, he writes after some fairly heavy varsity anecdotage, 'It was by outbreaks of animal spirits such as these that the monotony of collegiate life in those days was relieved, for the University supplied but little excitement of the mental kind'.[11]

He then returns to his main theme, the 'Ride from Bude to Boss' of himself and his friend Francis Jeune, and describes how early one morning they released all the pigs in Boss or Boscastle from their sties, to the understandable chagrin of their owners and the joy of the gilded young men. Fun at the expense of the lower orders, accompanied by copious rustic exclamation, was plainly fair game at Oxford and elsewhere.

He does however reflect later in his life on the more serious side of Oxford, implying that there was some 'excitement of the mental kind'. The Oxford Movement was hardly under way – Keble delivered his Assize Sermon in 1833; and Hawker's imagination may have contributed to this reminiscence in a letter written in 1861: 'How I recollect their faces and words – Newman – Pusey – Ward – Marriott – they used to be all in the common room every evening discussing, talking, reading.'[12]

Whether or no – alternatives one has to keep proffering when dealing with Robert Stephen Hawker – he was certainly writing poetry. 'Pompeii' (see Appendix), which won him the Newdigate Prize in 1827 and which was proudly reprinted in successive volumes of his verse, actually requires little attention. Such an exercise, with an imposed subject and a reading public of Oxford dons, is likely to produce a correct rather than an inspired response. Some original imagery breaks through the conventions of the time, for instance the pronouncement of doom over the people of the city.

> Yes! they must die: behold! yon gathering gloom
> Brings on the fearful silence of the tomb;
> Along Campania's sky yon murky cloud
> Spreads its dark form – a City's funeral shroud.

And the rhetorical question is strong as Vesuvius erupts.

> Oh! who shall paint, in that o'erwhelming hour,
> Death's varying forms, and Horror's withering power?

However, another poem from this stage of his life, 'The Song of the Western Men', is a different matter altogether. Its refrain is known the world over:

> And shall Trelawny die?
> Here's twenty thousand Cornish men
> Will know the reason why!

The poem, effectively adopted as Cornwall's national anthem, is undoubtedly the most famous that Hawker wrote, so it seems particularly cruel that it brought him little but grief. In 1826, with uncharacteristic modesty, he sent it anonymously to a Plymouth newspaper, where it was noticed by the Cornish historian and President of the Royal Society, Davies Gilbert. He apparently knew of and acknowledged Hawker's authorship, but then successively Walter Scott, Lord Macaulay and Charles Dickens took up the poem and admired it as a ballad contemporary with the event it commemorated. This was the imprisonment in the Tower in 1687 of Sir Jonathan Trelawny, Bishop of Bristol, one of the 'seven bishops', on the order of James II. Macaulay wrote in his *History of England*:

The people of Cornwall, a fierce, bold and athletic race, among whom there was a stronger provincial feeling than in any other part of the realm, were greatly moved at the danger of Trelawny, whom they reverenced less as a member of the Church than as the head of an honourable house, and the heir through twenty descents of ancestors who had been of great note before the Normans had set foot on English ground. All over the county the peasants chanted a ballad of which the burden is still remembered . . . [13]

THE SONG OF THE WESTERN MEN

With the exception of the choral lines, 'And shall Trelawny die? Here's twenty thousand Cornish men Will know the reason why!' and which have been, ever since the imprisonment by James the Second of the seven bishops – one of them Sir Jonathan Trelawny – a popular proverb throughout Cornwall, the whole of this song was composed by me in the year 1825. I wrote it under a stag-horned oak in Sir Beville's Walk in Stowe Wood. It was sent by me anonymously to a Plymouth paper, and there it attracted the notice of Mr Davies Gilbert, who reprinted it at his private press at Eastbourne under the avowed impression that it was the original ballad. It had the good fortune to win the eulogy of Sir Walter Scott, who also deemed it to be the ancient song. It was praised under the same persuasion by Lord Macaulay and by Mr Dickens, who inserted it at first as of genuine antiquity in his *Household Words*, but who afterwards acknowledged its actual paternity in the same publication.

R.S.H.

A good sword and a trusty hand!
    A merry heart and true!
King James's men shall understand
    What Cornish lads can do!

And have they fixed the where and when?
    And shall Trelawny die?
Here's twenty thousand Cornish men
    Will know the reason why!

Out spake their Captain brave and bold:
    A merry wight was he: –
"If London Tower were Michael's hold,
    We'd set Trelawny free!

We'll cross the Tamar, land to land:
    The Severn is no stay:
With 'one and all,' and hand in hand;
    And who shall bid us nay?

And when we come to London Wall,
  A pleasant sight to view,
Come forth! Come forth! Ye cowards all:
  Here's men as good as you.

Trelawny he's in keep and hold:
  Trelawny he may die:
But here's twenty thousand Cornish bold
  Will know the reason why!"

* ❧ * ❧ *

It seems likely that the 'burden' did have an earlier origin, but there need be no doubt that Hawker wrote the rest, on vacation in 1824 with his new wife at a delightful spot, Coombe Cottage, near Morwenstow. He complained eloquently, in a letter in 1862:

All these years the Song has been bought and sold, set to music and applauded, while I have lived on among these faraway rocks unprofited, unpraised and unknown. This is the epitome of my whole life. Others have drawn profit from my brain while I have been coolly relinquished to obscurity and unrequital and neglect.[14]

Here is another example of the depressive self-pitying Hawker, and it will not be the last, for such feelings often find expression in poems and letters. But it does seem most unfair that this splendidly vigorous poem, summing up the pride and independence of the Cornish, never brought Hawker the fame which he craved for and merited.

His time at Oxford remained a precious memory, and he made some lifelong friends there. He wrote thirty years later:

In 1825 three men in Oxford formed a friendship. They studied, read, walked and talked together from that date for three years there. Their names were Jeune, Jacobson and Hawker. Their college honours varied. Jeune had a first-class, Jacobson a second, Hawker the Newdigate Prize Poem. Their friendship still subsists – but their positions are not alike.[15]

Francis Jeune, his companion at Boscastle, became eventually

Bishop of Peterborough, and William Jacobson Bishop of Chester. 'And the third of these is now Vicar of Morwenstow.' They did not entirely forget him. Jeune and his wife came to see him in 1846: her reaction to Charlotte has been quoted. Jacobson and he were reunited at least once at Oxford. But still his successful clerical friends do not seem to have done much to alleviate his solitude. After the publication of 'The Quest of the Sangraal' in 1863 he wrote to a mutual friend, 'You mention Jacobson. Did you speak of the Sangraal to him? Any little word of encouragement from any source would be of real value to me - here alone . . .'[16]

It would be wrong however to assume that Hawker was left completely stranded and neglected at Morwenstow by the great and the good. For example, John Keble visited him there, as did Charles Kingsley. Tennyson paid a memorable call in 1848. The Earl of Harrowby was in Morwenstow in 1859, the Earl of Carlisle drew a sketch of him at his hut in 1863, and the Bishop of London came to see him in 1871. Edward Arnold, Matthew's younger brother, inspected the school, reporting very favourably, in 1874. His frequent assertion that he was forgotten 'among these rocks' needs to be kept in proportion. At the same time, these would have been summer visitors, spread over forty years, and Morwenstow winters are long.

Another distinguished friend was Lord Exmouth, son of the Admiral, who was involved in a vivid event in Hawker's limited social life. In 1864 he travelled to London, for the first time by train, to meet the mother of his prospective second wife. He leaned out of the carriage window and his hat blew off, whereupon he pulled the communication cord and demanded that it should be retrieved. The guard threatened to prosecute him, but he was more than a match for that. At the next stop, Salisbury, he insisted upon seeing the stationmaster, and required to know where he could buy a hat. He was told that there were no hat-shops on the station, and his reply has to be a classic of its kind, "Bless my soul, what a benighted place this is!" He wrapped a red handkerchief round his head, and since the rest of his dress was probably as eccentric as ever - a fisherman's jersey, a brown cassock 'the hue of Our Lady's hair', and sea-boots coming up to his knee - he must have formed an unusual spectacle when at the end of his dramatic journey he was due to meet Lord Exmouth for lunch at the Great Western Hotel. Exmouth expressed some surprise at his appearance, and Hawker said "No doubt you would rather see me dressed like the waiter with a black suit and white choker!" He seems to have been entirely confident about his strange dress and indeed behaviour, irrespective of where he was, and his reputation for eccentricity is understandable.

He was always thankful to be back at Morwenstow, particularly after such adventures. But his love of Oxford was never far from his mind. He expressed more than once the hope that he might be invited to become Head of a College: completely unrealistic, for his scholarship and his churchmanship were equally unsound. He wrote to J.G. Godwin, a close friend who was later (1879) to edit his poems:

I quite envy you the place you live in. Oxford always seemed to me a place 'sui generis' with its own pursuits and occupations, where amid the fine old architecture of the past the toil and turmoil cark and care of the present might be shaken off and forgotten.[17]

The high point of his career there, the winning of the Newdigate Prize, was to do him one piece of good. Following his ordination in October 1829, he was appointed curate of North Tamerton, in the same area of North Cornwall as Bude, Stratton and Morwenstow, and he was there for five years. Meanwhile Henry Phillpotts became Bishop of Exeter. Hawker wrote thirty years later:

H. Exon, then Rector of Stanhope, had told his son William to be sure to bring home with him the Prize Newdigate. He carried mine with him, and his father read it aloud to the family that evening. When he came to Exon, he said to me, "It gave me real delight to find your name entered in the diocese book by Bishop Carey, for early preferment".[18]

2

North Tamerton to Morwenstow, 1830-35

In the years between leaving Oxford and becoming Vicar of Morwenstow, Hawker wrote some of his finest poetry, most of it appearing in *Records of the Western Shore*, which was published in 1832. He had plenty of time. He was not vicar of North Tamerton, but one of a series of assistant curates who looked after the place between 1811 and 1850 when the actual vicar was 'non-resident'. North Tamerton is a remote scattered inland village, dominated by its fifteenth century church with a tall tower, which formed the model for a chimney at Morwenstow vicarage. The Hawkers lived two miles out of the village at Trebarrow, a cottage near the main road from Stratton to Launceston. A cross over the front door commemorates their time there. He was already beginning to cultivate eccentricity. A favourite Hawker story originating at this time involves a black pig called Gyp, which followed him everywhere like a dog. His sister Mrs Kingdon, wife of the vicar of Whitstone, protested when it followed him into the house, and he replied "He's as well behaved as any of your family". Dealings with his relatives tended to be tinged with an element of aggressiveness.

Before settling at North Tamerton, Hawker made with his friend Francis Jeune a tour of the coast and moors of North Cornwall, and the outcome, besides that 'Ride from Bude to Boss' which casts them in a relatively unengaging light, was a remarkable poem, 'A Rapture on the Cornish Hills'. In a note to the poem – as will become increasingly apparent, he rarely let his poems stand alone – he alludes to a landscape 'heaped with rude structures of various kinds', traceable back to 'the Patriarchal Religion' established, according to his rather free interpretation of ancient history, in the time of Jacob, who at Bethel was induced 'to rear a pillar there, and to pour oil thereon, and to call it the place of God.'

A RAPTURE ON THE CORNISH HILLS

There is a wide extent of hilly moorland stretching from Rough Tor to Carradon and heaped with rude structures of various kinds, that would reward the researches of an Antiquary. The cromlech, piled rocks, and unhewn pillar, are commonly referred to the times of Druidical worship. To me, they seem to claim a more ancient origin. A simple structure of stone was the usual altar and monument of the Patriarchal Religion. The same feelings would actuate the heirs of that creed in Cornwall as in Palestine; and the same motives would induce them to rear a pillar there, and to pour oil thereon, and to call it the Place of God.

R.S.H.

I stood at the foot of Rocky Carradon –
The massive monuments of a vast religion,
Piled by the strength of unknown hands, were there.
The everlasting hills, around, afar,
Uplifted their huge fronts, the natural altars
Reared by the Earth to its surrounding God.
I heard a Voice, as the sound of many waters: –
"What do'st thou here, Elijah?" And I said,
"What doth *he* here, Man that is born of woman?
The clouds may haunt these mountains; the fierce storm
Coiled in his caverned lair – that wild torrent
Leaps from a native land: but Man! O Lord!
What doth *he* here!"

Stranger
Did'st thou not fear the Voice?
The Bard
I could not, at the foot of Rocky Carradon.

It is unwise to attempt precision here. He simply seems to have been inspired by awe, a feeling that may be shared by anybody who stands in that huge primitive landscape. Caradon is a substantial rounded tor on the southern edge of Bodmin Moor, which has on its summit – along, in recent years, with a television mast which rather detracts from the magic – the greatest concentration of Bronze Age burial cairns to be found in Cornwall. Since Hawker's day the majority of these have been robbed, but they are still impressive.

Hawker concentrates in one poem the power of the prehistoric past – 'The massive monuments of a vast religion', and the more diffident approach of the Christian God: 'a voice, as of the sound of many waters', and the 'still small voice which asks "What dost thou here, Elijah?"' These, along with the elemental forces of fierce storm and wild torrent, confront two intensely vulnerable men for whom there seems no place in such company. 'The Stranger' must be Jeune, so called because he is not sharing the spiritual experience to which the poet lays claim, able just to ask the question "Didst thou not fear the Voice?" The confident reply of 'The Bard' implies that his faith, his confidence in the protective authority of the Voice, was strong enough to resist the pagan power of those massive monuments. As we shall find again in a moment, in 'The Silent Tower of Bottreaux', the sound echoes the sense admirably, with pagan, Christian and elemental power reflected in the description of the huge granite boulders which are such an imposing feature of that landscape, while the rough blank verse, which Hawker does not attempt elsewhere, recalls William Blake's *Prophetic Books*. The similarity of the first and last lines, with the significant difference that the poet finally could not fear, points a strong Christian moral.

To return to Trebarrow, and to a poem of that name, dated 1834, which contains some of the best and some of the least satisfying of Hawker's poetry. Again, he provides a note, which reveals the historical interests that gave rise to 'Trebarrow'.

This romanticising of history runs through the poem, but finally with a difference. Were Arthur and his knights fighting over this

TREBARROW

The word *tre* signifies in the ancient Cornish tongue 'the place of abode', and *barrow* means 'a burial mound'. The word ' Trebarrow' implies, therefore, 'a dwelling among the graves'; and my house at North Tamerton was so named by me because it was surrounded by these green heaps of the dead. Some of these I opened, and in the centre of one of them I found an urn of baked clay filled with human ashes, and a patera, which I still possess, of the same material. It denotes in all likelihood the entombment of a Keltic priest, and that of pre-Christian times.

R.S.H.

Did the wild blast of battle sound,
Of old, from yonder lonely mound?
Race of Pandrago! Did ye pour
On this dear earth your votive gore?

Did stern swords cleave along this plain
The loose rank of the roving Dane?
Or Norman charger's sounding tread
Smite the meek daisy's Saxon head?

The wayward winds no answer breathe,
No legend cometh from beneath
Of chief, with good sword at his side
Or Druid in his tomb of pride.

One quiet bird, that comes to make
Her lone nest in the scanty brake;
A nameless flower, a silent fern –
Lo! The dim stranger's storied urn.

Hark! On the cold wings of the blast
The future answereth to the past;
The bird, the flower, may gather still,
Thy voice shall cease upon the hill!

ground; closely followed by Danes and Normans? One is tempted to reply 'probably not', but there then occurs something of a miraculous transformation, a reflection of the subject matter. 'The dim stranger's storied urn' is at one with the bird and the flower, becoming part of the natural scene as 'The future answereth to the past', the pitiful human remains are cared for and by implication will be at peace after the 'wild blast' of past battles and brutalities. Those last two verses, complex and profound, must rank among the finest things that Hawker ever wrote.

Incongruously, there are signs in this group of poems that Hawker had an appetite for the life of a country gentleman. Perhaps his marriage into the I'ans family lifted his aspirations beyond those of his almost exclusively clerical forebears. 'Tetcott, 1831' (see Appendix) records the destruction and rebuilding of Tetcott House, ancestral home of the Molesworth family near North Tamerton, and also exalts hunting and its fraternity. Then at the latter end of his life, in 1865, he wrote a prose account of 'Black John', a ghastly-sounding individual who was part of the Molesworth household.[1] Black John used to amuse the assembled company with two parlour-tricks in particular, swallowing live mice, and 'sparrow-mumbling', which involved attaching a sparrow to his teeth with a cord and pulling off its feathers with his lips. There is a degree of ambivalence here, between Hawker's parading with apparent approval this favourite entertainer of the gentry on the one hand, and on the other his affectionate concern for animals, one of his most attractive characteristics. This eagerness to be at one with the gentry is further illustrated in 'An Election Song', where he redeploys 'The Song of the Western Men' for political purposes and adds a note which implies intimacy with 'the County'.

The bulk of the 1832 publication, *Records of the Western Shore*, comprises about a dozen short ballads. At least one, 'The Silent Tower of Bottreaux', is something of a triumph, and several have powerful moments; but an American student of Hawker, Sarah Dopp, is surely right to say that they tend to 'suffer because they are vague in

AN ELECTION SONG

Written when Sir Salusbury Trelawny contested the county in 1832, against my impulses and judgment, but I was subdued by Lady Trelawny in her peremptory way.   R.S.H.

And do they scorn Tre, Pol, and Pen?
    And shall Trelawny die?
Here's twenty thousand Cornish men
    Will know the reason why!

The former spirit is not fled,
    Where Cornish hearts combine,
We bow before the noble dead,
    And laud their living line!

Be chainless as yon rushing wave,
    Free as your native air;
But honour to the good and brave,
    And homage to the fair!

Think on the warrior's waving hand,
    The patriot's lasting fame,
And follow o'er the Rocky Land,
    The old Trelawny name!

Up with your hearts, Tre, Pol, and Pen!
    They bid Trelawny die:
But twenty thousand Cornish men
    Will know the reason why!

* * * * *

the very element they require most centrally, a narrative line'.[2] They need to be longer, to give the story and indeed its characters proper scope for development and credibility. They were probably as much as Hawker felt inclined to manage: he was never strong on sustained effort and also, lacking as he did critical company, let himself be too easily satisfied. For example in 'The Death Race', a mysterious ship comes ashore to collect the body of a young lady, Gwennah. As it sets sail her father, 'The grim Sir John', arrives in full armour just too late. Gwennah, now well out to sea, is raised from her death-like trance, and Fitz-Walter has won his Cornish bride. It is all a bit peremptory. Again, in 'Annot of Benallay' Lady Annot is buried wearing her rings, and as the 'ghastly caitiff sexton' is about to help himself she revives and marries Lord Harold. Two tales of wreckers, 'Mawgan of Melhuach' and 'Featherstone's Doom', are more effective, even if each requires a note from the author to clarify the story. Featherstone is set the task of making rope with sand, to avenge the time 'When thy stern hand no succour gave, The cable at thy side'. As for Mawgan, a boat comes to collect him, as he lies dying with a sore conscience. Voices speak with a lightly mocking authority.

> "Out with the boat there," some one cried, –
> "Will he never come? we shall lose the tide:
> His berth is trim and his cabin stored,
> He's a weary long time coming aboard."

In sharp contrast, the violence of Mawgan's words blends with the rolling tide:

> Wildly he shrieked as his eyes grew dim,
> "He was dead! he was dead! when I buried him."

'The Sisters of Glen Nectan', one of the less successful of these short ballads, tells the story of two mysterious sisters who came to live at this beautiful spot near Boscastle, named after the brother of St Morwenna who in Hawker's history book was the founder of

THE DEATH-RACE

Watch ye, and ward ye! a ship in sight,
And bearing down for Trebarra Height,
She folds her wings by that rocky strand:
Watch ye, and ward ye! a boat on land!

Hush! for they glide from yonder cave
To greet these strangers of the wave;
Wait! since they pace the seaward glen
With the measured tread of mourning men.

"Hold! masters, hold! ye tarry here,
What corpse is laid on your solemn bier?
Yon minster-ground were a calmer grave
Than the roving bark, or the weedy wave!"

"Strong vows we made to our sister dead
To hew in fair France her narrow bed;
And her angry ghost will win no rest
If your Cornish earth lie on her breast."

They rend that pall in the glaring light,
By St Michael of Carne! 'twas an awful sight!
For those folded hands were meekly laid
On the silent breast of a shrouded maid.

"God speed, my masters, your mournful way!
Go, bury your dead where best ye may!
But the Norroway barks are over the deep,
So we watch and ward from our guarded steep."

Who comes with weapon? Who comes with steed?
Ye may hear far off their clanking speed;
What knight in steel is thundering on?
Ye may know the voice of the grim Sir John.

"Saw ye my daughter, my Gwennah bright,
Borne out for dead at the deep of night?"
"Too late! too late!" cried the warder pale,
"Lo! the full deck, and the rushing sail!"

They have roused that maid from her trance of sleep,
They have spread their sails to the roaring deep;
Watch ye, and ward ye! with wind and tide,
Fitz-Walter hath won his Cornish bride.

ANNOT OF BENALLAY

At lone midnight the death-bell tolled,
　　To summon Annot's clay;
For common eyes must not behold
　　The griefs of Benallay.

Meek daughter of a haughty line,
　　Was Lady Annot born:
That light which was not long to shine,
　　The sun that set at morn.

They shrouded her in maiden white,
　　They buried her in pall;
And the ring *He* gave her faith to plight
　　Shines on her finger small.

The Curate reads the deadman's prayer,
　　The sullen Leech stands by:
The sob of voiceless love is here,
　　And sorrow's vacant eye.

'Tis over! Two and two they tread
   The churchyard's homeward way:
Farewell! farewell! Thou lovely dead:
   Thou Flower of Benallay.

The sexton stalks with tottering limb
   Along the chancel floor:
He waits, that old man grey and grim,
   To close the narrow door.

"Shame! Shame! These rings of stones and gold,"
   The ghastly caitiff said,
"Better that living hands should hold
   Than glisten on the dead."

The evil wish wrought evil deed,
   The pall is rent away:
And lo! beneath the shatter'd lid,
   The Flower of Benallay!

But life gleams from those opening eyes!
   Blood thrills that lifted hand!
And awful words are in her cries,
   Which none may understand!

Joy! 'tis the miracle of yore,
   Of the city calléd Nain:–
Lo! glad feet throng the sculptur'd floor
   To hail their dead again!

Joy in the halls of Benallay!
   A stately feast is spread;
Lord Harold is the bridegroom gay,
   The Bride th' arisen dead.

MAWGAN OF MELHUACH

Gilbert Mawgan, a noted wrecker, lived in a hut that stood by the sea shore at Melhuach, or The Vale of the Lark. Among other crimes it is said that he once buried the captain of a vessel, whom he found exhausted on the strand, alive! At the death of the old man, they told me that a vessel came up the Channel, made for Melhuach bay and lay-to amid a tremendous surf. When Mawgan ceased to breathe she stood out to sea and disappeared.

R.S.H.

'Twas a fierce night when old Mawgan died,
Men shuddered to hear the rolling tide:
The wreckers fled fast from the awful shore,
They had heard strange voices amid the roar.

"Out with the boat there," some one cried, –
"Will he never come? we shall lose the tide:
His berth is trim and his cabin stored,
He's a weary long time coming on board."

The old man struggled upon the bed:
He knew the words that the voices said;
Wildly he shriek'd as his eyes grew dim,
"He was dead! he was dead! when I buried him."

Hark yet again to the devilish roar!
"He was nimbler once with a ship on shore;
Come! come! old man, 'tis a vain delay,
We must make the offing by break of day."

Hard was the struggle, but at the last,
With a stormy pang old Mawgan pass'd,
And away, away, beneath their sight,
Gleam'd the red sail at pitch of night.

FEATHERSTONE'S DOOM

The Blackrock is a bold, dark, pillared mass of schist, which rises midway on the shore of Widemouth Bay, near Bude, and is held to be the lair of the troubled spirit of Featherstone the wrecker, imprisoned therein until he shall have accomplished his doom.

R.S.H.

Twist thou and twine! in light and gloom
A spell is on thine hand;
The wind shall be thy changeful loom,
Thy web the shifting sand.

Twine from this hour, in ceaseless toil,
On Blackrock's sullen shore;
Till cordage of the sand shall coil
Where crested surges roar.

'Tis for that hour, when, from the wave,
Near voices wildly cried;
When thy stern hand no succour gave,
The cable at thy side.

Twist thou and twine! in light and gloom
The spell is on thine hand;
The wind shall be thy changeful loom,
Thy web the shifting sand.

THE SISTERS OF GLEN NECTAN

It is from Nectan's mossy steep,
The foamy waters flash and leap:
It is where shrinking wild-flowers grow,
They lave the nymph that dwells below.

But wherefore in this far-off dell,
The reliques of a human cell?

Where the sad stream and lonely wind
Bring man no tidings of his kind.

"Long years agone," the old man said,
'Twas told him by his grandsire dead:
"One day two ancient sisters came:
None there could tell their race or name;

Their speech was not in Cornish phrase,
Their garb had signs of loftier days;
Slight food they took from hands of men,
They withered slowly in that glen.

One died – the other's sunken eye
Gushed till the fount of tears was dry;
A wild and withering thought had she,
'I shall have none to weep for me.'

They found her silent at the last,
Bent in the shape wherein she passed;
Where her lone seat long used to stand,
Her head upon her shrivelled hand."

Did fancy give this legend birth?
The grandame's tale for winter hearth:
Or some dead bard, by Nectan's stream,
People these banks with such a dream?

We know not: but it suits the scene,
To think such wild things here have been:
What spot more meet could grief or sin
Choose, at the last, to wither in?

❋ ❋ ❋ ❋ ❋

Morwenstow. One sister died, and the second mourned her and then died herself in the realisation that 'I shall have none to weep for me'. The story-line is none too strong, and the poem's most significant feature is actually Hawker's note:

There is a local legend linked with this ruined abode, which was told me on the spot; and which I expanded at the time into the above ballad. I have recognised the coinage of my brain in the prosaic paraphrases of Wilkie Collins, Walter White, and other subsequent writers; but with regard to any claimant for the original imagination, I must reply, in the language of John Cade, 'No, no; I invented it myself'.

This view of his, that he had a kind of copyright on legends which he invented, remained a matter of grievance. He simultaneously overlooks his own statement, that they were told him on the spot. Over twenty years later he writes about 'The Silent Tower of Bottreaux'.

The sole materials that I gathered on the spot were, that a certain church tower on the seashore, called in reality Forrabury, but by myself in poetic licence, Bottreaux, was devoid of bells: because they had been lost at sea. The remainder of the legend, the incidents and language of the pilot, the captain, the storm; if any man should suppose them to be historic, or claim them for his own use, I must encounter him . . . .[3]

. . .and again Jack Cade is invoked. This tells us something about his modes of composition, and also, unfortunately, about his capacity for making a fool of himself. He grumbled away in the isolation of Morwenstow, not always very sensibly.

'The Silent Tower of Bottreaux' tells a complete story, though the characters – boy, pilot, captain – are ciphers. Hawker's handling of variations on the refrain, half of each verse, is masterly. 'Come to thy God in time' is constant to each verse, 'Come to thy God at last' appears in six of the eight, 'Youth, manhood, old age past' in four, all combining with lines that we hear only once. It is evocative of change-ringing. One waits for a certain sequence which only rarely comes, but there is still a pattern, deriving here from the reiterated 'chime' at the end of each second line. The movement of the sea, from breeze to storm to 'sullen surges' after the event, seems to echo

THE SILENT TOWER OF BOTTREAUX

The rugged heights that line the seashore in the neighbourhood of Tintadgel Castle and Church are crested with towers. Among these, that of Bottreaux, or, as it is now written, Boscastle, is without bells. The silence of this wild and lonely churchyard on festive or solemn occasions is not a little striking. On inquiry I was told that the bells were once shipped for this church, but that when the vessel was within sight of the tower the blasphemy of her captain was punished in the manner related in the Poem. The bells, they told me, still lie in the bay, and announce by strange sounds the approach of a storm.

R.S.H.

Tintadgel bells ring o'er the tide,
The boy leans on his vessel's side;
He hears that sound, and dreams of home
Soothe the wild orphan of the foam.
    "Come to thy God in time!"
    Thus saith their pealing chime:
    "Youth, manhood, old age past,
    Come to thy God at last."

But why are Bottreaux' echoes still?
Her Tower stands proudly on the hill;
Yet the strange chough that home hath found,
The lamb lies sleeping on the ground.
    "Come to thy God in time!"
    Should be her answering chime:
    "Come to thy God at last!"
    Should echo on the blast.

The ship rode down with courses free,
The daughter of a distant sea:
Her sheet was loose, her anchor stored,
The merry Bottreaux bells on board.
    "Come to thy God in time!"
    Rung out Tintadgel chime;
    "Youth, manhood, old age past,
    Come to thy God at last!"

The pilot heard his native bells
Hang on the breeze in fitful swells;
"Thank God!" with reverent brow he cried,
"We'll make the shore with evening's tide."

"Come to thy God in time!"
It was his marriage chime:
"Youth, manhood, old age past,"
His bell must ring at last.

"Thank God, thou whining knave! on land,
But thank, at sea, the steersman's hand" –
The captain's voice above the gale –
"Thank the good ship and ready sail,"
        "Come to thy God in time!"
        Sad grew the boding chime:
        "Come to thy God at last!"
        Boom'd heavy on the blast.

Uprose that sea! as if it heard
The mighty Master's signal-word:
What thrills the captain's whitening lip?
The death-groans of his sinking ship.
        "Come to thy God in time!"
        Swung deep the funeral chime:
        "Grace, mercy, kindness past,
        "Come to thy God at last!"

Long did the resued pilot tell –
When grey hairs o'er his forehead fell,
While those around would hear and weep –
That fearful judgment of the deep,
        "Come to thy God in time!"
        He read his native chime:
        "Youth, manhood, old age past,"
        His bell rang out at last.

Still when the storm of Bottreaux waves
Is wakening in his weedy caves:
Those bells, that sullen surges hide,
Peal their deep notes beneath the tide:
        "Come to thy God in time!"
        Thus saith the ocean chime:
        "Storm, billow, whirlwind past,
        "Come to thy God at last!"

the peal of the bells, and altogether the ballad is a triumph of musical poetry, the sound echoing the sense and indeed comprising it. Not surprisingly, the refrain of the first verse has been inscribed on church bells in North Cornwall and beyond:

"Come to thy God in time!"
Thus saith their pealing chime:
"Youth, manhood, old age past,
Come to thy God at last."

Within these years we also have a recorded example of Hawker the preacher. These are rare: Byles tells us that he burned a lot of manuscripts and spread the ashes over a turnip field, reporting with some delight that there was not a single turnip more in that field than in any other, and in later years he generally preached extempore. Byles also transcribes a text at length. Two extracts should be enough to illustrate the man's power as an orator. The scene is his father's parish church in Stratton in 1831.

Brethren! we are gathered together this day to listen to an exceedingly bitter cry. The voice of famine from another land. The loud necessities of the Irish people. They are wild with hunger. How came this to pass is not a tale for this place. The shrunken hands of a nation are stretched forth unto us, and that is enough. Whole crowds have died, mad with want, and hardly was there anyone to bury them. You would see it as you passed along at this time. Men tottering, but not with age; frail in the midst of their days. You would shudder, on the one hand at the babe laid at the breast in vain, and on the other, at the woman that would fain deny the morsel to her child, and will not have compassion on the son of her womb! These things have been, are, and will be yet again. These men, covered with the sores of human life, the pain, the poverty, and the grief, are laid today at the gate of our hearts.

The givers will receive their reward on the Day of Judgment, and a different fate will be in store for those who fail to give.

Then choose you for this day's part how it shall be. If we will not melt – if we close our fingers upon the coin and hereafter pay it down for some indulgence of our own: we shall be very sorry on a certain time. The voice of many spirits will chide the selfish spirit hereafter. Sad and reproachful faces will move around him in the land of souls. Yes! there is a place where the keen remembrance of every neglect of the law of love will goad men for ever and ever – an awful scene! where there is neither day nor night to bring sweet change; nor storm nor cloud to vary the dismal blank; where the human food we keep back is clean out of mind, and the silver and gold we grasp have no name: where a man will say 'what is the hour?' and his neighbour will answer 'Eternity'.[4]

One cannot help feeling in passing a certain sympathy for his father's parishioners, who must have had precious little to spare themselves.

So we have our man, thirty-one years old, an accomplished poet and preacher, already a little eccentric, keen to mingle with the gentry, his pastoral capacities not yet full stretched; with his wife, twenty years older, probably a calming influence on him. On December 15th, 1834, a letter reached him from the Bishop of Exeter.

The Vicarage of Moorwinstow in your neighbourhood being vacant, I would offer to present you to it, did I not think that it is not a Parish suited to you. I would rather see you placed in some district where access to congenial society would be easy to you, and where you would be justly appreciated, and, by being more in tone with things around you, would also be more useful, with God's blessing, to others. I have not, however, bestowed the living elsewhere, so that if I am mistaken about you (which I think after our last conversation is not likely) inform me by an early post.

If Hawker shared these scruples at all he did not show it, and so his long ministry at Morwenstow began. He himself changed the spelling from that employed by the bishop, to fit with his insistence that St Morwenna, daughter of a ninth century Welsh king Brechin, had founded the church. He gives her words to speak, in the high-flown prose style which, regrettably, he fancied.

Very often, from my abode in wild Wales, have I watched across the waves until the westering sun fell red upon that Cornish rock, and I have said in my maiden vows, 'Alas! and would to God a font might be hewn and an altar built among the stones by yonder barbarous hill'. Give me then, as I beseech thee, my lord the king, a station for a messenger and a priest in that scenery of my early prayer, that so and through me the saying of Esaias the seer may come to pass, 'In the place of dragons, where each lay, there may be grass with reeds and rushes'.

Her voice was heard; her entreaty was fulfilled . . . [5]

A thousand years later, Robert Hawker approached Morwenstow in a similar frame of mind.

Morwenstow church and vicarage stand almost alone, in an austerely beautiful setting, with just two fields of glebe land between them and those awesome cliffs. Many Cornish villages have their churches established separate from the main concentration of homes, and one can visualise the origins of such separate foundations. In the fifth and sixth centuries of Christianity in particular, there was plainly an astonishing traffic across the Irish and Bristol Channels of so-called Celtic Saints, travelling from Wales and Ireland towards Brittany and pausing, often settling, in Cornwall. They would set up shrines outside villages in isolated settings, with a holy well nearby, as places of pilgrimage for their neighbours. The detail is bound to be vague at best, but it is not hard to visualise a Morwenna-figure establishing Morwenstow, perhaps accompanied by her brother Nectan. Canon Miles Brown in his book *The Church in Cornwall* provides a vivid and not unconvincing picture of the beginnings of such a place.

There would be a group of beehive-shaped huts . . . surrounded by a stone enclosure, formed of stones picked up from the moor and piled without mortar. In the midst would be a little oratory of wood or perhaps of stone . . . A well and a crudely carved granite cross would be within the enclosure. The huts are the cells of monks, who have come to study with the famous teacher and saint. He himself would be clad in a white tunic with a rough coat of fur over it . . . To us his appearance would be grotesque by reason of the Celtic tonsure. The head was shaved in front of a line drawn from ear to ear, the hair hanging down long behind. He would also wear a long beard. The rough stone oratory or wattle chapel built by the saint in his lifetime, or piously erected after his death, would enshrine his relics, and his mode of teaching and his scholarship would be carried on by those who had associated themselves with his work while he was alive. Such were the austerities of the enthusiastic Celts that the rule adopted by these men for themselves was often harsh. Little food, long periods of absolute fasting, and the recitation of the psalter while immersed up to the neck in some cold pool were common practice. The devotion and self-surrender of these heroes of the faith gave them a willingly-conceded power over the semi-civilised dwellers in the neighbourhood.[6]

Hawker would have liked to equate himself with this saint, and he shared his aspiration, as 'I would not be forgotten in this land'. Dress and hair-style differed, though his appearance was equally startling; and he would certainly not have cared for the cold pool. The final sentence applies in every detail.

'Semi-civilised' does seem a fair description of some at least of the people of Morwenstow in 1835. Smuggling was a popular pastime. Hawker himself is our best source, even given that capacity for exaggeration. He describes one of his parishioners, Tristram Pentire.

He was the last of the smugglers; and when I took possession of my glebe, I hired him as my servant-of-all-work, or rather no-work, about the house, and there he rollicked away the last few years of his careless existence, in all the pomp and idleness of 'The parson's man'.

He tried to encourage a change in Tristram, and managed to extract a bit of a concession.

"Well, sir, I do think, when I come to look back, and to consider what lives we used to live, - drunk all night and idle abed all day, cursing, swearing, fighting, gambling, lying, and always prepared to shoot the gauger, - I do really believe, sir, we surely was in sin!"

But the gaugers, the excisemen, remained fair game. He explains why no grass would grow on Will Pooly's grave.

"Why, you see, sir, they got poor Will down to Bodmin, all among strangers, and there was bribery, and false swearing; and an unjust judge came down - and the jury all bad rascals, tin-and-copper-men - and so they all agreed together, and they hanged poor Will. But his friends begged the body and brought the corpse home here to his own parish; and they turfed the grave, but 'twas all no use, nothing would ever grow - and he was hanged unjustly."

"Well, but, Tristram, you have not told me all this while what this man Pooly was accused of: what had he done?"

"Done, sir! Done? Nothing whatever but killed the exciseman!"

The glee, the chuckle, the cunning glance, were inimitably charac-

teristic of the hardened old smuggler; and then down went the spade
with a plunge of defiance . . . [7]

That kind of activity was just one side of life in Morwenstow in
the 1830s, but an important one, for two reasons. The smugglers,
Kipling's 'gentlemen', were only evading customs duty, which plenty
of people, not including the unfortunate gaugers, regarded as an
acceptable crime. Wreckers were several degrees worse, if they really
lured ships onto the rocks with false lights. Historical evidence is
lacking, as it would be, and in any case, on North Cornwall's coast
ships hardly needed to be lured.

> From Padstow Point to Lundy Light,
> Is a watery grave, by day and night.

A refinement upon wrecking, just as cruel in effect, undoubtedly
was practised. A wrecked cargo would belong to surviving members
of the crew, so it was important to ensure that there were no survivors.
We have already met Featherstone and Mawgan.

> Wildly he shrieked as his eyes grew dim,
> "He was dead! he was dead! when I buried him."

So the activity, practised by the men of Morwenstow, was brutal.
Secondly, it is important in our story because here is possibly Hawker's
greatest single achievement. He put a stop to such barbarism, at least
along his own stretch of coast, teaching his people that they must
rescue, and that if they were too late, bodies must be carried to
church for Christian burial.

Hawker's experiences with wrecks will come into the story again:
wrecks played a major part in his life. But before moving on to a
broader consideration of parish and parishioners, this is an
appropriate moment to look at his most moving poem on the subject,
'Death Song', written in 1835 but, surprisingly, not included in any
of the collections published in his lifetime. Perhaps it was just too
vivid for him to bear to recall, because here surely is an exceptionally
powerful piece of work. The first two lines set the scene, with the still

DEATH SONG

There lies a cold corpse upon the sands
Down by the rolling sea;
Close up the eyes and straighten the hands,
As a Christian man's should be.

Bury it deep, for the good of my soul,
Six feet below the ground;
Let the sexton come and the death-bell toll,
And good men stand around.

Lay it among the churchyard stones,
Where the priest hath blessed the clay;
I cannot leave the unburied bones,
And I fain would go my way.

✳ ✼ ✳ ✼ ✳

corpse beside the relentlessly moving sea, reiterated in the second verse, the solemn burial with its accompanying death-bell set against the poet's own perturbed soul, and again in verse three, the body resting in the consecrated earth while the priest's conscience wrestles with his abhorrence of the task demanded of him. Also reiterated are the imperatives, four of them, framed by the initial setting of the scene and the last two lines.

It also happens that this short poem contains the most glaring example of a major problem which confronts the student of Hawker's poetry: careless editing. The poem first appears in Godwin's edition, and he prints 'thy' for 'my' in the fifth line. It sounds as though the vicar is shouting brisk not to say threatening instructions to the gravediggers over the churchyard wall. Wallis substitutes 'my', and so converts the poem into a soliloquy, with an emphasis on the poet's horror at the wrecks and their desolate offerings. Save my soul, he

commands and implores, by burying the body deep so that it may
not haunt me. There is no consistency among subsequent editors.
Byles follows Wallis, and he would have had Hawker's daughter
looking over his shoulder. Drinkwater and Woolf in their selections
ignore the poem altogether, and Brendon includes it and reverts to
'thy'. O for a sight of the original manuscript! That small word makes
such a significant difference to the force of the poem.

Another masterly short poem, 'Datur Hora Quieti', is concerned
once more with the main theme of this chapter. That sonorous Latin
title, 'an hour of peace is given', seems to have been invented by
Wallis: it was originally called 'The Funeral Time', on its first
publication in 1836 in the Second Series of *Records of the Western
Shore*, and then 'The Burial Hour' in 1869. It was actually written in
1832 when Hawker was still at North Tamerton. It captures an
ordinary event in a young priest's life, the burial one evening of an
obscure farm labourer. But there is much more, all within eight lines:
the practical but also poignant country custom, 'because the bearers
have then left work'; the macrocosm of this humble occasion, as the
dead man waits for his wages from the Lord of the Vineyard; and the
overtones of the man's status, 'our hireling'. Wallis's title provides
one further element, the labourer's one hour of peace as he 'treads
his homeward way' from toil in the field to family responsibilities
and anxieties, life on 7/- a week. You could hardly ask more of two
short verses.

Hawker likened the shape of his parish to a horseshoe, its heels
on the seashore which stretched for five miles, its toe inland on the
road from Bideford to Bude, three and a half miles from the church,
embracing about seven hamlets, three manor houses and several
isolated farms. Byles describes North Cornwall as 'a spacious and
windswept land of bare hills and wooded valleys' and goes on:

One striking feature of the landscape is the scarcity of human habita-
tions. The lanes wind along between high-banked hedges for miles and
miles, with hardly a cottage to break the solitude. Morwenstow has a
particularly desolate appearance, because there is no central village.[8]

DATUR HORA QUIETI

To the MS of this Poem is the following note: "Why do you wish the burial to be at five o'clock?" – "Because it was the time at which he used to leave work."

"At eve should be the time," they said,
To close their brother's narrow bed:
'Tis at that pleasant hour of day
The labourer treads his homeward way.

His work was o'er, his toil was done,
And therefore with the set of sun,
To wait the wages of the dead,
We laid our hireling in his bed.

* * * * *

Nine hundred people were scattered around within this inhospitable setting. Most would have been very poor. That 7/- wage compares with 8/5d in the southern counties as a whole. In more prosperous areas, there were riots in the 1830s in response to the introduction of threshing machines, and against the operation of the New Poor Law. The Tolpuddle Martyrs were transported in 1834. None of this touched Morwenstow. The labourers simply accepted their lot, and left it to their vicar to be angry on their behalf. He wrote in 1868:

England has never prospered since the passage of the Poor Law Bill whereby such direct insult and injury were wrought upon the person of the Redeemer of Man. Whatsoever you do unto the least of my poor brethren you do it unto me. Lock him up. Give him 4 oz of bread.[9]

Twenty-five years earlier, he was already passionately opposed to the Poor Law and its most vivid effect, the Union Workhouse, and he published as a leaflet 'The Poor Man and his Parish Church'. In a pencilled note he claims that John Keble visited him at Morwenstow and said 'That ballad quite haunts me'.[10] He writes initially about the fellow-hirelings of the dead man in 'Datur Hora Quieti'. The first two verses have an imposing simplicity about them, especially the second.

> The poor men have their wedding-day:
> And children climb their knee:
> They have not many friends, for they
> Are in such misery.
> They sell their youth, their skill, their pains,
> For hire in hill and glen:
> The very blood within their veins,
> It flows for other men.

When they grow old, he goes on to say, they should have the dignity of independence in their own homes, and he gives the example of one such 'poor man' who prayed in his church morning and evening until he went blind, when he needed and obtained guidance.

> He died – he slept beneath the dew,
> In his own grassy mound:
> The corpse, within the coffin, knew
> That calm, that holy ground.

He compares the fate of inmates of the workhouse:

> And when they vaunt, that in those walls,
> They have their worship-day,
> Where the stern signal coldly calls
> The prisoned poor to pray, –
> I think upon that ancient home
> Beside the churchyard wall,
> Where roses round the porch would roam,
> And gentle jasmines fall.

THE POOR MAN AND HIS PARISH CHURCH
A *True Tale*

The poor have hands, and feet, and eyes,
　　Flesh, and a feeling mind:
They breathe the breath of mortal sighs,
　　They are of human kind.
They weep such tears as others shed,
　　And now and then they smile:-
For sweet to them is that poor bread,
　　They win with honest toil.

The poor men have their wedding-day:
　　And children climb their knee:
They have not many friends, for they
　　Are in such misery.
They sell their youth, their skill, their pains,
　　For hire in hill and glen:
The very blood within their veins,
　　It flows for other men.

They should have roofs to call their own,
　　When they grow old and bent:
Meek houses built of dark grey stone,
　　Worn labour's monument.
There should they dwell, beneath the thatch,
　　With threshold calm and free:
No stranger's hand should lift the latch,
　　To mark their poverty.

Fast by the church those walls should stand,
　　Her aisles in youth they trod:-
They have no home in all the land,
　　Like that old House of God.
There, there, the Sacrament was shed,
　　That gave them heavenly birth;
And lifted up the poor man's head
　　With princes of the earth.

There in the chancel's voice of praise,
   Their simple vows were poured;
And angels looked with equal gaze
   On Lazarus and his Lord.
There, too, at last, they calmly sleep,
   Where hallow'd blossoms bloom;
And eyes as fond and faithful weep
   As o'er the rich man's tomb.

They told me of an ancient home,
   Beside a churchyard wall,
Where roses round the porch would roam,
   And gentle jasmines fall;
There dwelt an old man, worn and blind,
   Poor, and of lowliest birth;
He seemed the last of all his kind –
   He had no friend on earth.

Men saw him till his eyes grew dim,
   At morn and evening tide
Pass, 'mid the graves, with tottering limb,
   To the grey chancel's side:
There knelt he down, and meekly prayed
   The prayers his youth had known:
Words by the old Apostles made,
   In tongues of ancient tone.

At matin-time, at evening hour,
   He bent with reverent knee:
The dial carved upon the tower
   Was not more true than he.
This lasted till the blindness fell
   In shadows round his bed;
And on those walls he loved so well,
   He looked, and they were fled.

Then would he watch, and fondly turn,
   If feet of men were there,
To tell them how his soul would yearn
   For the old place of prayer;
And some would lead him on to stand,
   While fast their tears would fall,
Until he felt beneath his hand
   The long-accustomed wall.

Then joy in those dim eyes would melt;
   Faith found the former tone;
His heart within his bosom felt
   The touch of every stone.
He died – he slept beneath the dew,
   In his own grassy mound:
The corpse, within the coffin, knew
   That calm, that holy ground.

I know not why – but when they tell
   Of houses fair and wide,
Where troops of poor men go to dwell
   In chambers side by side:–
I dream of that old cottage door,
   With garlands overgrown,
And wish the children of the poor
   Had flowers to call their own.

And when they vaunt, that in those walls
   They have their worship-day,
Where the stern signal coldly calls
   The prisoned poor to pray, –
I think upon that ancient home
   Beside the churchyard wall,
Where roses round the porch would roam,
   And gentle jasmines fall.

I see the old man of my lay,
    His grey head bowed and bare;
He kneels by one dear wall to pray,
    The sunlight in his hair.
Well! they may strive, as wise men will,
    To work with wit and gold:
I think my own dear Cornwall still
    Was happier of old.

O! for the poor man's church again,
    With one roof over all;
Where the true hearts of Cornish men
    Might beat beside the wall:
The altars where, in holier days,
    Our fathers were forgiven,
Who went, with meek and faithful ways,
    Through the old aisles to heaven.

* * * * *

He craves on behalf of his people for an idealised, indeed sentimentalised, past, but the power of his loving care comes through, and is a consistent theme in poems and letters throughout his life.

Well! they may strive, as wise men will,
To work with wit and gold:
I think my own dear Cornwall still
Was happier of old.

So the people of Morwenstow were fortunate in their vicar, especially after a hundred years without one. But they must have found him strange. The eccentricity of his dress is famous, more so probably than any of his poems apart from 'The Song of the Western Men'. Only his socks were clerical black, made with wool from his own black ewe, knitted by children in the school. He wore a brown cassock (the hue of Our Lady's hair, and her Blessed Son's), a fisherman's blue jersey (fisher of men) with a small red cross woven into it (to mark the entrance of the centurion's cruel spear), sea-boots, and a broad-brimmed hat. A carpenter's pencil, indicative of the Carpenter of Nazareth, was attached to his button-hole. He was nothing if not a symbolist, and he must have been a striking figure, striding round his scattered parish, or riding in his dog-cart, or mounted on his pony on the path to Welcombe, his second parish just over the Devon border of which he became curate in 1850.

His dress in church was also highly individual, at a time when the Church of England was agonising over whether vestments should be worn at all. A member of the Waddon Martyn family of Tonacombe Manor provides a description.

Mr Hawker christened my oldest son, in full vestments (as he always did) – alb – magnificent purple cope, fastened with a large sort of brooch – a white stole very richly worked in gold, an exact copy, he said, of St Cuthbert's, found on opening the coffin still preserved (in Durham Cathedral) . . . [11]

The church was of course the centre of his life, and he strove to draw his people to it, and save them from the 'Dissenters', of whom more will be heard. He did not expect them to attend his daily services of matins and evensong. 'I did not want them there', he said. 'God hears me; and they know I am praying for them, for I ring the bell.'[12] Often his wife was the only person in the congregation, and he would begin the service 'Dearly beloved Charlotte, the scripture moveth us in sundry places . . . '. Often he was alone.

The church provides a timely reminder that Morwenstow had a long history before Hawker appeared on the scene. Its most astonishing feature is the concentration of architecture in a relatively confined space: a Saxon font, and Norman, Early English, and Perpendicular arches, the first decorated with beak-head ornament which looks as though it was carved yesterday. Hawker expresses his reverence in 'Morwennae Statio', published in a slim volume of verse, *Ecclesia*, in 1840. It is greatly superior to his prose account of the church, called 'Morwenstow', in *Footprints of Former Men in Far Cornwall.* When a direct comparison can be made between his poetry and prose, the poetry version tends to be better. In his prose he was often diffuse, mannered, pseudo-archaic, too eager to please the reader. Much of it was written in the last ten years of his life, after his second marriage, when he had a family to support and was frantic to make money. His style of letter-writing tends to be more relaxed and more pleasing, frequently indeed brilliant.

'Morwennae Statio' celebrates first and foremost the church's Saxon builders, their strength and the strength of their creation.

> Huge, mighty, massive, hard, and strong,
> Were the choice stones they lifted then:
> The vision of their hope was long,
> They knew their God, those faithful men.
> They pitched no tent for change or death,
> No home to last man's shadowy day;
> There! – there! – the everlasting breath,
> Would breathe whole centuries away.

The church is a daughter of the rock, in the first and again in the last verse, recalling both the words of Jesus to Peter, and also the granite upon which it stands and of which it is built. Hawker was to become less enamoured of the granite landscape, 'I have lived long among these faraway rocks unprofited, unpraised and unknown'. But his main concern here, in his hopeful early days, is with physical power allied with holiness, notably in the third and fourth verses. The image that follows, of the nave resembling an inverted boat, is attractive but baffling. A note from Byles is helpful.

The Stow, or the place, of St Morwenna;
hence the Breviate, hodie, *Morwenstow*

My Saxon shrine! the only ground
    Wherein this weary heart hath rest:
What years the birds of God have found
    Along thy walls their sacred nest!
The storm – the blast – the tempest shock,
    Have beat upon those walls in vain;
She stands – a daughter of the rock –
    The changeless God's eternal fane.

Firm was their faith, the ancient bands
    The wise of heart in wood and stone:
Who reared, with stern and trusting hands,
    These dark grey towers of days unknown:
They fill'd these aisles with many a thought,
    They bade each nook some truth reveal:
The pillar'd arch its legends brought,
    A doctrine came with roof and wall.

Huge, mighty, massive, hard, and strong,
    Were the choice stones they lifted then:
The vision of their hope was long,
    They knew their God, those faithful men.
They pitch'd no tent for change or death,
    No home to last man's shadowy day;
There! there! the everlasting breath,
    Would breathe whole centuries away.

See now, along that pillar'd aisle,
    The graven arches, firm and fair;
They bend their shoulders to the toil,
    And lift the hollow roof in air.
A sign! beneath the ship we stand,
    The inverted vessel's arching side;
Forsaken – when the fisher-band
    Went forth to sweep a mightier tide.

Pace we the ground! Our footsteps tread
    A cross – the builder's holiest form:
That awful couch, where once was shed
    The blood, with man's forgiveness warm.
And here, just where His mighty breast
    Throb'd the last agony away,
They bade the voice of worship rest,
    And white-robed Levites pause and pray.

Mark! the rich rose of Sharon's bower
    Curves in the paten's mystic mould:
The lily, lady of the flower,
    Her shape must yonder chalice hold.
Types of the Mother and the Son,
    The twain in this dim chancel stand:
The badge of Norman banners, one
    And one a crest of English land.

How all things glow with life and thought,
    Where'er our faithful fathers trod!
The very ground with speech is fraught,
    The air is eloquent of God.
In vain would doubt or mockery hide
    The buried echoes of the past;
A voice of strength, a voice of pride,
    Here dwells amid the storm and blast.

Still points the tower, and pleads the bell;
    The solemn arches breathe in stone;
Window and wall have lips to tell
    The mighty faith of days unknown.
Yea! Flood, and breeze, and battle-shock
    Shall beat upon this church in vain:
She stands, a daughter of the rock,
    The changeless God's eternal fane.

Several inverted boats, cast up at different times, formerly lay upon the graves of shipwrecked sailors. They typified to Hawker's mind the safety of the Ark, 'the Ark of Christ's Church', so he was fond of saying. These boats have long since rotted away.[13]

Next, down on the church floor, comes the concept of the cruciform church bearing the body of Christ, so that his heart died where the priest stands, at the bottom of the chancel steps. Hawker frequently drew his reader, and probably still more his listener, to the human physical Jesus. Then before again extolling the church and its builders, he describes the small details of the patten and the chalice, 'Types of the Mother and the Son'. And so to the penultimate verse, which must be among his finest.

> How all things glow with life and thought,
> Where'er our faithful fathers trod!
> The very ground with speech is fraught,
> The air is eloquent of God.
> In vain would doubt and mockery hide
> The buried echoes of the past;
> A voice of strength, a voice of pride,
> Here dwells amid the storm and blast.

I have been trying with a few daubs of the brush to portray Morwenstow as Hawker found it in 1835: the traditions of smuggling and wrecking, the scattered geography of the place, the poverty, the church. I have also tried to describe how Morwenstow might have viewed its new vicar. Before embarking on a chronological account of his long ministry, let me quote a description of the man by Byles, helped no doubt by his wife, the vicar's daughter.

The Vicar of Morwenstow was a tall and strongly built man, with fair hair, blue eyes, and a ruddy complexion. His voice was rich and power-ful. He could be heard all over his glebe, and would sometimes carry on a conversation with his neighbours at a farm across the valley.[14]

The people of Morwenstow must indeed have been surprised.

3

Dissenters, and Poetry, into the 1840s

Any attempt at understanding Robert Stephen Hawker must face up to his apparently profound, certainly very vigorously expressed, aversion to 'Dissenters': not simply Methodists, followers of John Wesley, but members of the various groups which separated and then formed after his death in 1791, and in particular the Bryanites, or Bible Christians, who were notably active in North Cornwall. Hawker tended to lump them all together under that one name, and confuses the issue further by sometimes calling them 'Protestants' – a term which plainly in his book did not include Anglicans. Another baffling element is that several of his leading parishioners were in fact dissenters, and he was often on the best of terms with them. This conflict ran through the forty years of Hawker's ministry, so before pursuing it further, more should be said about his and his wife's activities in their first few years at Morwenstow.

The new vicar and his wife needed somewhere to live. There had not been a resident incumbent for more than a century, and the vicarage was a ruin. 'I ought not to build a shoppy residence', Hawker wrote, and he did not, if we take 'shoppy' to mean typically and unimaginatively professional. Morwenstow Vicarage is highly original, a fine spacious building folded in to a relatively sheltered spot just below the church with a splendid view down a steep-sided valley to the cliffs and the sea. The strange chimneys have already been remarked upon. The front door is another striking feature, with a verse carved above it:

> A House, a Glebe, a Pound a Day;
> A pleasant Place to Watch and Pray.
> Be True to Church, be Kind to Poor,
> O Minister! For Evermore.

The vicarage took nearly five years to complete, and for that time the Hawkers lived 'in a hired cottage of two rooms'. This did not however cramp the vicar's style. He rapidly embarked on a series of building projects. In the Coombe Valley, near the savage mouth with the gentle name of Duckpool, the coast road to Bude ran through a marshy area, vulnerable to dangerous flooding. Within a year he had inspired and supervised the building of a new bridge, which still stands, known as King William's Bridge because William IV contributed £20 towards the expense. Throughout his life Hawker was adept at approaching royalty cap in hand.

His principal benefactor was not however his king, but his wife. The expense of constructing the bridge, the vicarage, and (in 1843) the school, was borne principally by the vicar, and he could not have managed it on a pound a day. Charlotte's private means inherited from her father seem to have been largely absorbed into these admirable but perhaps excessively ambitious building schemes. Consequently, almost from those early beginnings, Hawker's years at Morwenstow were dogged by debt and financial anxieties. His son-in-law once again puts it well.

He was too lavish, too generous; doing everything as he considered it *ought* to be done, and never pausing to reflect whether he could afford it. But while this principle was fatal to himself, there was no doubt that it was very beneficial to the parish and the living.[1]

That continues to apply, nearly a hundred years after Byles was writing. All three – vicarage, bridge, school – stand strong today. A boy at the school, Kingsley Bryant, contributed a brisk couplet to a poetry competition in 1975, the centenary of Hawker's death:

> Our school was built in the form of a cross,
> For Reverend Hawker was the boss.[2]

Reverend Hawker certainly intended to be the boss, indeed no alternative would have entered his mind. Morwenstow in 1835 conspicuously failed to conform to the standard pattern of an English rural community: 'The parson was a member of the ruling class. In the country the squire and he were the natural lords of the village. Between the squire and the villagers, even the poorest, he was the natural mediator'.[3]

There had been no resident vicar for a hundred years; and there was effectively no squire. The Waddon Martyn family of Tonacombe Manor barely qualified, because they were frequently absent, and they were also sympathetic to the dissenter cause themselves. Hawker, the 'natural lord', summed up his natural vassals.

My people were a mixed multitude of smugglers, wreckers, and dissenters of various hue. A few simple-hearted farmers clung to the grey old sanctuary of the church and the tower that looked along the sea; but the bulk of the people, in the absence of a resident vicar, had become the followers of the great preacher of the last century who came down into Cornwall and persuaded the people to alter their sins. I was assured, soon after my arrival, by one of his disciples, who led the foray among my flock, that my "parish was so rich in resources for his benefit, that he called it, sir, the garden of our circuit".[4]

Wesley was also to be blamed for the apparent degeneration of the Cornish. The Bude lifeboat failed to put out to help a shipwreck in 1864, and this was why:

John Wesley years ago corrupted and degraded the Cornish Character, found them wrestlers, caused them to change their sins and called it conversion. With my last breath I protest that the man Wesley corrupted and depraved instead of improving the West of England, indeed all the land. He found the miners and the fishermen an upstanding rollicking courageous people. He left them a downlooking lying selfish-hearted throng.[5]

It is only fair to add that when he wrote this he was very agitated, and having gone on for some time in the same vein he concludes, 'Well, well. I have written in haste as you may see an account of the wreck. So now farewell.'

John Wesley's influence on England and Wales was of course very considerable, and in Cornwall it was peculiarly intense. In 1851 there were 265 Anglican churches in the county, and 839 nonconformist places of worship, of which 737 were Methodist.[6] Wesley himself had never wished for or intended a break away from the Church of England, despite his heroic claim that 'All the world is my parish'. But he was seen, with justification, as a threat to the church's authority, and time and again as he rode round the country he arrived at churches to find them locked against him. Typically, he approached North Tamerton in 1750: 'when we came, we found no notice had been given, and the key of the church was a mile off, so I preached in a large room adjoining to it'.[7]

It is surprising to think that he visited that remote little church, where Hawker eighty years later was to be curate. He never actually came to Morwenstow, despite its becoming 'the garden of our circuit'. Meanwhile, a clergyman of Redruth replied to a request by his bishop to report on this new phenomenon of Methodism in practice.

In their private devotions I am told that they have been sometimes overheard to make use of rapturous expressions, and seem to be in a kind of ecstasy.

In public prayer I hear they frequently shed tears especially in singing their hymns.

They are very constant attenders at Church and the Sacrament, and when there seem very attentive and much affected.[8]

We have here a paradox. These dangerous radicals were often simultaneously the most loyal and devout churchgoers that the Church could claim. It has of course to be borne in mind that the Church retained for some time the monopoly of baptisms, weddings and funerals. For instance, a hundred years later in 1852, Hawker describes opposition to his choice of wardens, and the account is made vivid by his quoting his opponent's reply.

I told John Venning he had no business there, that he was a Meetinger, as he was, he had never been in Church since 1849 when the window was put in. Said he never would till he was brought in as a corpse . . . [9]

To return to Wesley, as a loyal Anglican he had cause for concern at the effect of his preaching: for instance in Bristol in 1739.

Immediately one that stood by (to our no small surprise) cried out aloud with the utmost vehemence, even as in the agonies of death . . . Soon after other persons were seized with strong pain, and constrained to 'roar for the disquietness of their heart'.[10]

Forty years later, he could be sceptical about a notable feature of Methodist practice, extempore prayer.

It has no determinate meaning. Let but a pert, self-sufficient animal, that has neither sense nor grace, bawl out something about Christ and his blood or justification by faith, and his hearers cry out, "What a fine gospel sermon!"[11]

Nevertheless, ten years on again, two years before his death, he writes of Methodism: 'It requires of its members no conformity, either in opinions or modes of worship, but barely this one thing, to fear God, and work righteousness'.[12]

One is left wondering whether John Wesley actually knew what he was starting. Hawker had no doubt, as a few quotations from his Thought Books will show.

Nothing ever conceived in the Roman Catholic church ever approached the tremendous blasphemies of Methodism.

Methodism. A man's own feelings save him. It is salvation made easy, or every man his own Redeemer.

Compare the Turning and Howling Dervishes of Turkey with our Jumpers and Ranters of Cornwall.[13]

And in a letter he describes

. . . that spasm of the ganglions which the Methodist calls the witness of the Spirit, or assurance of the sensual perception of the forgiveness of sin, the badge and shibboleth of the Wesleyan all over the world and here in Cornwall the solitary doctrine of this vile sect.[14]

Much of this is of course outrageous, and barely defensible even in the context of sectarian controversy in the mid-nineteenth century. But he plainly did see Wesley as personifying a fundamental attack on everything he held dear, especially the authority of the Church and the Priesthood in general, and of himself in his parish in particular, beleaguered as he felt 'among these rocks' with the greater part of his parishioners infected by Dissent. The independence which Wesley bestowed on the individual worried him above all, and the loosening of sexual mores which he judged to be a consequence. 'I swear that I never once in all my life married a Dissenting wife who was not about to become a mother', he wrote to Mrs Watson in 1863. One needs to remember that despite all his voluminous correspondence with that lady, he and she never actually met, so he could exaggerate confidently and with impunity.

An extraordinary feature of Hawker's pronouncements about Dissenters is that he seems to have made no distinction between, on the one side, his parishioners who quietly attended, perhaps, chapel in the morning and church in the afternoon; and on the other, the wilder and more excitable sub-sects which broke away from the main body of the Methodist Church after John Wesley's death in 1791. Of these most notable were the Bible Christians, or Bryanites, founded in North Devon by William O'Bryan in 1815. Here were his turners and howlers. Baring-Gould is probably no more reliable a witness of Bryanite behaviour than he is about the life of the vicar of Morwenstow, but his account of them would have produced a sympathetic belly-laugh from an Anglican colleague:

A favourite performance in a Bryanite meeting, according to popular report, is to 'hunt the devil out'. The preacher having worked the people up into a great state of excitement, they are provided with sticks, and the lights are extinguished. A general melée ensues. Everyone who hits thinks he is dealing the Devil his death-blow; and every one who receives a blow believes it is a butt from the Devil's horns.[15]

A more stern comment is provided by Francis Gribble.

Hawker's notorious animus against Dissenters is amply understood by the peculiarities of the particular Dissenters with whom he mostly came in contact. They were Bryanites, and Bryanism is neither more nor less than an attempt to reconcile religious fervour with loose living.[16]

I have no wish to comment on the accuracy or justice of these comments on the Bible Christians in Hawker's time and beyond: simply to suggest that they were probably typical of the views of the Church of England, and as such were likely to be shared with interest by a bellicose character like Hawker.

Some of Hawker's remarks about Dissenters were relatively cheerful, almost sympathetic with a touch of the sardonic. You are sometimes left wondering whether he really meant it all. 'I like to give them a little comfort in this world, for I know what discomfort awaits them in the next'[17] might or might not have been found comforting; and his relatively simple parishioners would have been puzzled by his reply to the question, whether he had any objection to burying Dissenters in his churchyard, 'None at all, I should be only too glad to bury you all'.[18] In 1865, when his second wife was expecting their first child, he found himself in a dilemma.

We have a sad domestic trouble. We have taken a very good cook, a Wesleyan. She asked leave to go and meet her brother at Woodford, and there is a parish rumour that she went to the conventicle. If this is verified, we must of course dismiss her, a sad loss because she is a very good servant and a time is at hand when it will not do to have a bad one.[19]

The girl's fate is not recorded. More impressively, Hawker writes to Mrs Watson describing a fire at the vicarage. 'Anything more noble than the conduct of the people was never seen. They risked life and limb and the Dissenters were conspicuous among them all for vigour and zeal.'[20]

Most admirable of all is this tribute to Hawker after his death in 1875.

I was chosen, at his request, upwards of twenty years since to be church-warden, though a Wesleyan and local preacher . . . For forty years I have known him as one of my best and dearest friends. He never reproached me for being a Wesleyan, but I had every encouragement to virtue . . . [21]

So, not for the first or the last time, we are faced with inconsistency. It is an over-simplification – apart from the doubtful applicability of the term – to say that he loved the sinner but hated the sin. The irony of it is that he also seems to have had a lot in common with these dreadful Dissenters. Comparisons between his style of preaching and that of Billy Bray, the best known of the Cornish dissenting preachers, are illuminating. First, a local newspaper quotes a Bray sermon, predictably reporting in dialect.

If you have a lot you'm affeared you'll lose it – my prayer is you'll all find the price of the high calling. Amen, hallelujah, glory be to God. I have it – it's mine – mine in death – mine after death – and it may be your'n too (cries of 'Amen, Hallelujah', and 'God be praised').[22]

The comparison with a passage from one of Hawker's sermons is not entirely fair because Hawker can be quoted at greater length and is more respectfully recorded.

Am I alone? Not so. There are horses and chariots of fire about me. There are angels around us on every side!
      You do not see them. You ask me, "Do you?"
      And I answer, "Yes, I do."
      Am I weak? An angel stays me up. Do my hands falter? An angel sustains them. Am I weary to death with disappointment? My head rests on an angel's bosom, and an angel's arms encircle me. And believe me, as long as one stone stands upon another of Morwenna's church, so long will there be a priest to answer God's call, and so long will there be an angel to stay him up in his agony and weakness, and to meet his adversary with the sword of challenge.[23]

There is a lot in common between the resonant periods of the High Anglican priest-poet, and the exciting and excited utterance of the revivalist preacher. Of course here are sharp differences too. A sermon in Morwenstow church would hardly have offered scope for audience participation: significantly, Hawker plays both parts, himself and his congregation. At Bray's prayer meeting, according to the same report, 'such ravings, such groanings and prostrations we never before witnessed in persons professedly in possession of sane minds'. We are still left with the common ground. Two more passages merit setting side by side. This passage of Hawker has already been quoted, as he visualises the fate of anyone who failed to give to the starving Irish.

. . . an awful scene! where there is neither day nor night to bring sweet change; nor storm nor cloud to vary the dismal blank; where the human food we keep back is clean out of mind, and the silver and gold we grasp have no name: where a man will say "what is the hour?" and his neighbour will answer "Eternity".[24]

Billy Bray is also in the business of describing Hell.

After a hundred years one comes up and hollers out "what a clock es a?" And the ould devil lays hold of 'un and says "There bean't no clock, no time here – thes es eternity", and pitches um back again into the brimstone.[25]

Hawker would not have cared to be thought of in the same breath as Billy Bray and his ilk, indeed he took pride in being their avowed enemy. But they had in common a wonderful gift for dramatic fervour, and skill in its implementation.

It is time to return to Hawker's poetry, with the publication of a volume drably entitled *Ecclesia* in 1840. First, a critical overview by a fellow-poet merits quotation. John Drinkwater was a poet and dramatist of the 1920s, now out of fashion but admired in his day. In 1922 he edited a selection of Hawker's poetry, published in the United States. In his introduction he summed up Hawker's achievement, in a patronising not to say niggardly spirit but nonetheless with some accuracy.

To call him an unlettered poet would be absurd, but he was a poet who wrote away from the world of letters. At his best he was none the worse for that, but when the pressure of his gift was low he was not very exacting with himself, and there was no 'neighbourly authority', as it were, to keep him up to standard. So that at times he wrote verse much as another parson might compile his parish magazine. Even so, Hawker's magazine would be a superior one, but we would hardly want to turn over its pages again. A good deal of his verse is, in short, commonplace. But a little of it is anything but commonplace . . . [26]

It must be acknowledged that the lack of a 'neighbourly authority' did have a detrimental effect on his work: a critical audience comprising principally Charlotte would have lacked edge. But a very substantial quantity of his verse was, at the very least, 'anything but commonplace'.

'Modryb Marya – Aunt Mary' (1838) provides a welcome antidote

MODRYB MARYA – AUNT MARY

A Christmas Chant

Now of all the trees by the king's highway,
    Which do you love the best?
O! the one that is green upon Christmas Day,
    The bush with the bleeding breast.
Now the holly with her drops of blood for me:
For that is our dear Aunt Mary's tree.

Its leaves are sweet with our Saviour's Name,
    'Tis a plant that loves the poor:
Summer and winter it shines the same,
    Beside the cottage door.
O! the holly with her drops of blood for me:
For that is our kind Aunt Mary's tree.

'Tis a bush that the birds will never leave:
    They sing in it all day long;
But sweetest of all upon Christmas Eve,
    Is to hear the robin's song.
'Tis the merriest sound upon earth and sea:
For it comes from our own Aunt Mary's tree.

So, of all that grow by the king's highway,
    I love that tree the best;
'Tis a bower for the birds upon Christmas Day,
    The bush of the bleeding breast.
O! the holly with her drops of blood for me:
For that is our sweet Aunt Mary's tree.

*   *   *   *   *

to all that carping about Dissenters, offering as it does a warmth and simplicity to match the relationship that Hawker hoped to establish with his new parishioners. With its cheerful rhythm, and slightly varied refrain that so well suits a carol, it takes as its theme the symbolism of the holly tree in Christian folklore, embracing the hedgerow's uniquely bright bounty at Christmas, there for everyone including the poor. It is also evergreen, emblematic of eternal life, and spattered with berries, like blood falling from the crucified body of Christ onto his mother standing below. Meanwhile the robin, his breast reddened from the same source, sings on Christmas Eve, and shelter is given to all the birds especially on Christmas Day. There is a hint of the poet's favourite habit of equating birds with angels, '*Ubi aves ibi angeli*', where birds are, there are angels. The name 'Aunt Mary's Tree' becomes entirely appropriate. The same symbolism is taken a stage further in the much better known carol 'The Holly and the Ivy', with the thorns of the holly representing the pain of Mary's childbirth and of Jesus on the cross. Hawker's lovely carol has never achieved such popularity. Presumably the title, and his translation of it, provides too much of a local emphasis.

A more ambitious poem, at least in terms of length, is 'Minster Church and the Confirmation Day, August XVII, MDCCCXXXVI'. An unusual feature of 'Minster Church', as his editors understandably came to call it, is that an earlier and shorter version exists, which makes no reference to the culminating event of the published poem, the visit of Bishop Phillpotts. It bears the title 'A Sketch for Mrs F', and is a more modest affair altogether. The lady must have been Mrs Fortescue, a friend in those early years. Verse 1 of the longer, published, version does not appear, the poem starting quite comfortably with verse 2; verse 6 takes a different form, designed to conclude the poem; and verses 7, 8 and 9 have no place either, naturally as they concern the bishop. This shorter version, it should be added, was never published, which makes the addition of the first verse in the published version all the more interesting. It does not after all have anything to do with the bishop. It is the first record of Hawker's frustration, his sense of being stranded at Morwenstow. In a manner which echoes Milton's 'Lycidas', and also recalls Wordsworth's Lucy, 'A violet by

MINSTER CHURCH AND THE CONFIRMATION DAY

August XVII, MDCCCXXXVI

Hang not the harp upon the willow-bough,
But teach thy native echoes one more song
Though fame withhold her sigil from thy brow,
And years half yield thee to the unnoted throng.
Doth not the linnet her meek lay prolong
In the lone depths of some deserted wood?
Springs not the violet coarse weeds among,
Where no fond voice shall praise her solitude?
Happy that bird and flower, though there be few intrude!

The Minster of the Trees! A lonely dell
Deep with old oaks, and 'mid their quiet shade,
Grey with the moss of years, yon antique cell!
Sad are those walls: the cloister lowly laid
Where pacing monks at solemn evening made
Their chanted orisons; and as the breeze
Came up the vale, by rock and tree delay'd,
They heard the awful voice of many seas
Blend with thy pausing hymn – thou Minster of the Trees!

The thoughts of days long past lie buried here;
Scenes of the former men my soul surround;
Lo! A dark priest, who bends with solemn ear –
A warrior prostrate on the awful ground,
Hark! By stern promise is Lord Bottreaux bound
To spread for Palestine his contrite sail;
In distant dreams to hear the vesper sound
Of that sweet bell; but never more to hail
Amidst those native trees, the Minster of the Vale!

Gaze yet again! A maid with hooded brow
Glides like a shadow through the cloister'd wood;
'Tis not to breathe Saint Ursula's stony vow

She haunts at eve that dreamy solitude;-
Yon gnarléd oak was young, when there they stood,
The lady and the priest - they met to sigh:
For who be they with sudden grasp intrude?
They sever them in haste - yet not to die.
Hark! From yon stifled wall a low and frequent cry!

Long generations! lo, a ghastly man
Is leaning there, bent with the weight of days!
His cell was shattered by the reckless ban
Of a hard monarch - hush'd the voice of praise.
He had gone forth - strange faces met his gaze:
Ailric was dead, and cold was Edith's eye;
He had return'd - no sheltering roof to raise,
But 'mid the ruins of his love to die -
To pass from that worn frame into his native sky.

Wake! Dreamer of the Past; - no fairer grace
Dwelt in the vale or glided o'er the plain.
Heaven's changeless smile is here - earth's constant face;
The mingling sighs of woodland and the main.
Here, at lone eve, still seek this simple fane
Hearts that would cherish, 'midst their native trees,
A deathless faith - a hope that is not vain;
The tones that gather'd on the ancient breeze;
The Minster's pausing psalm; the chorus of the seas.

And lo! 'tis Holy Day! - through vale and wood
Beat joyful hearts; and white-rob'd forms are seen
Peopling with life the leafy solitude;
For He, of aspect mild yet stately mien,
The master-soul of a far loftier scene,
Hath come, beside that low-roof'd wall to stand,
Where the meek minster loves her bowers of green,
To breathe the Blessing on that rural band;
Proudly they hear those tones and see that lifted hand!

And we, who gaze and ponder, have we not
Thoughts new and strange, for fancy's future hour?
Shall no glad visions haunt this storied spot,
Glide from those boughs, and rest by yonder tower?
Yes; there shall be a spell of mightiest power
Breath'd o'er that ground – him will these groves recall
Who saw, unbent, the deadly battle lower,
Fair Sion's turrets shake, her bulwarks fall;
And foremost mann'd the breach and latest left the wall.

Fane of the woods, farewell! an holier thought
Henceforth be thine; with added beauty blest!
The presence of this day hath surely wrought
A charm immortal for thy home of rest.
Long may the swallow find her wonted nest
On thy grey walls; long may the breezes bear
The sounds of worship from thy happy breast;
The mind that shook whole senates hath been there;
Strong be the soul of faith, and firm the voice of prayer.

* * * * *

a mossy stone, Half hidden from the eye', he half-heartedly resigns
himself to obscurity.

Doth not the linnet her meek lay prolong
In the lone depths of some deserted wood?
Springs not the violet coarse weeds among,
Where no fond voice shall praise her solitude?
Happy that bird and flower, though there be few intrude!

That final line has a curious history of its own. 'Minster Church'
was initially published as a pamphlet, presumably to accompany the
occasion. In that original form, and again in *Records of the Western
Shore*, the line ends with a question mark. Was this simply careless? It

is certainly awkward to read. Or was Hawker questioning his own acceptance of insignificance, having it both ways? For its third printing in *Ecclesia* the question mark is replaced with an exclamation mark, surely more appropriate even if it does imply a submissiveness that was hardly applicable at any stage of his life and particularly not when he was only thirty-two. For good measure his editors vary, Godwin preferring the exclamation and Willis and Byles the question.

There is another intriguing variation between the published version and the earlier 'Sketch for Mrs F'. To explain it, verse 3 of the 'Sketch' and the corresponding verse 4 of 'Minster Church' both need to be quoted in full.

A *Sketch for Mrs F* (unpublished)

A change! Long years! a maid of sunny brow
Glides like a shadow through the cloister'd wood;
'Tis not to break Saint Ursula's stony vow
She haunts at eve that dreamy solitude;
Yon gnarlèd oak was fresh, when there they stood,
The lady and the priest - they met to sigh:
But who be they with sudden grasp intrude?
They sever them in haste - yet not to die.
Hark! from yon stifled wall a low and frequent cry!

'Minster Church' (as in *Ballads and Other Poems*)

Gaze yet again! A maid with hooded brow
Glides like a shadow through the cloister'd wood;
'Tis not to breathe Saint Ursula's stony vow
She haunts at eve that dreamy solitude;
Yon gnarlèd oak was young, when there they stood,
The lady and the priest - they met to sigh:
For who be they with sudden grasp intrude?
They sever them with haste - yet not to die.
Hark! from yon stifled wall a low and frequent cry!

For good measure, in *Ecclesia*, where it was first published, in line six 'met' becomes 'meet' and in line seven 'For' (or 'But') becomes 'And'. But there is already enough to contend with.

The small differences completely alter the point of this gruesome little tale. Mrs F.'s maid, even though her brow is sunny rather than hooded (and yon gnarled oak fresh rather than simply young), plans to emulate St Ursula, to keep her virginity. She and the priest will sigh and then, by implication, part. But intruders interpret otherwise. The fate of maid and priest, a slow death by immurement, is not only appalling but undeserved. In the published version, she has no plans even to 'breathe', let alone to model herself upon, St Ursula: her intentions are quite otherwise. So (and this is intensified with the 'meet' in *Ecclesia*) the consequence of their meeting is a future given over to sighing, and quite right too, our stern moralising poet seems to be telling his readers.

The published form, 'Minster Church', was not reprinted by Hawker in the collection which he made in 1869: understandably, he must have been in quite a muddle with it. Nor does it appear in any of the selections made since the last complete *Ballads and Poems* edited by Byles in 1908. This is more surprising, because much merit remains. Hawker deploys the Spenserian Stanza with considerable skill. As the verses are rounded off with six-foot iambic alexandrines, they lend themselves to a series of pictures, linked but each complete in itself, as in 'The Faerie Queen', Keats's 'Eve of St Agnes', and Byron's 'Childe Harold'. The tales of Lord Bottreaux, the priest and the maid, and the ancient monk returning after the dissolution of the monastery, are entirely Hawker's inventions and may seem far-fetched and heavily Victorian-Romantic. But they do not seem so remote, let alone absurd, to a visitor to Minster Church, which stands in a solitary and beautiful setting in the woods above Boscastle. The adulation of the Bishop of Exeter, Henry Phillpotts, can safely be described as heartfelt – Hawker would have wanted to acknowledge at this early stage of his ministry that he owed him a great deal. Nor was there any reason why the bishop should ever know that this imposing eulogy comprised the sprucing up and adornment of an earlier poem. And after all, why not? The economy of effort arguably makes good sense: why write two poems when one will do? It is just something that I for one have not come across before.

Meanwhile, he and his wife were settling in to Morwenstow, and

66   I WOULD NOT BE FORGOTTEN

this undated statement of his daily routine might have been written at almost any time between their arrival in 1835 and her death in 1863, but probably before his hut was built in about 1843: otherwise their evening visits there would surely have had a place.

> All working days. Sundays included.
> I see my animals and glebe and people who call, until eleven.
> Then into parish with Mrs H., or alone as she can or not.
>   Home. Dine at once. About one o'clock.
>   Till three o'clock, read and write.
>   Church again.
>   Walk by sea.
>   Home again, reading and writing till ten.
>   To Mrs H. and bed.
>   Read until midnight.[27]

Those walks, and his times in the hut, must have provided direct inspiration for the numerous poems he wrote about the sea. His affection for the sea, his craving indeed when he was away at boarding school, was apparent in *Tendrils*. He wrote a fine sonnet in 1835, 'Pater Vester Pascit Illa' ('Your father cares for her'), or as he originally more matter-of-factly entitled it 'A Bird Shot At Sea'. One is immediately impressed by the tautness and control: an exultant family in a boat far out at sea, 'wide around, The wandering wave', and the excitement of shooting the bird, which is plucked from the sea by its 'lank wing'. Still within the octave, by contrast, the dead creature will be desperately missed somewhere far away. The sestet echoes this back, with the power and violence of the Creation, macrocosm of the bounding boat and the gun, set against the love of a creator who provides a home for 'this nameless bird', victim of a thoughtless deed. I find it a marvel of construction.

It is not however a marvel of editing. Here again is the inexplicable problem. People like his son-in-law, and his close friend J. G. Godwin, who cared intensely about Hawker and admired him as a poet so much that they took pains to put together collections of his poems, could print them with mistakes in the text which wrench the meaning awry or, as in this case, leave that text completely meaningless. Even more astonishing, Hawker himself in his 1869 edition could leave

'PATER VESTER PASCIT ILLA'

Our bark is on the waters! wide around,
The wandering wave; above, the lonely sky.
Hush! A young sea-bird floats, and that quick cry
Shrieks to the levelled weapon's echoing sound:
Grasp its lank wing, and on, with reckless bound!
Yet, creature of the surf, a sheltering breast
To-night shall haunt in vain thy far-off nest,
A call unanswered search the rocky ground.
Lord of Leviathan! When Ocean heard
Thy gathering voice, and sought his native breeze;
When whales first plunged with life, and the proud deep
Felt unborn tempests heave in troubled sleep;
Thou didst provide, e'en for this nameless bird,
Home, and a natural love, amid the surging seas.

❊ ❊ ❊ ❊ ❊

patent errors in his own work uncorrected. Here, the text printed in
Ecclesia in 1840 under the further choice of title, 'Sonnet of the Sea',
is surely accurate.

> Hush! a young sea-bird floats, and that quick cry
> Shrieks to the levelled weapon's echoing sound:
> Grasp its lank wing, and on! with reckless bound.

'Grasp its lank wing' is an order, from within the boat. However,
every edition that follows *Ecclesia* provides a comma rather than a
colon at the end of the previous line and then reads

> Grasps its lank wing, and on, with reckless bound!

I challenge anyone to make sense of it, with that 's' crept in at the
end of 'grasp'. Just conceivably, 'that quick cry' could be the subject

of 'grasps', the person who cries also grasping the wing. But the cry is the bird's, dramatically simultaneous with the sound of the gun, and in any event, when did a cry last grasp anything? One might perhaps work harder at such an interpretation, were the poem not printed in a way that makes admirable sense in *Ecclesia*. More likely, one would lose interest and give up, because it is irritating to read a poem that is incomprehensible. One begins to wonder whether the neglect of Hawker the poet might be principally the fault of his editors, and to feel thoroughly disgruntled with them.

Calm of mind can be restored by a modest poem of three verses, published in 1836, called 'The Western Shore' – originally 'Cornwall'. Here is Hawker in a humble, gentle, contented mood, loving his native land and rejoicing that he lives within it. He has given up ambition, time's cold touch controls the volcano of his soul, he is happy to be lost to the world, incorporated with the 'wild rock and lonely shore, Where round my days dark seas shall roar'. This calm of mind may or may not have been genuine but was certainly short of staying power, perhaps understandably so, given a poet of thirty-three with a wife in her fifties. It is interesting that he produced an altered version of the poem, entitled 'Lava', in 1864, the time of his second marriage. The volcano discovered new energy.

First however, a poem in a different mood, but still not divorced from calm, deserves to be looked at. It is actually about a very savage sea, but Hawker paradoxically implies a contentedness with his fate, as he looks out over the amazing seascape from Morwenstow's cliffs. It is called 'The Storm', and describes just that, with an overlay of personification which finally transmutes into an utterance of praise to God. Unusually, among poems about a stormy sea, it is not simultaneously about the poet. Everyone – surely? – responds to a stormy sea. Certainly it is a common sight on the North Cornish coast, people who may not habitually pause for contemplation staring as if mesmerised at the waves crashing on the rocks. The sea inspires thoughtfulness, perhaps of the human's puniness in the face of it: indeed as the human's awareness intensifies he may involuntarily take a step back. Certainly the observer, thinker, poet, is relating the spectacle to himself. This is true for example of Byron:

THE WESTERN SHORE

Thou lovely land! where, kindling, throng
Scenes that should breathe the soul of song;
Home of high hopes that once were mine
Of loftier verse and nobler line!

'Tis past – the quench'd volcano's tide
Sleeps well within the mountain-side;
Henceforth shall time's cold touch control
The warring Hecla of my soul.

Welcome! wild rock and lonely shore,
Where round my days dark seas shall roar;
And thy gray fane, Morwenna, stand
The beacon of the Eternal Land!

❀　❀　❀　❀　❀

There is society, where none intrudes,
By the deep sea, and music in its roar.[28]

Similarly John Betjeman, who wrote so memorably about
Cornwall, and acknowledged Hawker as 'a magnificent sea-poet, a
poet of storms and crises', describes a scene which might even suggest
that he had been reading 'The Storm':

Tide after tide by night and day
The breakers battle with the land
And rounded smooth along the bay
The faithful rocks protecting stand.

Then Betjeman brings in himself:

> But in a dream the other night
> I saw this coastline from the sea
> And felt the breakers plunging white
> Their weight of waters over me.[29]

Of course it is very well done, but comparatively it is self-indulgent. Hawker is describing what he sees. He moralises briefly, seeing the rocks as symbols of faith (so much stronger than Betjeman's 'faithful rocks protecting'). But his main image, set in the first line, is of eternal warfare. He uses his favourite device of alliteration to some effect:

> They come! and shall they not prevail,
> The seething surge, the gathering gale?

In the third verse he introduces an ingenious antithesis to contrast the limits of the waves with that common anxiety that they will exceed those limits: perhaps a slight personal element here, the almost involuntary step back:

> Thus far, incalculable main!

He sets the hugeness and multitude of the waves against the insignificant lichen, which is quite unmoved by their attack, and personifies them, agonising in their failure to win the war. Finally, with marvellous skill, he introduces the sudden calm which can surprise the watcher and claims it as a sign of God's power, leaving the way open nonetheless for a continuation of the mystery:

> O Lord, thy footsteps are not known!

He never mentions himself, and perhaps this self-effacement explains why an exceptionally fine poem on a popular subject has never found fame. Hawker was himself justifiably pleased with it, publishing it four times in his lifetime.

This modesty, among the personal poems included in *Ecclesia*,

THE STORM

War, 'mid the ocean and the land!
The battle-field, Morwenna's strand,
Where rock and ridge the bulwark keep,
The giant-warders of the deep.

They come! and shall they not prevail,
The seething surge, the gathering gale?
They fling their wild flag to the breeze,
The banner of a thousand seas.

They come – they mount – they charge in vain,
Thus far, incalculable main!
No more! thine hosts have not o'erthrown
The lichen on the barrier stone.

Have the rocks faith, that thus they stand,
Unmoved, a grim and stately band,
And look, like warriors tried and brave,
Stern, silent, reckless, o'er the wave?

Have the proud billows thoughts and life,
To feel the glory of the strife;
And trust, one day, in battle bold,
To win the foeman's haughty hold?

Mark where they writhe with pride and shame,
Fierce valour, and the zeal of fame!
Hear how their din of madness raves,
The baffled army of the waves!

Thy way, O God, is in the sea,
Thy paths, where awful waters be;
Thy spirit thrills the conscious stone:
O Lord, thy footsteps are not known!

was not due to last, nor indeed was the calm of mind in whatever form. The poems concerned with Christian teaching, of which 'Modryb Marya' was designed to be a foretaste, are a different matter and will be looked at separately. First we ought to consider two more in the 'personal' category, in which Hawker's capacity for self-pity, first noticed in 'Minster Church', breaks the surface. 'The Token Stream of Tidna Combe' relates to the river, or stream, Tidna, which runs down a steep valley into the sea half a mile down the coast from Morwenstow. Looking inland from the dramatically named Tidna Shute where it forms a spectacular waterfall over the cliffs, one can see most of the river's short course. So it lends itself particularly to the purposes of a poet who wishes to see his life in symbolic or token terms, even though it is now too overgrown to enable one to check, if one had a mind to, the accuracy of the stages which he describes.

The first three verses contain some of the finest and least effective of Hawker's poetry. Consistency was not a quality that he admired, nor did he practise it, in either the expression of his ideas or the quality of his poetry. The lack of Drinkwater's 'neighbourly authority' is nowhere more apparent. He sets the scene of a childhood paradise. The most timid creature, needing complete quiet and lack of threat, will find it.

> The loneliest bird, that flees to waste or wild,
> Might fold its feathers here in peace to drink.

The sensuous detail of the second line recalls his affection for birds and his exaltation of them, *ubi aves ibi angeli*, and offers a wonderfully appropriate emblem of peace. Then in the very next verse he recalls 'When earth looked e'en on me with tranquil mien', and takes us back at least a century in stylistic terms, to Thomas Gray's statement that 'The language of the age can never be the language of poetry': admirably practised by Gray, disastrously imitated by so many of his successors, and Hawker is on the list. This may seem a lot of opprobrium to inflict on one poor line, but alas, he wrote plenty like it, and one has to acknowledge that his poetry at its least satisfactory must have seemed anachronistic in his own time.

THE TOKEN STREAM OF TIDNA COMBE

A source of gentle waters, mute and mild,
    A few calm reeds around the sedgy brink,
The loneliest bird, that flees to waste or wild,
    Might fold its feathers here in peace to drink.

I do remember me of such a scene,
    Far in the depths of memory's glimmering hour,
When earth looked e'en on me with tranquil mien,
    And life gushed, like this fountain in her bower.

But lo! A little on, a gliding stream,
    Fed with fresh rills from fields before unknown,
Where the glad roses on its banks may dream
    The watery mirror spreads for them alone.

Ah! Woe is me! that flood, those flowers, recall
    A gleaming glimpse of Time's departed shore,
Where now no dews descend, no sunbeams fall,
    And leaf and blossom burst, no more, no more!

See now! With heart more stern, and statelier force,
    Through Tidna's vale the river leaps along;
The strength of many trees shall guard its course,
    Birds in the branches soothe it with their song.

O type of a far scene! The lovely land
    Where youth wins many a friend, and I had one;
Still do thy bulwarks, dear old Oxford, stand?
    Yet, Isis, do thy thoughtful waters run?

But hush! A spell is o'er thy conscious wave,
    Pause and move onward with obedient tread;
At yonder wheel they bind thee for their slave,
    Hireling of man, they use thy toil for bread.

Still is thy stream an image of the days
    At duty's loneliest labour meekly bound;
The foot of joy is hush'd, the voice of praise,
     We twain have reached the stern and anxious
                    ground.

And now what hills shall smile, what depths remain,
    Thou tamed and chastened wanderer, for thee?
A rocky path, a solitary plain
    Must be thy broken channel to the sea.

Come then, sad river, let our footsteps blend
    Onward, by silent bank, and nameless stone:
Our years began alike, so let them end, -
    We live with many men, we die alone.

Why dost thou slowly wind and sadly turn,
    As loth to leave e'en this most joyless shore?
Doth thy heart fail thee? Do thy waters yearn
    For the far fields of memory once more?

Ah me! My soul, and thou art treacherous too,
    Linked to this fatal flesh, a fettered thrall:
The sin, the sorrow, why would'st thou renew?
    The past, the perish'd, vain and idle all!

Away! Behold at last the torrent leap,
    Glad, glad to mingle with yon foamy brine;
Free and unmourn'd the cataract cleaves the steep –
    O river of the rocks, thy fate is mine!

* * * * *

He descends into a gloom, realising that those days can never be recalled, but as the Tidna gathers pace he commemorates the happiness of Oxford. After that we move immediately and relentlessly into the slow indeterminate slavery of his ministry:

> The foot of joy is hush'd, the voice of praise,
> We twain have reached the stern and anxious ground.

We twain, poet and stream, can expect no further happiness, as we reach 'a solitary plain', realising that 'We live with many men, we die alone'. Charlotte, waiting at home, is forgotten, as the serious tedium sets in. Death is not easily available at the age of thirty-seven, so he visualises a course of remaining life which will 'slowly wind and sadly turn, As loth to leave e'en this most joyless shore'.

One can mock the subject matter of a poet who is surely a little young to be so obsessed with this particular brand of misery. But the quality of the poetry, despite the odd anachronistic lapse heavily noted earlier, principally demands respect. For example in the last two verses Hawker, having up to that point blended his life with its 'token', turns exclusively upon himself, the treachery of his soul, slave (repeating an earlier image) of his body which insists on continuing to live as the stream postpones its final plunge. He seems savagely angry with himself for recalling nostalgically 'The sin, the sorrow': the past is dead, and so to final death,

> Free and unmourn'd, the cataract cleaves the steep –
> O river of the rocks, thy fate is mine!

One might hope that a poem written at much the same time with the bounding title 'Home Once More!' might be a little more cheerful, but alas, no. Hawker is returning to Morwenstow after a period of absence, an unusual circumstance in itself. While welcoming the familiar scene, he finds that he has changed from the dynamic young man who first came there. The signs of vigour 'are fled – and in their room Thought thickens all things into gloom'. He compares himself to Bishop Ridley, waiting in prison to be burnt at the stake:

HOME ONCE MORE!

Home! home once more! and every tree
Looks with familiar face on me:
A smile comes o'er the accustomed hill,
A voice of welcome from the rill.

Home! home once more! but where are now
The bounding breast and brightening brow,
The footstep firm, the bearing bold,
Wherewith I trod these scenes of old?

These all are fled – and in their room
Thought thickens all things into gloom;
Along this path the listener hears
Feet heavy with the toil of years.

Yet cleaves my soul to this dear glen,
The old remembrance lives again,
The scene sighs with its former breath,
Like that old Ridley loved in death.

Here did I chaunt to many a wind,
The themes of God's eternal mind;
While the deep stream and thrilling birds
Made music 'mid those mighty words.

Here, oracles an echo found
Breathed, far away on Syrian ground,
By prophet-bards to whom were given
The lore and poetry of Heaven.

Here, too, would dreamy thoughts recall
Gesture and tone of saintly Paul,
Till fancy heard the iron bands
That shook upon his lifted hands.

All, all is gone – no longer roll
Vision and dream around my soul:
But, in their stead, float down the wind
These fragments of a broken mind.

Still, home once more; for in this dell
The dust of love will fondly dwell;
And scenes so dear in life shall hide
The hearts that death could not divide.

✻　✻　✻　✻　✻

a hint presumably of his own impending demise. The epigraph from Jeremiah comprises in *Ecclesia* the poem's title, 'They shall flee every one to his own land'. This is puzzling. It is part of a passage in which Jeremiah foresees the imminent destruction of Babylon and exhorts the Children of Israel, in exile there, to depart before the invasion by 'an assembly of great nations from the north country'. In Hawker's cosmology, as becomes apparent in 'The Quest of the Sangraal', the north was inhabited by demons, so it appears that Babylon is due to be replaced by something worse. Is he equating Morwenstow with Babylon? He is finding a refuge there, from a wicked and also dangerously threatened world, but he is returning in a state of enfeeblement and distress, 'All, all is gone'. However one interprets it, one is left with a desperately unhappy poem. The final verse provides rare involvement of his first wife Charlotte. They will die together, among 'scenes so dear to life'. When at the age of sixty he met his twenty year old second wife Pauline, he wrote some very attractive, indeed positively racy, love poems to and about her. Charlotte was twenty years older than he, and admirable and devoted woman as she undoubtedly was, her company does not appear to have been a persistent source of invigoration. This will not have helped.

The chapter should end on a more optimistic note, albeit an ambivalent one. In 1922 Hawker's son-in-law and biographer C. E.

Byles edited a small book entitled *Stones Broken from the Rocks, Extracts from the Manuscript Note-books of Robert Stephen Hawker, Vicar of Morwenstow 1834-1875*. These note-books, or Thought Books as Hawker himself preferred to call them, will need more attention, but at this moment the title is significant. In 'Home Once More!' he wrote of 'These fragments of a broken mind' replacing the visions of his younger days, and he returned to the phrase more than once later, in gloomy moments, particularly relating to his Thought Books: 'Perhaps one day they may be read and printed as the "Fragments of a broken mind"'. But in 1846 he wrote more cheerfully, '"Stones Broken from the Rocks" – a good title for these MSS', and in due course Byles must have been happy to comply. Here is exemplified both Hawker's violent vacillations of mood which caused him such unhappiness, and more precisely his recurrent concern with rocks, matching those vacillations, symbolising his feelings of exile, and also of the strength, security, comfort almost, with which Morwenstow provided him. He wrote of 'The Song of the Western Men', 'All these years the Song has been bought and sold, set to music and applauded, while I have lived on among these faraway rocks unprofited, unpraised and unknown'. But in 'The Storm' the rocks fight back the sea and protect the land, they are 'The giant-warders of the deep'; and most notably of all, in 'Morwennae Statio' he describes his church as 'a daughter of the rock', founded upon it, built with it, and conjoined with Christ's charge to St Peter, 'Thou art Peter, and upon this rock I will build my church'. In the third verse Hawker writes of Morwenstow's builders:

> Huge, mighty, massive, hard, and strong,
> Were the choice stones they lifted then:
> The vision of their hope was long,
> They knew their God, those faithful men.

The Vicar of Morwenstow was profoundly aware of this inheritance, and much of his poetry, especially in *Ecclesia*, takes up the theme.

4

The Churchman and the Mystic

Nicholas Ross, an outstanding student of Hawker's work, wrote in 1963 to Hawker's bibliographer Cecil Woolf, 'He was thinking as a Roman Catholic from about 1845'. In that very year Hawker described, with an originality and vividness remarkable even for him, the effect on a communicant of the Eucharist:

After it is swallowed down He remains with us – permeates – imbues and imbathes, glides through our bodily frame as the light within a crystal lamp will beam all over the glass. Thus as we walk from the chancel the angels behold in every one of us a lamp kindled within and without with the presence of God.[1]

Such richness of description is actually much more. We cannot begin to understand Hawker unless we appreciate that he believed himself to be constantly surrounded by spiritual beings, providing for him almost tangible evidence of the truth of his Christian convictions. Nor was he diffident about proclaiming the fact. From this belief derives much of his reputation for eccentricity. It simultaneously bears witness to the totality of his faith.

The first of a set of religious poems which will be considered in this chapter, all but one published in 1840 in *Ecclesia*, is entitled 'Ephphatha'. The word is Hebrew and means 'be opened, be made clear', hence 'knowledge'. Twelve years later Hawker described a vision that came to him in the chancel of Morwenstow church, where he habitually conferred with angels.

Deep in thought I saw, not with eyes, but with my whole body, a grave calm noble form in white. He said, or breathed, this phrase, 'Ephphatha is good but Amen is better still'. I went away with this saying in my mind for long before I understood its force. At last in chancel too it came to me that in the Mysteries 'be opened', 'be made clear', is not so churchlike or so happy for a Christian mind as 'so it is', 'so let it be'. 'Knowledge', in this portal of the Church Universal, Life, is not so desirable as 'Acquiescence'.[2]

He goes on to define more generally the value to him of these visionary moments.

I live afar off from books and society of men. Beyond the boundary of Morwenstow I very seldom go. My own volumes are but few. And yet, strange to say, there is hardly a point of doctrine which I am fain to know but I receive it in clear and beautiful words as the lightning leaps from the dark cloud suddenly.

More will need to be said about this spectacular means of acquiring scholarship: first, to return to the poem of the name, 'Ephphatha'. It is not actually one of the poet's more successful efforts although one might not agree with Margaret Burrows that 'it would be difficult to find a more unenterprising verse than the first one of 'Ephphatha".[3] Hawker seems not to have been happy writing couplets, achieving an easier flow with more complex rhyme schemes. The setting is confusing. We are not in a church, we are in a hall, setting for a lady and her 'youthful page' Ronald, but 'the Baptist's festival' is being celebrated, and the patron saints of Morwenstow church are jointly Morwenna and John the Baptist, with St John's Well standing nearby. On a more positive note, the poem exemplifies Hawker's ability to encapsulate in a Christian context the pathos, allied with the wisdom, of old age, contrasted as it is here with the carelessness of youth. Ronald must have wished that he had never opened his mouth.

Very much more significantly, the light, 'the glorious radiance', shining first on the old man's bread and water and then on Ronald's bread and wine as he takes communion, constitutes 'the Real Presence'. If this is not clear in the poem, Hawker characteristically employs a footnote to spell it out, or to be precise he employs two, one in *Ecclesia* in 1840, one in *Echoes from Old Cornwall* six years later. The overall effect is doctrinally baffling. Both notes need to be quoted, first from *Ecclesia*.

I have sought in these verses, to suggest a shadow of the beautiful instruction to Christian men, the actual and spiritual presence of our Lord in the second sacrament of his church; a primal and perpetual doctrine in the faith once delivered to the Saints. How sadly the simplicity

EPHPHATHA

High matins now in bower and hall!
It is the Baptist's festival:
What showers of gold the sunbeams rain,
Through the tall window's purple pane!
What rich hues on the pavement lie,
A molten rainbow from the sky!

But light and shadow loveliest fall
Yonder, along the southward wall,
Where ceased, e'en now, the chaunted hymn
Of that grey man whose eyes are dim:
'Twas an old legend, quaintly sung,
Caught from some far barbaric tongue.

He asks, and bread of wheat they bring;
He thirsts for water from the spring
Which flowed of old and still flows on,
With name and memory of St John:
So fares the pilgrim in that hall,
E'en on the Baptist's festival.

"How sad a sight is blind old age!"
Thus said the lady's youthful page:
"He eats, but sees not on that bread
What glorious radiance there is shed;
He drinks from out that chalice fair,
Nor marks the sunlight glancing there."

"Watch! Gentle Ronald, watch and pray!
And hear once more an old man's lay:
I cannot see the morning pour'd
Ruddy and rich on this gay board;
I may not trace the noonday light,
Wherewith my bread and bowl are bright:

But thou, whose words are sooth, hast said,
That brightness falls on this fair bread;
Thou sayest – and thy tones be true –
This cup is tinged with heaven's own hue:
I trust thy voice; I know from thee
That which I cannot hear nor see.

Watch! gentle Ronald, watch and pray!
It is the Baptist's holy day!
Go, where in old Morwenna's shrine,
They break the bread and bless the wine;
There meekly bend thy trusting knee,
And touch what sight can never see.

Thou wilt behold, thy lips may share
All that the cup and paten bear;
But life unseen moves o'er that bread,
A glory on that wine is shed;
A light comes down to breathe and be,
Though hid, like summer suns, from me.

Watch! gentle Ronald, watch and pray!
Day oft is night and night is day:
The arrowy glance of lady fair
Beholds not things that throng the air;
The clear bright eye of youthful page
Hath duller ken than blind old age."

'Tis evensong in bower and hall
On the bold Baptist's festival;
The harp is husht and mute the hymn,
The guest is gone whose eyes are dim,
But evermore to Ronald clung
That mystic measure, quaintly sung.

of this hath and has been distorted by the gross and sensuous notion of a carnal presence introduced by the Romish innovators of the eleventh century!

By 1846 it appears that, as Nicholas Ross suggests, Hawker has begun his long journey towards the Roman Catholic church. 'The Romish innovators' are no longer taken to task, and Hawker expresses himself more briefly and, superficially, more simply.

I have sought in these verses, to suggest the manner of that miraculous event, the actual and etherial presence of Our Lord in the second sacrament of his church.

Actually it is if anything more baffling, not more simple. The 'carnal presence', the miraculous transformation of the bread and wine into the body and blood of Jesus Christ, is surely a fundamental doctrine of the Roman Catholic church, and a matter of fundamental dispute with for example the Church of England with its belief in 'the spiritual food'. Hawker, it seems, equates the two: 'actual and spiritual', 'actual and etherial'. This blithe melding together of two such disputatious views suggests something like high-handed doctrinal carelessness. It must also have simplified his deathbed conversion.

High-handed and careless he may have been, or more sympathetically one can describe him, again, as very much his own man. As such he was outwardly confident, in most respects and certainly over doctrinal matters, whether his knowledge was acquired from angels in the chancel or from his limited supply of books. In broader terms one sometimes senses the lack of Drinkwater's 'neighbourly authority' – someone among his rocks, an intellectual equal, to question his certainties.

To return to the chapter's starting point, whatever he may have meant by the Real Presence he certainly believed most fervently in the presence of Christ at the Eucharist. He would never preach then, 'in my Master's presence', and he expressed himself strongly if obliquely about priests who did so. It was the priest's task first and foremost to present the Host to each communicant, and those who encouraged the custom of passing the bread and wine down the line at the altar-rail were simply finding a means of saving time so as to enable them to preach, which they had no business to do. He was never too charitable about the motives of clergy whose observances differed from his. Since that amounted to every clergyman within his range, his letters in particular are filled with such deprecatory comments, which are often of course very entertaining.

Anyone capable of writing 'The Signals of Levi' might perhaps be forgiven for looking a little loftily at his clerical colleagues. Here is an immensely successful poem. Yet it is neglected, like most of the rest whether good bad or indifferent, never for example being selected for an anthology of Victorian verse, though Hawker does generally achieve meagre representation. The poem, in its three parts, is a celebration of the first and second coming of Christ. The setting in each part is the same, a watchman in Jerusalem at dawn looking out for the moment when Hebron, twenty miles to the south, became visible, then giving the signal for the daily oblation or sacrifice to begin. In 'Signal the First' the watchman is a Levite, and the scene is raucous, as 'both prince and priest' assemble to rejoice that the Messiah had not been born that night, the time foretold: so the throne is left for Herod and the sacrifice, the party, can begin. 'Signal the Second', predictably but with wonderful sensitivity, announces that he has been born, in Bethlehem which stands between Jerusalem and Hebron. The last verse of the one and the first of the other can be quoted to mark the contrast, made by a poetic craftsman.

> How they throng the cloistered ground
> Mid Judah's shame and sin:
> Hark to the trumpet-sound!
> Let the sacrifice begin.
>
> There is light on Hebron's towers,
> Day dawns o'er Jordan's stream,
> And it floats where Bethlehem's bowers
> Of the blessed morning dream.

Then in 'Signal the Third' it seems that we all, poet and readers, are asking the 'Christian soldier', no longer the Levite, what he sees as day dawns and he describes a heaven on earth, the Second Coming.

THE SIGNALS OF LEVI

Signal the First

There is light on Hebron now:
    Hark to the trumpet din!
Day dawns on Hebron's brow,
    Let the sacrifice begin.

Hear ye the gathering sound!
    How the lute and harp rejoice,
'Mid the roar of oxen bound,
    And the lamb's beseeching voice.

This day both prince and priest
    Will hold at Salem's shrine
A high and haughty feast
    Of flesh and the ruddy wine.

For a perilous hour is fled,
    And the fear is vain at last,
Though foretold by sages dead,
    And sworn by the Prophets past.

They said that a mortal birth
    E'en now would a Name unfold
That should rule the wide, wide earth,
    And quench the thrones of old.

But no sound, nor voice, nor word,
    The tale of travail brings;
Not an infant cry is heard
    In the palaces of kings.

Blossom and branch are bare
    On Jesse's stately stem:
So they bid swart Edom wear
    Fallen Israel's diadem.

How they throng the cloistered ground
    'Mid Judah's shame and sin:
Hark to the trumpet-sound!
    Let the sacrifice begin.

Signal the Second

There is light on Hebron's towers,
　Day dawns o'er Jordan's stream,
And it floats where Bethlehem's bowers
　Of the blessèd morning dream.

Yet it wakes no kingly halls,
　It cleaves no purple room;
The soft, calm radiance falls
　On a cavern's vaulted gloom.

But there, where the oxen rest
　When the weary day is done,
How that maiden-mother's breast
　Thrills with her Awful Son!

A cave where the fatlings roam,
　By the ruddy heifer trod,
Yea! The mountain's rifted home
　Is the birthplace of a God!

This is He! the mystic birth
　By the sign and voice foretold;
He shall rule the wide, wide earth,
　And quench the thrones of old.

The Child of Judah's line,
　The son of Abraham's fame:
Arise, ye lands! and shine
　With the blessèd Jesu's name.

This is the glorious dawn:
　So fades the night of sin;
Lo! the gloom of death is gone,
　Let the sacrifice begin.

Signal the Third

"Oh! watchman! what of the night?
　Tell, Christian soldier, tell:
Are Hebron's towers in sight?
　Hast thou watched and warded well?"

"Yea; we have paced the wall
　Till the day-star's glimmering birth;
And we breathed our trumpet-call
　When the sunlight waked the earth."

"What sawest thou with the dawn?
　Say, Christian warder, say:
When the mists of night were gone,
　And the hills grew soft with day?"

"We beheld the morning swell
　Bright o'er the eastern sea;
Till the rushing sunbeams fell
　Where the westward waters be.

City and bulwark lay
　Rich with the orient blaze,
And rocks, at the touch of day,
　Gave out a sound of praise.

No hill remained in cloud,
　There lurked no darkling glen;
And the voice of God was loud
　Upon every tongue of men.

There shall never more be night
　With this eternal sun;
There be Hebrons many in sight,
　And the sacrifice is done!"

No hill remained in cloud,
   There lurked no darkling glen;
And the voice of God was loud
   Upon every tongue of men.

* * * * *

This poem bears comparison with anything of its scale written in the great age of English religious poetry which begins with Donne and moves through the seventeenth century taking in Milton, Herbert and Crashaw among others. Between them, it might be thought, they must have approached the Christian story from every conceivable angle. Yet here we have poor neglected Hawker two hundred years later expressing in a totally original way the achievement of Jesus Christ. Can anyone ask for more?

Another poem from *Ecclesia* that merits praise, at a more modest level, is ' "I Am the Resurrection and the Life!" Saith the Lord.' Hawker the humble parish priest is presiding over a funeral 'By fair Morwenna's walls of grey'. The cry of a cuckoo accompanies the words of the service: symbol and herald of the Resurrection as it is heard again every spring. Hawker is in resolutely moralistic mood, 'A doctrine dwells in that deep tone; A truth is borne on yonder wing'. Probably for that reason, and because of its clumsy title, the poem has never been popular. The title is in fact confused as well as clumsy. In *Ecclesia* there is an exclamation mark after 'Life', which is plainly right and which is retained by Godwin in 1879, but first Wallis in 1899 and then Byles in 1904 substitute a question mark, introducing a ludicrously inappropriate element of doubt, apparently in the mind of the Almighty. Here is a further example of Hawker's editors failing to take proper care of his poetry in print. One can only add that succeeding generations have effectively ignored it altogether.

The first three verses in particular invite comparison with Wordsworth's 'To the Cuckoo', written thirty-six years earlier: the same surprise, the same 'tale Of visionary hours', with the difference that Hawker's vision is of actual physical resurrection, while Wordsworth is less precise. His cuckoo is 'No bird, but an invisible

' "I AM THE RESURRECTION AND THE LIFE"
SAITH THE LORD!' May, 1840

We stood beside an opening grave,
By fair Morwenna's walls of grey:
Our hearts were hush'd – the God who gave
Had called a sister-soul away.
    Hark! What wild tones around us float:
    The chaunting cuckoo's double note!

We uttered there the solemn sound –
"Man that is born from flesh of Eve,
The banished flower of Eden's ground,
Hath but a little time to live;" –
    And still, amid each pausing word,
    The strange cry of that secret bird.

"Ashes to ashes – dust to dust" –
The last farewell we sadly said.
Our mighty hope – our certain trust –
The resurrection of the dead.
    Again, all air, it glides around,
    A voice! – the spirit of a sound.

A doctrine dwells in that deep tone;
A truth is borne on yonder wing;
Long years! long years! The note is known –
The blessèd messenger of spring!
    Thus saith that pilgrim of the skies:
    "Lo! all which dieth shall arise!"

Rejoice! though dull with wintry gloom
Love's sepulchre and sorrow's night,
The sun shall visit depth and tomb
A season of eternal light!
    Like the glad bosom of the rose,
    The mound shall burst – the grave unclose!

Yea! soothed by that unvarying song
What generations here have trod!
What winds have breathed that sound along,
Fit signal of the changeless God!
    Hark! yet again the echoes float,
    The chaunting cuckoo's double note!

thing, A voice, a mystery', while Hawker, retaining the mystery – 'the secret bird', 'the spirit of a sound' – enrols the bird to express a Christian doctrine. Such overt didacticism is unlikely to have a wide appeal, even though the doctrine is hopeful and joyful, supported by a vivid simile of a flowering rose and an opening grave. Wordsworth's simple childlike romantic poem is by contrast a universal favourite. To employ a modern concept one is left wondering, if Hawker had handled his public relations as effectively as Wordsworth did, would this poem too have lasted?

He remained a country priest, in a corner of England which is still remote. It is indeed an irony that such fame as it has derives from him. His poetry and more notably his letters often depict a tumultuously frustrated and discontented man, yet for much of the time he attended reverently to his calling, caring for his parish and its people as season followed season and year followed year. Hawker the parish priest and pastor has received attention already in earlier chapters and will receive more, because this was his principal preoccupation for forty years of his life. Hawker the visionary, who met and spoke with angels in his church, was briefly glimpsed early in this chapter, 'Ephphatha is good but Amen is better still'. The two, dutiful priest and mystical visionary, came together with particular vividness when he conducted baptisms. A member of his congregation provides a picture of him in 1874, a year before he died.

Mr Hawker's sermons on Sundays made a deep impression on us, they were so out of the common, and under them all lay that feeling and belief in spiritual beings and existences to which I referred. I remember, at Morwenstow, I stood as sponsor for a child at baptism, and afterwards Mr Hawker preached on the baptism – his subject was guardian angels – he described most vividly a scene in heaven as a guardian angel was chosen to care for the newly baptised infant – the descent of the angel – his hovering round the font at the baptism – it was all so vividly described that you felt it was something the vicar had seen himself, and one involuntarily glanced round to look for the presence of the angelic being.[4]

Hawker himself described these visionary proceedings in a passage from a Thought Book, designed no doubt for incorporation in a sermon.

You bring within your arms a little child, the offspring of parents on earth, overshadowed with the hue of original guilt – angels enter with your concourse at the door, and one ministering angel unassigned. One by one, as the introductory prayers are said, angelic movements occur. They glide in their courses along the aisles and roof. The angel of the church is in command. In their eyes, the child is dark, the waters dull and dim.

But at Consecration light flashes around the font and flows from the water like a sudden radiance of dawn. At the instant of Baptism the water falls gleamy with God upon the infant brow. The babe grows bright. The halo of the baptised surrounds its voiceless form. The angel touches its lip and clings to it with guardian wing.[5]

One must add here in parenthesis that the mention of an angel's wing is surprising, since elsewhere Hawker is very specific:

Angels have no wings: not a single feather. Whensoever in the Old Testament or the New Testament they actually appear, they are expressly said to be 'young men in white garments': not to be distinguished by the patriarchs from other youthful guests, and so entertained unawares . . . Wings, moreover, are to me destructive of all poetry of motion from place to place. They imply effort. The angels glide on the chariots and horses of their own desires. One in Syria is fain to be in Egypt, and immediately is there; just as we think in one scene of a distant spot, and at once our minds behold it without consciousness of the space between.[6]

In his only poem exclusively about angels, in *Ecclesia*, a distressingly feeble brief effort called 'Are They Not All Ministering Spirits?', wings are in fact included; but in one of the finest verses of his greatest poetic achievement, 'The Quest of the Sangraal', there is no doubt. The angels, the young men, are wingless, as their presence in the home of Joseph of Arimathea is described.

> He dwelt in Orient Syria: God's own land:
> The ladder foot of heaven – where shadowy shapes
> In white apparel glided up and down.
> His home was like a garner, full of corn,
> And wine and oil; a granary of God!
> Young men, that no one knew, went in and out,
> With a far look in their eternal eyes!
> All things were strange and rare . . .

'ARE THEY NOT ALL MINISTERING SPIRITS?'

We see them not – we cannot hear
 The music of their wing –
Yet know we that they sojourn near,
 The Angels of the spring!

They glide along this lovely ground,
 When the first violet grows;
Their graceful hands have just unbound
 The zone of yonder rose!

I gather it for thy dear breast,
 From stain and shadow free,
That which an Angel's touch hath blest
 Is meet, my love, for thee!

❊　❊　❊　❊　❊

So, wings or no wings? It is surprising that his accounts of these
creatures, so precious to him, lack consistency, but Hawker never set
much store on that particular virtue, indeed he wrote '. . . no man
can be called [inconsistent] unless he adopts two conflicting opinions
at the same time; if he allows five minutes to intervene . . . then he is
only contrasting his sentiments to avoid monotony, which is always
vapid and tiresome'.[7] Byles adds rather sternly after quoting that
passage, 'There is many a true word spoken in jest, and in this confession
of faith as regards consistency we may find the key to Hawker's clerical
career'. One can alternatively treat it as manageable, and part of his
charm. Even his descents into patent untruth are by no means always
serious. But a wary eye must be kept open.

He was consistent in his belief in a world of spirits, constantly
surrounding him: 'I firmly believe that the daily affairs of us all are
discussed among spirits and angels, and are helped or hindered by

them as usually as one earthly friend helps another. The angels hear what we say; read what we write. One is looking over my shoulder now.'[8] Equally precisely he writes:

. . . all the while we know, for it is revealed, that myriads of shapes, nothing but soul, come down, go up, glide close so as to touch us, occupy the arch of air, watch and ward us by command . . . How anyone can waver in this belief, or rather knowledge, if he reads the New Testament, to me is marvellous.[9]

He himself could not only see them, in his church and elsewhere. He describes in his Thought Books how they appeal to his other senses, writing of 'scented presence, lilied fragrance', and again, under the heading 'Faith':

We stretch forth our hands to feel the air and to find out what the ethereal space around us contains. At first there is nothing, our fingers close on our empty palms. By and by there is something soft and warm, we perceive that it is the touch of an angel.[10]

Demons were also vivid to him, 'They have a pitching place in the air, where an atmosphere of gloom expands like a vast tent. Thence they glide; thither return to recount the exploits of their sinful journey. Thence, perchance, pay periodic visits to their victims of Earth.'[11] Their manner of visitation is predictably more aggressive than that of their angelic counterparts. He describes a moment on a ride along the cliffs upon his pony Carrow: 'As I entered the gulf between the vallies today, a storm leaped from the sea and rushed at me roaring – I recognised a Demon and put Carrow into a gallop and so escaped. But it was perilous work.'[12] One Sunday morning in 1856, at the same spot, he saw something else:

That day the sky was silent with heat, and the whole scene was like a place where all was so lonely that hardly God was there; when all at once a swift, brown, rough shape started up among the gorse bushes, and rushed or glided towards the stream. I felt myself flush and then grow pale; but, remembering St Thomas's word that every creature must crouch to the Sign, I made it in the air, and rode as fast as I could urge the mare towards it. I saw its head disappear down the bank, and although I looked along the river and followed its course I caught sight of it no more. It was a kind of nameless and indefinable sensation, rather than the sight, that assured me it was preternatural: at least, so I thought, and think.[13]

It is a relief to find him writing to his friend William Maskell in the same year:

You tax me with being pixy-taught: 'I wish I war'. As once I said to an ancient woman, "They tell me you are a witch". "I wish I war," was the answer; "some on 'em should suffer."[14]

He was also not above employing his apparent power over demons to achieve his own ends.

My usual Xmas duties have received this year [1852] the addition of a vile rebellion in my parish of five farmers who have made a fruitless attempt to diminish the Church Rate. A Vestry was convened, over which I read the Exorcistic Service of the western church, in Latin of course. They knew not the meaning of the voice, but those who inhab-ited them did. The five fled from the room howling, as my deacon will attest, and my rate was forthwith carried by a majority of 24 to 1.[15]

Two further dimensions of Hawker the mystic and the visionary await description: both a great deal more impressive than the one just illustrated. First, he had a wonderful capacity for describing the human Jesus, as a child and as a growing man, in his family setting talking to his mother; and also for describing Mary, living with St John after the crucifixion. The passages concerned are not easy to find. He never published them: they are hidden in his Thought Books. There is one exception, a marvellous poem, 'Aishah Schechinah', of which more will be said in a moment. But a curious feature of Hawker's employment of his literary talent is that he offered very little for publication on certain themes which plainly were of profound importance to him. One is secular, the subject of shipwrecks, which will be dealt with in a separate chapter. Among religious themes, his devotion to Mary is recorded in 'Modryb Marya' which was discussed at the beginning of the last chapter; 'Aisha Schechinah' is about the incarnation and birth of Jesus, not about him as a boy; and 'Are They Not All Ministering Spirits?' deserves to be consigned to the parish magazine as John Drinkwater recommended. The second aspect of the mystic and visionary which calls for attention is his ecclesiography, his employment of the design of the church and its various parts to express symbolically the presence of God.

His insights into the family life of Jesus and Mary have a poignancy which is hard to find elsewhere. Yet they are scarcely known. The first passage to be quoted has been published, in *Stones Broken from the Rocks*, in the Preface to which C. E. Byles writes, 'Should this book find favour, it is hoped to publish further selections from the same source, and possibly a small volume of Hawker's extant sermons'. It did not find favour. Other examples, including the longer quotation, are to be found in the unpublished Thought Books lodged in the Bodleian Library. He may have used them in sermons in Morwenstow and Welcombe, but perhaps thought the descriptions too unsophisticated for the readers he hoped to find for his poetry in London and Oxford. If so, the more's the pity. Mary watches the child:

She watched him as he slept, and saw those infant arms howsoever she had placed them on the couch evermore move into the shape of the cross in dreams. And always as she knelt by the bed and hushed her very heart to listen for his breath she was aware that another life was awake in the room.[16]

Mary talks to Jesus about his nature, and then, when she lives with St John, recalls the conversation:

It was on a day when Our Lady sat by her wheel and span, and Lord Jesu for pastime was framing as his usage was a simple cross of the cedar and cypress wood that lay in fragments along the floor, that Mary looked up and said suddenly, 'Jesu, my son, in that faraway life of thine, whereof thou art wont to discourse, before there were any stars, when thou wert nothing but God, what was thy name?' Said the Lord tenderly and lovingly, 'Aisha, my nature was my name. I was he amid the Trinity through whom glided into life that which men call thought and utterance and deed. It was my ethereal essence which like a seashore bankless and boundless rolled into space, replenished with the thoughts and utterance of all of Godhead. Through me these travelled out of the Godhead into space. I was the mould of our imagery, the vesture, its sound and the very channel of its life. As thy thought O my mother is embodied in

thy mind and is then delivered to thy voice and will come forth, a thing
of life living and breathing as a word, even so in the Godhead came
forth the embodiment which was I. If there had been the language of
Adam, because Memra would have been our thought and our utterance
flowing into life through me only, my nature, Memra would have been
my name.'

Long years had passed. The cross had been lifted and lowered
again, and in the house of St John at Ephesus once more Our Lady
sat by her wheel and span. Now in her converse with the son of
Zebedee that disciple had searched her memory deeply and often for
the sayings of her son. But chiefly did he the Eagle of Galilee yearn
for tidings of that eternal and former existence which he had when
he was merely a God. And so it was that on a day she had rehearsed
to the listening evangelist the former nature and the eternal name
of the Lord Memra before he took the manhood into God, that then
said St John, these things are an oracle and must be revealed in the
Greek tongue. So they searched the language until they found the
phrase that would signify in Greek Memra the Hebrew name. It was
Logos verbum. The word alive. Thought and thing in blended imagery. Language and utterance beneath one native name.[17]

This same intimacy carries Hawker towards the centre of one of
the greatest Christian mysteries in 'Aishah Schechinah', written in
1859. He himself describes it as 'that poem wherein I am said to
have rehearsed the Incarnation in a way not yet found in the language'[18],
and his staunch friend and biographer F. G. Lee comments, 'Anything
more theologically accurate or poetically perfect could not be
conceived. In the whole range of English religious poetry I know
nothing at all to be compared to it.'[19]

The title calls for elucidation. It comprises two Hebrew words.
The meaning of Aisha, 'the happy name of Eve in the days of
innocence', is vividly defined by Hawker in his note on the poem,
which also contains another entrancing piece of dialogue between
Jesus and Mary. Schechinah is a more complex term. Hawker
associates it with numein, or numyne, which again needs definition.

They say it was a stately pillar, or column of soft and fleecy cloud, which
took ever and anon, as to Elias upon Carmel, the outline of a human
shape or form, vestigium hominis. Within its breast sojourned the glory of
the Presence, as in a tent.

At much this time he wrote to his neighbour Sir Thomas Acland:

Now my own element, mine by discovery: Numyne illustrates such a field of thought, that sacramental essence which pervades the cone of space, the woof of Schechinah and the atmosphere wherewithal angels fold their visible forms, the substance semi-material, semi-divine, the element which encompasses and pervades the universe, wherein light undulates and air glides, a network of spiritual and conscious life with gossamer threads that thrill with the attributes, the field or realm wherein mind and matter meet, the first created thing, caelum in the book of Genesis, i.e. spiritualises nature, said St Augustine. But this is a theme too vast for a note.[20]

Sir Thomas was probably not surprised; he must have known his man, they corresponded a good deal. Whether he comprehended is another matter. An unidentified visitor to Morwenstow was simply bewildered.

On one of our visits I was walking with the old man along the edge of the cliffs; it was getting latish in the summer and the stunted furze bushes were thickly draped with cobwebs. I observed to him that evidently the spiders had been busy. He stopped short, faced me and said, "My young friend, all that gossamer is not the work of spiders. This is the substance called numein, of which the angels' drapery is made." I never knew whether it was jest, or poetry, or credulity that prompted these quaint utterances.[21]

It may in this case have been a testy response to an inane remark. Numeyn or schechinah seems to mean the substance of the insubstantial, or the atmosphere, visible or not, in which a body with divine attributes is clothed.

Hawker in 'Aishah Schechinah' tackles a mystery the beginning and culmination of which, the Annunciation and the newborn Jesus with his mother, have persistently attracted artists. He seems to attempt more than they, to describe what happened in between. Immediately in the first verses he brings together the spiritual and the carnal, heaven and earth, God and Man, Mary who 'link'd' and 'blent' and was 'A chancel for the sky', the way to the altar and so to God. The unique gentleness of the process of gestation and birth is summed up in the repeated word 'folded', supported by the reiteration of soft consonant

AISHAH SCHECHINAH

A shape, like folded light, embodied air,
　　Yet wreath'd with flesh and warm;
All that of heaven is feminine and fair,
　　Moulded in visible form.

She stood, the Lady Schechinah of earth,
　　A chancel for the sky;
Where woke, to breath and beauty, God's own birth,
　　For men to see Him by.

Round her, too pure to mingle with the day,
　　Light, that was life, abode;
Folded within her fibres meekly lay
　　The link of boundless God.

So link'd, so blent, that when, with pulse fulfill'd,
　　Moved but that infant hand,
Far, far away, His conscious Godhead thrill'd,
　　And stars might understand.

Lo! where they pause, with intergathering rest,
　　The Threefold and the One!
And lo!　He binds them to her orient breast,
　　His Manhood girded on.

The Zone, where two glad worlds for ever meet,
　　Beneath that bosom ran:
Deep in that womb, the conquering Paraclete
　　Smote Godhead on to man!

Sole scene among the stars, where, yearning, glide
　　The Threefold and the One:
Her God upon her lap, the Virgin-Bride,
　　Her Awful Child, her Son.

sounds, and is then transformed into vigour with the marvellous concept of the child in the womb moving his hand for the first time, to be connected with his own divinity. Then, apparently at a specific moment, the third person of the Trinity makes God and child one, 'Deep in that womb the conquering Paraclete Smote Godhead on to man'. At the moment of birth the only thing that is happening in the universe is 'Her God upon her lap', the mystery which Lancelot Andrewes reached for, over two hundred years earlier, '*Verbum infans*, the Word without a word, unable to speak a word'.[22]

Surely, 'Aisha Schechinah' is a major piece of Christian poetry. Yet again we search for it in vain in anthologies.

Before moving on from the theme of 'The Churchman and the Mystic' – so far as one ever can, given that these components of Hawker's complex personality were central to his life – a relatively minor poem called 'The Vine' demands attention: both on its merits, as a well turned sonnet, but also as a means of introducing Hawker's ecclesiography, his employment of the church's design and its various features to express symbolically the presence of God.

Ecclesiography is a familiar component of religious poetry, definable as a form of allegory, and expressed at its most basic by John Betjeman writing of a favourite Cornish church, 'Why does St Endellion seem to go on praying when there is no one in it?'[23] George Herbert three hundred years earlier had found plentiful symbolism within a church, for example seeing Christian virtues in the pattern of the paving stones:

> Mark you the floore? that square and speckled stone,
> Which looks so firm and strong,
> Is Patience:
> And th' other black and grave, wherewith each one
> Is checker'd all along,
> Humilitie . . .[24]

William Wordsworth took up the theme in the early nineteenth century, with the difference that he was describing the design of his own work rather than that of the Almighty. Hawker would probably have found this amusing, for he lacked respect for the great man, expressing himself succinctly in his Thought Book of 1856, 'Wordsworth sought popularity'. Certainly, as has been suggested, Wordsworth's public relations were very much more effective than those of the Vicar of Morwenstow. He wrote in the Preface to 'The Excursion' (1814):

The two Works ['The Recluse' and 'The Excursion'] have the same kind of relation to each other, if he may so express himself, as the ante-chapel to the body of a gothic church. Continuing this allusion, he may be permitted to add, that his minor Pieces, which have been long before the public, when they shall be properly arranged, will be found by the attentive reader to have such connection with the main Work as may give them claim to be likened to the little cells, oratories, and sepulchral recesses, ordinarily included in such edifices.

The scene was set for the invention of this unlovely word, ecclesiography, and Hawker can claim to have been its inventor, though the OED records its first use in 1881. 'The Vine' when published in 1843 was actually entitled 'Ecclesiography', becoming 'The Stem and the Boughs' in 1846 and only acquiring in 1869 the name which it kept. As a poem it is nothing if not didactic, with the reader invited twice to hearken and once to heed the sign. It describes a feature of Morwenstow church, 'Amid the carved work of the roof, a vine', and develops an allegory of Christian life, the vine's roots by the altar, its foliage growing down the length of the building, producing more and more grapes until in the final couplet 'gather' carries a double meaning:

> So let a meek and faithful heart be thine,
> And gather from that tree a parable divine.

Here indeed is a prime example of ecclesiography, and several strands of Christian thought and expression seem to converge, which require consideration first before Hawker can be seen as a significant element in an important tradition.

Jesus taught through parables both as a means of clarifying his mission and also, as it were, to deflect from his listeners the effect of

THE VINE

Hearken! There is in old Morwenna's shrine,
    (A lonely sanctuary of the Saxon days,
    Rear'd by the Severn sea for prayer and praise,)
Amid the carved work of the roof, a vine;
    Its root is where the eastern sunbeams fall,
    First in the chancel, then along the wall
Slowly it travels on, a leafy line,
    With here and there a cluster, and anon
    More and more grapes, until the growth hath gone
Through arch and aisle. Hearken! and heed the sign.
    See! at the altar-side the steadfast root,
    Mark well the branches, count the summer fruit:
So let a meek and faithful heart be thine,
And gather from that tree a parable divine.

the full force of God's presence, which caused Moses to hide his face, and Isaiah to despair: 'Then said I, woe is me! for I am undone; because I am a man of unclean lips, and I dwell in the midst of a people of unclean lips: for mine eyes have seen the King, the Lord of hosts'.[25] Simultaneously, however critical he may have been of them – 'O ye of little faith' – Jesus gave to his immediate followers the privilege of understanding his teaching direct, without the need for parable, allegory, analogy, ecclesiography: 'It is given unto you to know the mysteries of the kingdom of heaven, but to them it is not given'.[26]

Priests and preachers through successive generations have addressed their congregations in such dichotomous terms: 'you are special because you are here in front of me, but nonetheless you (and if he is a modest priest 'and I') must appreciate that you/we have hardly even begun. I can talk to you straight, but to reach those who are not here, we must find an adapted simpler message, based perhaps on parable, allegory, analogy, ecclesiography …' It is not usually expressed with such rawness. However, Hawker's contemporaries, the

Tractarians, did not shirk the issue.

Hawker's links with the Tractarians, proponents of the Oxford Movement with its aim of reviving Catholic doctrine and observance within the Church of England, were at most tenuous. He admired and corresponded with the most famous of the leaders of the Oxford Movement, John Henry Newman, and indeed like Newman became a Roman Catholic, albeit in controversial circumstances on his deathbed. Nicholas Ross has already been quoted, 'He was thinking as a Roman Catholic from about 1845'. As ever, he was very much his own man. As Byles put it, 'He was adamantly independent. Throughout his life he was always too idiosyncratic to accept the role of orthodox discipleship'.[27] This accounts both for his attractiveness and also, along with his geographical isolation, for his lack of influence.

A figure who was far more influential among his contemporaries than Hawker is now more forgotten than he. Isaac Williams was a leading Tractarian, a poet, and in a sense the ultimate ecclesiographer. He was the author of Tract 80, 'On Reserve in Communicating Religious Knowledge', expounding a doctrine which was far from popular with the more forthright Evangelicals of the time. It has been well defined as meaning that 'both the sacredness and the complexity of the subject of religious truth are such that they require a holding back and a gradual revelation as the disposition and understanding of the recipient mature'.[28] He allied it with the doctrine of Analogy, teaching through symbols and parables in the manner of Christ, and in his collection of poetry called *The Cathedral*:

He has undertaken to do nothing less than write poems for all the features of a vast Gothic cathedral, taking the reader through four main aspects of the structure, the exterior, the nave, the choir, and finally the pillars and windows. He has provided a ground plan of such a building that identifies each part of the structure in terms of what it symbolises, and has included engravings of the appropriate portions of various existing cathedrals, English and French.[29]

Hawker had less scope at Morwenstow than he would have had with a cathedral, but that did not daunt him. Any parallel with Isaac Williams's work cannot be taken far, for Hawker expressed his scrutiny of symbols with a localised Christian intimacy which Williams lacks and which is hard to find elsewhere. In 'Morwennae Statio' not only does the church form a cross, but the floor at the chancel steps signifies the holiest place of all, where Christ died:

> Pace we the ground! our footsteps tread
> A cross – the builder's holiest form:
> That awful couch, where once was shed
> The blood, with man's forgiveness warm.
> And here, just where his mighty breast
> Throb'd the last agony away,
> They bade the voice of worship rest,
> And white-robed Levites pause and pray.

In his prose description of the church, 'Morwenstow', he takes the analogy as far as it can reasonably go: perhaps further.

Before we proceed to descend the three steps of the chancel floor, so obviously typical of Faith, Hope, and Charity, let us look westward through the tower-arch; and as we look we discover that the builders, either by chance or design, have turned aside or set out of proportional place the western window of the tower. Is this really so, or does the wall of the chancel swerve? The deviation was intended, nor without an error could we render the crooked straight. And the reason is said to be this: when our Redeemer died, at the utterance of the words 'It is done!' his head declined towards his right shoulder, and in that attitude he chose to die. Now it was to commemorate this dropping of the Saviour's head, to record in stone this eloquent gesture of our Lord, that the 'wise in heart', who traced this church in the actual outline of a cross, departed from the precise rules of architect and carpenter.[30]

There is still more in his Thought Books, centring on the chancel steps. He quotes the text, 'When he was come down from the mountain great multitudes folowed him' and adds: 'He descended from the mysteries to instruct the people. He went from the chancel down into the church.'

He writes a year later (1845), under the heading 'Death', 'You only pass thereby from the nave to the chancel in the communion of saints.'

So he sees the salvation of his parishioners in symbolic terms, as they move through his church, not through a vast Gothic cathedral such as Williams depicts. His symbolism by contrast is close and intimate. There is a special place for him in the rich and strange pattern of mid-Victorian devotional literature, acknowledged by an authority on the Oxford Movement:

From *Ecclesia* onwards, Hawker writes poetry imbued with a sense of the Church as a mystical body and preoccupied with an awareness of specific places as repositories of sanctity . . . It is Hawker who gives this Tractarian practice a specific local habitation and a name from British antiquity. His poetry seizes upon a Tractarian devotional idea and finds it operative in the daily life of rural people.[31]

Morwenstow Church meant to Hawker a gathering place for angels, especially at a service of baptism though he could communicate with two in particular at any time. The carved vine was a symbol of Christian life. The church was not simply cross-shaped, it was consciously designed to represent Christ's position at the moment of his death. As his humble parishioners moved up the steps from the nave to the chancel, they partook of God's mysteries in death as in life.

5

A Corpse Ashore Sir

There is a problem about dividing Hawker's biography neatly into decades, summed up by Byles: 'A long life passed in one remote place does not lend itself easily to narrative'.[1] The main upheaval in that life still lies well ahead, the death of his first wife Charlotte in 1863. Otherwise the years of his ministry at Morwenstow tend not to be marked with substantial milestones.

It also happens that chronology in these pages has already been sabotaged, by my introduction to the preceding chapter of 'Aisha Schechinah' which was not actually written until 1859. It would have been perverse to omit this masterpiece of his from a chapter about Hawker the mystic.

By his standards, he published a lot of poetry between 1843 and 1846. Three slim volumes appeared, *Reeds Shaken by the Wind* (1843), *Second Cluster* (1844), and *Echoes from Old Cornwall* (1846). Nor was he just occupied as a poet. Wrecks on the shore, and conflicts on dry land, kept him busy, again by his standards. The most stark and poignant of these events were the shipwrecks. Shipwrecks, and anticipation of them, must have dominated his life. Yet, as has been remarked, he wrote very little poetry on the subject. The marvellous short poem 'Death Song' is dated 1835, his first year in Morwenstow, before he had become directly involved with wrecks. Its last two lines could provide an epigraph for this chapter:

> I cannot leave the unburied bones,
> And I fain would go my way.

But the only poem of direct local significance is 'The Figure-Head of the *Caledonia* at her Captain's Grave' commemorating the wreck of the *Caledonia* in 1842 (the poem is dated by his editors 1841, further evidence of their collective carelessness). The most vivid accounts of shipwrecks are those written shortly after the events, in

THE FIGURE-HEAD OF THE *CALEDONIA*
AT HER CAPTAIN'S GRAVE

We laid them in their lowly rest,
 The strangers of a distant shore;
We smoothed the green turf on their breast,
 'Mid baffled Ocean's angry roar;
And there, the relique of the storm,
 We fixed fair Scotland's figured form.

She watches by her bold, her brave,
 Her shield towards the fatal sea:
Their cherished lady of the wave
 Is guardian of their memory.
Stern is her look, but calm, for there
 No gale can rend or billow bear.

Stand, silent image! stately stand,
 Where sighs shall breathe and tears be shed,
And many a heart of Cornish land,
 Will soften for the stranger dead.
They came in paths of storm; they found
 This quiet home in Christian ground.

* ❖ * ❖ *

letters. Those which he incorporated in 'The Remembrances of a Cornish Vicar,' published in 1865 and reprinted in *Footprints of Former Men in Far Cornwall*, tend to be less satisfactory. He was writing for a London public, desperately trying to make money to support his new family, and he consequently let his capacity for dramatic elaboration come into full play. It is a great shame that by such means he spoiled many a good story.

Anyone visiting Morwenstow church for the first time will be surprised to see, high on the bank to the left as he steps down through the churchyard, an incongruous white object like a small statue, a bonneted and kilted Scottish lass in aggressive stance carrying a sword and shield: the figurehead of the wrecked *Caledonia*. Her captain's body lies below, and nearby are buried the corpses, entire or in part, of more than forty sailors. The figurehead represents an astonishing facet of the life of Morwenstow and its vicar, and it also bears testimony to perhaps his greatest achievement, the weaning of his parishioners away from their appetite for wrecking.

Some definition of the term, 'wrecking', is required here. There is no evidence that the custom, vividly described by Daphne Du Maurier in *Jamaica Inn*, of luring ships onto the rocks with false lights, was still being practised by the time Hawker came to Morwenstow. There is actually precious little evidence that it was ever practised. However, there is no doubt that the cargoes of wrecked ships could provide a most welcome supplement to the miserable incomes of Cornishmen living near the coast. A prayer composed by a parish priest from the far west is often quoted, 'Dear God, we pray not that wrecks should happen, but if it be thy will that they do, we pray let them be for the benefit of thy poor people of Scilly'. The instinct still prevails. Quite recently a barge being towed up the Bristol Channel broke away and ran aground at a remote spot on the coast of North Cornwall, and in no time at all the shore was black with people carrying the cargo home, stripping the boat bare. Whatever the rights and wrongs, and popular sympathy is likely to go one way, this is pretty harmless behaviour compared with our ancestors' habit of ensuring that no member of the crew of a wrecked ship survived to claim rights of salvage. When he was still at North Tamerton Hawker, as we have seen, wrote some brief ballads about wreckers of this kind. It was 'Featherstone's Doom' to make a rope from sand:

> 'Tis for that hour, when, from the wave,
> Near voices wildly cried;
> When thy stern hand no succour gave,
> The cable at thy side.

Mawgan of Melhuach 'once buried the captain of a vessel, whom he found exhausted on the strand, alive!':

Wildly he shriek'd as his eyes grew dim,
"He was dead! he was dead! when I buried him."

These are strong stories, but Hawker did not persist with writing them when within a few years he was up against the reality, of savage men on a savage coast dispatching their victims among the rocks and crashing waves in circumstances of barely imaginable terror. Instead, he asserted the full strength of his powerful personality, not only protecting the occasional survivor of wrecks on his stretch of coastline and beyond, but also, despite his physical aversion to the task, collecting the bodies of drowned sailors and giving them Christian burial.

In 1848 Alfred Tennyson, soon to meet Robert Stephen Hawker, expressed a wish to visit Bude, having heard that the waves were larger there than anywhere on the coast. The combination of these waves, the gales which whipped them up, the currents of the Severn Sea as Hawker called it, and the reefs which he watched from his hut, made this also the most dangerous of coastlines for the seafarer. In the fifty years 1824-74, over eighty ships were carried ashore between Bude and Morwenstow.

Hawker described the wreck of the *Caledonia* nearly thirty years after the event, and while that capacity for exaggeration must be borne in mind, anyone who has looked down from those cliffs on a stormy day will find his account very credible.

It was, indeed, a terrible scene. The vessel, a brig of five hundred tons, had struck, as we afterwards found, at three o'clock that morning, and by the time the wreck was discovered she had been shattered into broken pieces by the fury of the sea. The rocks and the water bristled with fragments of mast and spar and rent timbers; the cordage lay about in tangled masses. The rollers tumbled in volumes of corn, the wheaten cargo; and amidst it all the bodies of the helpless dead – that a few brief hours before had walked the deck the stalwart masters of their ship – turned their poor disfigured faces to the sky, pleading for sepulture.[3]

This particular event is remarkably well documented. We also have an account written by the only survivor, Edward Le Dain, dated September 22nd, 1842. After describing the ship's voyage from 'Rio

Janeiro', round the Mediterranean, to Falmouth, he goes on:

We then stood up the Bristol Channel with a fair wind until about 9
o'clock, when a sudden squall of wind and rain came on, and all hands
were called to shorten sail. The weather continued foul. All hands were
kept on deck, and a good lookout forward for the Light Houses. About
eleven we saw land on the starboard bow. We tacked ship, but from the
violence of the storm we could make no way to windward. About one
o'clock on the Thursday morning it blew a hurricane. Just at that time
we carried away our square mainsail, our foresail, and our topsail sheets.
About half-past two we saw that danger was very great indeed. The crew
were quite sober. The Captain only served out grog twice during the
night. About half-past two we saw the point of land on which the vessel
afterwards struck. We tried to weather it; we could not get the ship
about. There was nothing said by the crew one to another except about
the ship's work. Just before the ship struck I was going forwards, and I
met David Macdonald going aft. He took me by the hand and said,
"Where are we?" He was much moved. And then the ship struck. The
Captain sent us to the main rigging. We went. We were there about a
quarter of an hour. No one spoke, except once, when I saw the long boat
was gone, I said to the Captain, "Sir, our long boat is gone". But he
made no answer. Soon after the mast went overboard with the rigging
and we in it. A heavy sea poured over us, and I was washed towards the
land. Several seas struck me onwards. At last I felt a rock. I held on. I
looked for my companions: they were not to be seen. The ship was
going to pieces. I then climbed onto another rock, and then upwards,
until I felt some grass, and then I rested and looked down to the sea for
the crew. But there was no one to be seen. I then climbed higher, feeling
my way. When morning came I found myself on top of a very high cliff,
but I was very much exhausted, and did not then think I should live.
But by God's great mercy I am alive.[4]

Edward Le Dain, a native of Jersey, remained a close friend. He
named his son Edward Robert Hawker, and whenever the vicar needed
a Jersey cow, 'the family and friends of Le Dain rejoiced to ransack
the island until they had found the sleekiest, loveliest, best of that
beautiful breed'.[5]

David Macdonald, among Le Dain's drowned shipmates, had a
fine epitaph. His father wrote to Hawker from Arbroath, the
Caledonia's home port, and his 'reply to your mournful letter' merits
quoting.

I write to inform you that, although the body of David Macdonald was much disfigured by injuries received while dashed by the waves among the rocks, yet it was not so much so but that Edward Le Dain, the survivor, could recognise it. The corpse was prepared for burial by a very motherly woman, my sexton's wife. I did not suffer any of the bodies to be gazed at by the common people, but they were treated with as much decency and respect as if they had died at home. The four found up to this date lie buried side by side in my churchyard, and their graves have been dressed, as the custom is with us, with flowers. The figure-head of their ship stands fixed in their midst. I have sent to the owners by this post Le Dain's statement of the voyage and wreck, to which I refer you for information. You will find much in it which should be a comfort to you. Le Dain frequently speaks of David, who with him used to attend on the Captain in the cabin more than the rest. He constantly says to me, "David was a good quiet lad as could be in a ship". I think the crew perished about half-past three on the morning of the 8th of September. In conclusion, I hope that you will patiently bear your Heavenly Father's will. God took them – the day of their death was God's time. He is too good to have taken them when he did if there would have been a fitter day. We are in his hands, and by ourselves do nothing.[6]

He was a wonderfully sensitive provider of spiritual comfort. It is all the more disappointing that the commemorative poem, 'The Figure-Head of the Caledonia at her Captain's Grave', is stiff and formal, a dutiful performance. There is patently self-conscious alliteration, 'We fix'd fair Scotland's figured form', and a studied contrast in each of the three verses between 'the paths of storm' where the men died and 'This quiet home in Christian ground'. One is also left asking the tiresome question, can 'baffled ocean's angry roar' ever be heard from the churchyard even in stormy conditions. The cliffs are so high and sheer that in my experience you have to reach the very edge before you can hear the waves on the rocks below. Hawker did not publish the poem until 1869, which suggests that he was none too pleased with it himself.

There is another curious aspect of this sparseness of poetry on shipwrecks, given that the subject drew so deeply on Hawker's emotions. He did actually publish two poems about disasters at sea of a public and national as opposed to a local kind, in which he can hardly have been emotionally involved. Both are in my judgment unmemorable, not meriting further commentary. They were set pieces for, he hoped, public consumption. One, called 'The Lost Ship: *The President*', concerns the fate of a ship which disappeared in the Atlantic in 1841, just a year before the wreck of the *Caledonia*. The second, 'The Fatal Ship', is about an early ironclad, HMS *Captain*, which foundered in the Bay of Biscay in 1870. Apparently poetry was only appropriate on state occasions.

Meanwhile shipwrecks continued to occur throughout his time at Morwenstow, and the task which he imposed upon himself and his parishioners was a grim one. Bodies collected from the shore had often been torn apart as the waves flung them about on the sharp rocks. Hawker spares his readers nothing.

. . . the victims of our cruel sea are seldom drowned, but beaten to death by violence and the wrath of the billows. We gathered one poor fellow in five parts; his limbs had been wrenched off, and his body rent. During our search for his remains, a man came up to me with something in his hand, inquiring, "Can you tell me, sir, what is this? Is it a part of a man?" It was the mangled seaman's heart, and we restored it reverently to its place, where it had once beat high with life and courage, with thrilling hope and sickening fear. Two or three of the dead were not discovered for four or five weeks after the wreck, and these had become so loathsome from decay, that it was at peril of health and life to perform the last duties we owe to our brother-men.[7]

In a letter to Sir Thomas Acland following the wreck of the *Bencoolen* in 1862, Hawker sets together sublime and horrific aspects of this strange element in his life:

. . . the too accustomed message arrived at my door: 'a corpse ashore Sir, at Stanbury Mouth', – a little creek a mile south of the church. My staff went about their work. Six bearers with a rude bier were called to bring the dead. A letter written and sent by a policeman to the coroner, and my lych-gate-house on the vicarage premises got ready. At six o'clock notice came that they were nigh and I went out into the moonlight to greet them. I receive the dead sailor at my gate and with the sentence, 'I am the Resurrection and the Life'. And it always moves me to soothing thoughts, that no sooner is the bruised and broken and nameless stranger cast up by the seas than the Church greets him as a son and proclaims his right to inherit a glorified body and a life everlasting . . .

If we could have had a visit from the coroner next day, the work of mercy would be done. But we are always obliged to wait for the tardy proceedings of that official person, Mr Good, who forgets that a body already a fortnight dead and, as our people graphically say, 'looking for the earth long ago', must try our nerves and nostrils very cruelly . . . At last, on Thursday at noon, arrived a policeman with the letter from Mr Good and a warrant to bury. So we laid him in his rest not far from that oak tree, making my group of silent seamen twenty-eight!

> They came in paths of storm,
> They found this quiet home
> In Christian ground.[8]

Beside all this activity on his own shoreline, Hawker acquired a reputation up and down the coast as the champion of sailors in danger, in particular denouncing the lifeboatmen who in his probably unfair judgment failed to perform their duty when the *Bencoolen* was wrecked off Bude:

On Tuesday at two o'clock afternoon a hull was seen off Bude wallowing in the billows. All rushed to the shore. At three she struck on the sand close to the breakwater – not 300 yards from the rocks. Manby's apparatus was brought down – a rocket fired and a rope was carried over the ship. The mate sprang to clutch it – missed – and fell into the sea to be seen no more alive. 'Another rope!' was the cry. But from the mismanagement of those in charge there was no other there. They then saw the poor fellows – 34 – (two lost before) constructing a raft and launching it. A call for the Life Boat, one of large cost provided with all good gear kept close by. She was run down to the water. A shout for men – none – a few of the hovellers, pilot men, got on board, but refused to put off . . .

So his graphic account continues, as all but six of the crew are drowned, and Byles fails for a moment in his role of loyal son-in-law when he mentions that Hawker was 'not an eye-witness'. The story is completed and Hawker adds:

The country rings with cries of shame on the dastards of Bude . . . Ten years since the *Alonso* of Stockton-on-Tees came ashore at Bude

– one mile from shore – I was there watching her. I had the life boat launched. I offered a sovereign each to get men, and I offered to go myself with them. I went on board and challenged them to come with me. Only one man came at my call – next day the sea was lulled and a calm – the scoundrels went on board with the same boat and robbed the vessel.[9]

A year later the *Margaret Quayle* was dismasted off Morwenstow and drifted up the coast to Clovelly, with Hawker and some companions anxiously watching its course. The men of Clovelly did no better in Hawker's view than their *confrères* of Bude. Appledore lifeboat set off 'on wheels with ten horses!!', and although they arrived too late to be useful, as the crew had already succeeded in reaching shore, they were spared denunciation:

Tried every effort to induce Clovelly men to go off in a skiff – sneaking Wesleyan cowards – offered any sum they might ask – we to indemnify loss of skiff. No help . . . Gossett and the Appledore men behaved nobly – Bude and Clovelly like thoroughly Wesleyan sneaks.[10]

The letter continues with the remarkable passage quoted earlier, 'John Wesley years ago corrupted and degraded the Cornish character . . .' So that was where the fault lay, with Wesley: if indeed fault there were. As Tennyson noted, the largest waves on the British coast come to shore at Bude. They are massive and frightening to watch. An authority on North Cornish wrecks, quoted by Byles, writes, probably with Hawker in mind, 'It is sometimes asked, why did not the lifeboat go out? But I do not think that this question is put by any sensible man who has seen the awful possibilities of a Bude sea'.[11] It was not a sensible place to station a lifeboat. Hawker made no such concessions. He had still not finished with Bude's Wesleyan lifeboatmen. In a period of his life when he was publishing very little if any new poetry, he wrote a bitter poem called 'A Croon on Hennacliff', a dialogue between a raven and its mate about appetising possibilities available nearby in Bude Haven.

A CROON ON HENNACLIFF

Thus said the rushing raven,
     Unto his hungry mate:
"Ho! gossip! for Bude Haven:
     There be corpses six or eight.
Cawk! cawk! the crew and skipper
     Are wallowing in the sea:
So there's a savoury supper
     For my old dame and me."

"Cawk! gaffer! thou art dreaming,
     The shore hath wreckers bold;
Would rend the yelling seamen
     From the clutching billows' hold.
Cawk! cawk! they'd bound for booty
     Into the dragon's den:
And shout, for 'death or duty,'
     If the prey were drowning men."

Loud laughed the listening surges,
     At the guess our granddame gave:
You might call them Boanerges,
     From the thunder of their wave.
And mockery followed after
     The sea-bird's jeering brood:
That filled the skies with laughter,
     From Lundy Light to Bude.

"Cawk! cawk!" then said the raven,
     "I am fourscore years and ten:
Yet never in Bude Haven
     Did I croak for rescued men. –
They will save the Captain's girdle,
     And shirt, if shirt there be:
But leave their blood to curdle,
     For my old dame and me."

So said the rushing raven
    Unto his hungry mate:
"Ho! gossip! for Bude Haven:
    There be corpses six or eight.
Cawk! cawk! the crew and skipper
    Are wallowing in the sea:
O what a savoury supper
    For my old dame and me."

* * * * *

There is a vindictiveness here, which can charitably be seen as a tribute to Hawker's profound concern 'for those in peril on the sea', and perhaps derives in part from his desperate concern about Charlotte a year before she died, but is nonetheless unbecoming to say the least, especially when he brings in his obsessive suspicion of Wesleyans. He did not always forgive easily.

It is more appropriate to return to Hawker's work on Morwenstow's shore, comprising as it surely does a series of outstanding acts of Christian charity, symbolised by the figurehead in the churchyard. He wrote in a letter in 1865

We are surrounded by shipwreck and storm. Things of value, cotton bales, chests of tea &c. float ashore, but thank God no corpses yet. I have suffered so much from their burial in former times that I hear in every gust of the gale a dying sailor's cry.[12]

6

The Eighteen-Forties: Poetry and Conflicts

In spite of the shipwrecks, Hawker's fourth decade was on balance a good one. In fact very little remains on record about him between 1837, when the vicarage was completed, and 1842, the year of the wreck of the *Caledonia*. That year also marked the death of one of his parishioners of whom he was plainly very fond, Richard Cann. The family as a whole meant much to him. Richard's brother Thomas was his churchwarden during most of his time at Morwenstow, and seems to have been a constant companion and support, helping him harvest his glebe and comforting him when Charlotte died.

Hawker wrote a poem called first, when published in *Reeds Shaken by the Wind*, 'A Cornish Death Song', then more tersely in later editions 'The Dirge', with a note that provides a vivid commentary:

The first line of these verses haunted the memory and the lips of a good and blameless young farmer who died in my parish some years ago. It was, as I conceive, a fragment of some forgotten dirge of which he could remember no more. But it was his strong desire that 'the words' should be 'put upon his headstone', and he also wished me to write 'some other words, to make it complete'. I fulfilled his entreaty, and the stranger who visits my churchyard will find this dirge carven in stone, 'in sweet remembrance of the just', and to the praise of the dead, Richard Cann, whose soul was carried by the angels into Paradise on the 15th of February, 1842.[1]

It must be the most cheerful dirge ever written, a splendidly hopeful and uplifting poem, swinging along to the music of the church band. 'Sing from the chamber to the grave' is the command, the first line, remembered by the young man, and 'sing' is repeated five times, along with at least one word in each of the six verses betokening music and song, interspersed with words of happiness: sweet, lovely, gentle, pleasant. So the funeral procession is to be envisaged making its way from the dead man's home to the church and thence to the graveside. Finally:

> My soul shall sing among the just
> Until the judgment day.

THE DIRGE

"Sing from the chamber to the grave!"
    Thus did the dead man say:
"A sound of melody I crave,
    Upon my burial-day.

Bring forth some tuneful instrument,
    And let your voices rise:
My spirit listened, as it went,
    To music of the skies.

Sing sweetly while you travel on,
    And keep the funeral slow:-
The angels sing where I am gone,
    And you should sing below.

Sing from the threshold to the porch,
    Until you hear the bell;
And sing you loudly in the church
    The Psalms I love so well.

Then bear me gently to my grave,
    And as you pass along,
Remember, 'twas my wish to have
    A pleasant funeral song.

So earth to earth, and dust to dust!
    And though my flesh decay,
My soul shall sing among the just
    Until the Judgment-day."

✣ ✣ ✣ ✣ ✣

The poem can still be read today carved on Richard Cann's gravestone.

In that same year Hawker wrote one of his more ambitious ballads, 'Genoveva' (see Appendix), based on a German legend. Probably Charlotte helped with it. As has already been noted she was fluent in German, and her own published work, notably 'The Manger of the Holy Night' (1847), derived mainly from German sources. The 392 lines of 'Genoveva' take up a substantial proportion of successive slim volumes: only the incomplete 'Quest of the Sangraal', which comprises the high point of his poetic achievement, is longer. The ballad's story follows a predictable pattern. The noble and excellent maid Genoveva marries Lord Siegfried, and all is blissful until he finds himself obliged to go and fight the Moors in Spain, leaving his wife in the care of his castellain. Fortunately there are angels keeping an eye as well, because the castellain having failed to seduce her packs Genoveva off to the forest with two caitiffs who are to murder her. She persuades them to let her live as she bears Siegfried's child. She duly gives birth, to 'Ben-oni, sorrow's son', but having no milk must leave the child to die. A doe discovers and suckles him. The three of them live 'in peace, if not in joy', and she teaches Ben-oni about Jesus. He deduces that death must be preferable to life, and she appears to agree and to plan accordingly. Meanwhile Siegfried is back from the war. He is most distressed to hear that Genoveva is dead. By way of diversion from his misery, he goes hunting. His lost wife and son rescue the doe from his hounds, and happiness reigns once more over all.

Hawker rated his ballads high. The very title of his collected poems of 1869, The Cornish Ballads and Other Poems of the Rev R. S. Hawker, Vicar of Morwenstow, is designed to emphasise their significance. He wrote in 1862, when he was having difficulty finding a publisher, 'Hereafter my verses will be sought after sold read aye and extolled to the very echo. The Ballads will be called by every noble name – and then will come the ower-true tale: "In his lifetime they could find no printer brave enough to shed his ink in their behalf and so they died"'.[2] What he meant by 'ower' must remain a puzzle, perhaps one of his own archaisms meaning 'over' but 'over-true' does not seem right. In any event, he was wrong on both counts. His ballads, in particular 'Genoveva', have not necessarily died but have undeniably been dormant. I can find no mention of this substantial piece of work among critical commentaries on his poetry, such as there are.

Does it deserve oblivion? The story is pretty silly, but that could be said equally of ballads which have lasted better. On the other hand, the characters who claim our sympathies, Genoveva and Ben-oni, project in their conversations a purity and innocence which Hawker applies in his Thought Books to Jesus and his mother. The description of their home in the wood has a matching simplicity, for instance when Genoveva finds the place after her potential murderers have spared her:

> They melted at the voice they heard,
> They left her lonely there!
> The holy angels helped her word –
> There is such force in prayer.
> Then wandered she, where that wild wood
> A tangled pathway gave,
> Till lo! in secret solitude,
> A deep and mossy cave.

This is not a comforting place, far from Wordsworth's nature that 'never did betray The heart that loved her', closer to Hardy's grim indifferent nature:

> Good angels! 'twas a sight to see
> That cavern dark and wild;
> The nameless stream – the silent tree,
> The mother and her child.

There are other vivid moments, but it is not easy to make out a consistent case for 'Genoveva'. Much of it seems suitable material for John Drinkwater's parish magazine, and one wishes again for that 'neighbourly authority' which might have encouraged in Hawker a capacity to prune and trim and generally take pains. But can ballads, or indeed epics, as literary genres ever claim consistent excellence? Homer nods, Coleridge nods, Hawker sometimes seems to nod off altogether.

He was more successful with shorter ballads, for example the early stories of wreckers like Featherstone and Mawgan of Melhuach. In this later period of his writing life, 'A Legend of the Hive' invites attention, combining as it does a primitive Christian legend, an equally primitive setting which is still plainly his own Morwenstow, an admiration for bees that matches or even exceeds his love of birds and animals, and also an apparent sympathy with villainous indeed sinful behaviour which might be totally surprising if one did not find it elsewhere. In *Ecclesia* with its strong Christian emphasis he includes a poem, 'Isha Cherioth', spoken by Judas Iscariot's lover:

> And there, where clustering vineyards rest,
> And palms look forth above,
> He kindled in my maiden-breast
> The glory of his love!
>
> He left me – but with holier thought,
> Bound for a mightier scene;
> In proud Capernaum's path he sought
> The noble Nazarene!

Judas went wrong later, but it still seems incongruous that Hawker, the stern moralist, should write charitably about Christ's betrayer. At a less drastic level, his approval of the wicked old Tristram Pentire provides another example. Perhaps a connection can also be traced with that youthful delight in practical joking, and the persistent urge to be unconventional: all matching up with the deed of the 'ancient woman, worn and bent' of 'A Legend of the Hive' who stole the communion bread hoping to fulfil the legend and lure back the bees which had deserted her garden. Indeed 'Twas a wild wish, a thought unblest, Some evil legend of the west'. But it worked! This deplorable old woman had her bees restored to her, and the feeble moral is drawn that

ISHA CHERIOTH

They say his sin was dark and deep,
  Men shudder at his name –
They spurn at me because I weep,
  They call my sorrow, shame.

I know not! I remember well
  Our city's native street,
The path – the olive trees – the dell
  Where Cherioth's daughters meet:

And there, where clustering vineyards rest,
  And palms look forth above,
He kindled in my maiden-breast
  The glory of his love!

He left me – but with holier thought,
  Bound for a mightier scene;
In proud Capernaum's path he sought
  The noble Nazarene!

They tell of treachery bought and sold –
  Perchance their words be truth –
I only see the scenes of old;
  I hear his voice in youth.

And I sit, as Rizpah sate,
  Where life and hope are fled,
I sought him not in happier state,
  I will not leave my dead!

No! I must weep, though all around
  Be hatred and despair;
One sigh shall soothe this fatal ground,
  A Cherioth maiden's prayer!

A LEGEND OF THE HIVE

Behold those wingèd images,
  Bound for their evening bowers:
They are the nation of the bees,
  Born from the breath of flowers.
Strange people they! a mystic race,
In life, in food, and dwelling-place.

They first were seen on earth, 'tis said,
  When the rose breathes in spring:
Men thought her blushing bosom shed
  These children of the wing.
But lo! their hosts went down the wind,
Filled with the thoughts of God's own mind.

They built them houses made with hands,
  And there alone they dwell:
No man to this day understands
  The mystery of their cell.
Your mighty sages cannot see
The deep foundations of the bee.

Low in the violet's breast of blue,
  For treasured food they sink;
They know the flowers that hold the dew,
  For their small race to drink.
They glide – King Solomon might gaze
With wonder on their awful ways.

And once – it is a grandame's tale,
  Yet filled with secret lore –
There dwelt within a woodland vale,
  Fast by old Cornwall's shore,
An ancient woman, worn and bent,
Fallen nature's mournful monument.

A home had they, the clustering race,
    Beside her garden wall:
All blossoms breathed around the place,
    And sunbeams fain would fall.
The lily loved that combe the best
Of all the valleys of the west.

But so it was, that on a day
    When summer built her bowers,
The waxen wanderers ceased to play
    Around the cottage flowers.
No hum was heard, no wing would roam:
They dwelt within their cloister'd home.

This lasted long – no tongue could tell
    Their pastime or their toil;
What binds the soldier to his cell?
    Who should divide the spoil?
It lasted long – it fain would last,
Till autumn rustled on the blast.

Then sternly went that woman old,
    She sought the chancel floor,
And there, with purpose bad and bold,
    Knelt down amid the poor.
She took – she hid – that blessèd bread,
Whereon the Invisible is shed.

She bore it to her distant home,
    She laid it by the hive:
To lure the wanderers forth to roam,
    That so her store might thrive.
'Twas a wild wish, a thought unblest,
Some evil legend of the west.

But lo! at morning tide, a sign
  For wondering eyes to trace:
They found above that bread, a shrine
  Reared by the harmless race.
They brought their walls from bud and flower,
They built bright roof and beamy tower.

Was it a dream? or did they hear,
  Float from those golden cells,
A sound as of some psaltery near,
  Or soft and silvery bells;
A low sweet psalm that grieved within,
In mournful memory of the sin.

Was it a dream? 'tis sweet no less:
  Set not the vision free,
Long let the lingering legend bless
  The nation of the bee.
So shall they bear upon their wings
A parable of sacred things.

So shall they teach, when men blaspheme
  Or sacrament or shrine,
That humbler things may fondly dream
  Of mysteries divine;
And holier hearts than his may beat
Beneath the bold blasphemer's feet.

* * * * *

they recognised something sacred even when it was being mishandled, attracted as they apparently were by the sound of 'A low sweet psalm that grieved within, In mournful memory of the sin'.

Adulation of bees is the main theme of this engaging ballad. Every verse, apart from those that describe the woman's machinations in the bees' absence, marvels at their strange powers and offers them the highest praise.

> They are the nation of the bees
> Born from the breath of flowers.
> Strange people they! a mystic race,
> In life, in food, in dwelling place.

They are 'filled with the thoughts of God's own mind', 'King Solomon might gaze With wonder at their awful ways', and so on. Ten years later, in a letter to Sir Thomas Acland, Hawker solemnly credited them with astonishing ingenuity:

Mrs Hawker proffers for Lady Acland's acceptance a little honeycomb. It was gathered from the heath and furze blossoms of Hennacliff; and when our bees, on forage, are caught there by a sudden storm, they stoop down, gather up a small pebble or stone for ballast in the wind, and so glide safely home to their hive, where they drop it at the door. This is one of the bits of natural history which one gathers from an out-of-door life by the sea.[3]

So the eccentric purveyor of quaint tales, never absent for long, reappears. But this was only one facet of his complex nature, whatever may be stressed by many of the people, notably Sabine Baring-Gould, who have written about him.

In the 1840s he emerges as a powerful controversialist, locally and even nationally. In 1843 he won a court case concerning the ownership of a thirteenth century holy well, dedicated to St John the Baptist: a fine specimen of its kind which stands in a pretty orchard close to the church. He described the event.

The well and the ground whereon it stands having been unlawfully claimed by Sir J. Y. Buller in the year 1843, the Right of the Church was sustained by the present Vicar, and after a lawsuit which lasted two whole days at the Assizes held at Bodmin, wherein all that wealth and rank and power could accomplish were brought to bear against the Church, a triumphant verdict in the Vicar's favour was returned with costs.[4]

He had first sought divine intervention, in the form of a printed leaflet which reads in part:

A SECRET PRAYER

Offered up at the Altar of Morwenstow Church thrice every day in
Lent (1843) until March 27th

All-mighty and Most Merciful God! The Protector of all that trust in
Thee! We humbly beseech Thee that thou wouldest be pleased to stretch
forth Thy Right Hand to rescue and defend the possessions of this Thy
Sanctuary from the Envy and Violence of wicked and covetous Men!
Let not any Adversary despoil thine Inheritance, neither suffer Thou
The Evil Man to approach the Waters that flow softly for thy Blessed
Baptism from the well of Thy Servant Saint John.[5]

The efficacy of such militant, hardly secret, prayer was duly proved,
and the vicar returned from Bodmin in triumph. There was joy in
Morwenstow, bells ringing, flags flying, the choir singing at the top
of the tower; and one false witness, old Nicky, afterwards lost the
sight of one eye, 'and Parson said 'twas the Lord's judgment upon
him'.[6] He was always happy to see divine retribution meted out on
his adversaries. Sir John Buller however was more gently treated.
Hawker wrote some years later, 'I hope Sir John has quite forgiven
me. He told the bishop that I had never used a single harsh word or
done any crafty thing in the lawsuit, and that he could not blame me
for defending the rights of the church.'[6] One detects again an element
of weakness for the aristocracy.

In that same year the building of Morwenstow School was
completed, to join the bridge and the vicarage as a memorial to Hawker,
and the stamp of his authority was soon apparent:

THE VICAR will attend at Saint Mark's Schoolroom, every FRIDAY at
THREE o'clock, to catechise the scholars, and at the Sunday School at
the USUAL HOUR. He will not from henceforth show the same kindness to those parents who keep their children from school, as he will to
those who send them. 'Thou shalt not seethe a kid in his mother's milk'
– Exodus xxiii 19

THE VICARAGE, MORWENSTOW
Festival of St Swithin, Saint and Bishop, 1845.[7]

The parents must have been puzzled by his quotation from Exodus, and all the more respectful.

Also in 1843, Hawker made a small mark on history as a pioneer of Harvest Festivals. There are of course countless customs relating to the harvest, and some, which Hawker himself delighted in, were still practised at Morwenstow. But he was one of the first parish priests to institute a specifically Christian celebration. An announcement 'To the Parishioners of Morwenstow' dated September 13th, 1843, calling them to church, reads in part:

Brethren, God has been merciful to us this year also. He hath filled our garners with increase, and satisfied our poor with bread. He hath opened his hand, and filled all things living with plenteousness. Let us offer a sacrifice of thanksgiving among such as keep Holy Day. Let us gather together in the chancel of our church on the first Sunday of next month, and there receive, in the bread of the new corn, that blessed sacrament which was ordained to strengthen and refresh our souls . . . Furthermore, let us remember that, as a multitude of grains of wheat are mingled into one loaf, so we, being many, are intended to be joined together into one, in that holy sacrament of the Church of Jesus Christ.[8]

This modest plan is some way from the demonstrative harvest festival services practised in churches today, but it does seem to have been one of the first such special occasions. Hawker was of course a farmer himself, with a substantial area of glebe land to look after, and also he saw the process of growth and harvest as a form of holiness. 'Hearken to the shooting of the corn on a still night', he wrote in his Thought Book in 1848, and in a letter of 1864 he describes how he addressed his congregation. They, he said, simply sow the seed and 'their work is over and their work is done. They can fulfil no more.'

But God and his angels then enter the field – a mighty power broods over the grain, and the life below begins to move, and first the blade cometh up, and then the stalk, and then the ear, and then the full corn in the ear arises into light and growth beneath the silent touch of God.[9]

It must have been quite an amazing experience to hear his sermons.

In 1844 he set in motion two further innovations. In his capacity as Rural Dean of Trigg Major and with the support of his bishop he organised a Rural Synod, a meeting in Morwenstow church of all the clergy in the deanery, and later published a pamphlet on the subject. This included a memorable exposition on the appropriateness of their meeting place:

For my own part I hold the solemnity of such a scene to be a most salutary check on all levity of language, on all warmth and infirmity of temper, on the common tendency of mutual discussion to kindle or harass the human mind. The solemn roof which now bends over us, the image of that invisible shelter which has been our refuge from one generation to another; that single sacred font, the memorial that we have all been baptised into one body by one spirit; the simple and soli-tary altar at which, century after century, so many ministers have 'said the same thing'; the silence of these ancient aisles, that have grown old with the worship of past generations; all these are so many pledges to me of the propriety of our thought and language in this 'city of our solemnities', where we come to take sweet counsel together, and to walk in the House of God as friends.[10]

It is an impressive list of initiatives, by one vicar of an obscure and distant country parish: harvest festivals, rural synods, and the restoration as part of the church service of a weekly offertory for the benefit of the poor. This custom was no longer practised in the church as a whole, on the grounds, it seems, that employers would use it as an excuse to reduce wages. The establishment of 'outdoor relief' as part of the 1834 Poor Law may also have had to do with it. The mid-Victorians tended to be ambivalent about the relief of poverty. They acknowledged, as they rather had to, that the gospels enjoined them to give to the poor. But they were also persistently anxious that only the deserving poor should be helped, and that nothing should be allowed to slip into the hands of the undeserving except through the tightly controlled and calculatedly unsympathetic operation of the Poor Law. Hawker, who detested that piece of legislation and simply knew that most of his parishioners were very poor, was attacked personally in *The Times* as a champion of the offertory, and replied directly to the newspaper's proprietor, John Walter, in terms which were forceful even by his standards, not necessarily in keeping with the 'propriety of our thought and language' expected of his fellow-clergy:

... This practice of alms, whereunto the heavenly Head of the Church annexed a specific reward – this necessity, we are told, is become obsolete. A Christian duty become, by desuetude, obsolete! As well might a man infer that any other religious excellence ceased to be obligatory because it had been disused. The virtue of humility, for example, which has been so long in abeyance among certain of the laity, shall no longer, therefore, be a Christian grace! The blessing on the meek shall cease in 1844! Voluntary kindness and alms have been rendered unnecessary by the compulsory payments enacted by the New Poor Law! ...

And now, sir, I conclude with one or two parting admonitions to yourself. You are, I am told, an elderly man, fast approaching the end of all things, and, ere many years have passed, about to stand a separated soul among the awful mysteries of the spiritual world. I counsel you to beware lest the remembrance of these attempts to diminish the pence of the poor, and to impede the charitable duties of the rich, should assuage your happiness in that abode where the strifes and triumphs of controversy are unknown, 'Because thou hast done this thing, and because thou hadst no pity'. And lastly, I advise you not again to assail our rural parishes with such publications, and to harass and unsettle the minds of our faithful people. We, the Cornish clergy, are a humble and undistinguished race; but we are apt, when unjustly assailed, to defend ourselves in straightforward language, and to utter plain admonitions, such as, on this occasion, I have thought it my duty to address to yourself.[11]

Hawker must have sent a copy to the Bishop of Exeter, because Henry Phillpotts, no mean controversialist himself, expressed strong approval, 'If he has any sense of shame, he ought to feel deeply the exposure'.[12]

Here again, as with the lawsuit, poetry provided little more than a footnote. He dated 'The Oblation' Christmas Day 1843. There has to be some uncertainty about its subject matter, because it seems principally interested in celebrating the instalment of an altar-cloth made by a lady, indeed it was originally entitled 'The Lady's Offering'. But the third verse leaves no doubt as to what else was on his mind.

> We *offer'd* it to Him: – scorn not the phrase,
> Ye proud and stately magnates of the land;
> Grudge not the poor their pence, nor God his praise,
> Though as our simple fathers stood, we stand,
> And render thus our gifts with meek and votive hand.

THE OBLATION

A web of woven wool, fringed all around,
  Ruddy and rich in hue, like Syrian wine;
With golden leaves inlaid on that dark ground,
  That seemed just shed from some o'ershadowing vine:
Such was the lady's offering at Morwenna's shrine.

We laid it on the altar, while the word
  Lingered in echoes o'er the unconscious wall;
The voice that prophesied our God had heard
  The sound of alms, and would remember all;
'Twas the Child Jesu's day, the Bethlehem Festival.

We *offer'd it* to Him: - scorn not the phrase
  Ye proud and stately magnates of the land;
Grudge not the poor their pence, nor God His praise,
  Though as our simple fathers stood, we stand,
And render thus our gifts with meek and votive hand.

We left it in that chancel deck'd with flowers,
  And boughs that blossom'd like old Aaron's rod;
For faithful hands had built them leafy bowers
  Along our aisles, such as the angels trod
When Moses saw the bush, and Abraham talked
                              with God.

* * * * *

It is otherwise a pleasant domestic poem, describing with warm charm the decoration of the church at Christmas.

He was at least as profoundly concerned with the doctrines of the Church of England, at a time when the turmoil deriving from the

Oxford Movement was reaching, for the many thousands who cared about it, an agonising stage. In 1845, a few months before John Henry Newman's secession to Rome, Hawker preached the Visitation Sermon in Launceston parish church in the presence of the bishop, who, as will be seen further in a moment, was such a significant figure in his life. Hawker did not in fact deliver the sermon himself; it was read for him in his absence, because his father had just died. He did however have it published, and it is an enthralling document, the only one of his sermons to be thus recorded: most of them were delivered extempore, at least in the later stages of his career, and we are left mainly with the colourful notes in his Thought Books and some fragments preserved by Byles, one of which was quoted earlier. A cryptic note at the end of the Visitation Sermon reads 'The Bishop did not desire that this sermon should be printed', and Hawker's defiance is surprising, because one of the few people whom he unreservedly respected was Henry Phillpotts. The bishop had to tread carefully, though he did not always do so, and there must have been a difference of emphasis over the treatment of the seceders. However that may be, as an exposition of Hawker's views at this time, bearing in mind his deathbed conversion to Rome, this sermon entitled 'The Field of Rephidim' is of great importance.

The convert of 1875 makes clear his hostility to Rome thirty years earlier, strongly supporting the apostolic succession, while at the same time pronouncing by way of a personal gloss upon the variegated origins of the Anglican church.

So is it a function likewise of the chief shepherds to defend the flock from the secret or open ravages of heresy and schism; more especially here in England, and in these our troublous times, it behoves them to watch and ward against all attempted return to the old innovation by the see and Bishop of Rome. For the transit of our apostolic lineage through Romish times in England, is like the temporary passage of a well-known foreign river through one circumfluent lake; wherein, although the waters intermingle a little as they glide, yet the course of the mighty Rhone is visible throughout, in distinct and unbroken existence! So it is with us who have inherited the genealogy of the Apostles in these lands. We came from British fountains, we flowed in Saxon channels, we glided through Romish waters – but we were not, we are

not, we will not be of Rome; for we will preserve, God willing, the
unconquered courses of our own ancestral stream![13]

His sympathy with the seceders is plain, expressed in a manner
which seems to epitomise Christian charity.

Moreover, they who have departed from us have yet a rightful claim to
our constant sympathy and continual regard. Whether they confess or
deny it, they belong to us still. Yea, though Jacob be ignorant of us, and
Israel acknowledge us not, the baptised all over the land are our own.
We inhabit their ancient and their native house; and though they may
have gone into a far country, they can remember themselves still, and if
they do, they have a right to the very last, because of their baptism, to
come home and to lift once more the latch of their Heavenly Father's
gate. So that until the sun is gone down, and the door shut, our loving-
kindness should follow them all the days of their life.[14]

In the same vein he goes on to bring right home to Cornwall a
longing that the seceders should return.

God forbid, also, that we should sin in ceasing to pray for them. A man
may wage fierce war with a doctrine, and yet he may cherish all the
while a most affectionate anxiety for the everlasting welfare of those that
hold it. Now, the breath of love is prayer. We should pray for these our
kinsfolk that are afar off, continually; and the supplications should be
earnest and strong, that they may, after all, return one day to the heart
and home of the mother of their people. I, for one, will not only entreat,
but believe, that an hour may not be far off, when the old loving-kind-
ness for the Church will throb once more throughout the soul of dear
and native Cornwall, and that the ancient spirit will breathe yet again
along the land that is indeed our own land . . . [15]

Nicholas Ross's comment merits repeating, 'He was thinking as a
Roman Catholic from about 1845', the very year of the Visitation
Sermon.

Again, a poem provides a footnote, and only a doubtful one in
this case. 'The Night Cometh' is dated in Godwin's edition very
specifically, 'The Festival of St Andrew 1842', but Byles points out
that it was first printed in 1836. Hawker could well have revised the
date to suit the conflicts of the 1840s, a form of adaptation which he
employed with 'Minster Church'. This time there was no need to

THE NIGHT COMETH

When darkness fills the western sky,
And sleep, the twin of death, is nigh,
What soothes the soul at set of sun?
The pleasant thought of duty done.

Yet must the pastoral slumbers be
The shepherd's by the eastern tree,
Broken and brief - with dreams that tell
Of ravaged flock and poisoned well!

Be still, my soul! fast wears the night -
Soon shall day dawn in holier light:
Old faces - ancient hearts - be there,
And well known voices thrill the air!

change the words. The theme may originally have been more general:
things are due to be bad but will with God's help improve, but they
suited the new theme. Morwenstow is peaceful, but elsewhere slumbers are 'Broken and brief, with dreams that tell Of ravaged flock and
poisoned well!' All will be well at dawn, 'Old voices - ancient hearts
- be there, And well known voices thrill the air!' There is an echo in
the sermon, 'the ancient spirit will breed yet again along the land
that is indeed our own land'. But given either interpretation, or
both, this is a strained and undistinguished poem, and if he really
redeployed it in the manner suggested, one is left wishing that he had
managed to write something fresh, to express in verse the feelings
that must have come across so powerfully from the pulpit in
Launceston.

At the end of the decade Hawker became involved on the fringes of a major confrontation between high church and evangelical interests in Plymouth. At the centre stood the Bishop of Exeter, Henry Phillpotts, and before describing this event I propose to take a closer look at the remarkable man who, from the moment when he expressed approval of the Newdigate Prize Poem, exercised such an influence on Hawker's life.

Henry Phillpotts was nothing if not a political churchman. Before becoming bishop he worked closely with the Duke of Wellington when he was prime minister, and was well known as an ardent opponent of any extension of the rights of Roman Catholics. But when Wellington's intensely conservative government engaged in a dramatic change of policy and introduced the Roman Catholic Relief Act of 1829, Phillpotts changed his mind too, and shortly afterwards was appointed to Exeter. Violent feelings were aroused. Canon Sydney Smith expressed himself with customary vividness, 'I must believe in the apostolic succession, there being no other way of accounting for the descent of the Bishop of Exeter from Judas Iscariot'.[16] Once in office he was more single-minded, every inch a high church man. His biographer writes, 'He was the implacable foe of liberalism in every form, and no clergyman holding such views was willingly admitted to his diocese'.[17] This of course suited Hawker, whose manner of dressing and conducting himself in church would hardly have been acceptable in a more evangelically inclined diocese.

During the late 1840s Bishop Phillpotts instigated a 'church versus state' conflict which caused a considerable stir, known as 'the Gorham Judgment'. The details are at best of marginal relevance to the life of Hawker and need not delay us. George Gorham was a priest with Calvinist sympathies, believing that a baptised infant was only regenerate, freed from original sin, if it was already 'one of the elect'. Phillpotts wanted no truck with predestination and refused to permit Gorham to take up the living of Bramford Speke in Devon. Gorham appealed to the Privy Council and the bishop's verdict was overturned. The two men were eventually reconciled, but as well as being a significant event in the history of the Church of England, the Gorham Judgment was a cruel blow to the bishop's considerable pride. Hawker was not directly involved, but managed to be on good terms with both men, which suggests in him a breadth of sympathy which is not always apparent. Gorham visited him, and they discovered a shared interest:

The young seedpods (of the cudweed) outgrow the parent stem - hence its name Herba Impia, the undutiful plant. When Gorham came to Morwenstow, he, being curious in botany, asked me its name, and I gave it, whereupon he suspected some covert allusion to his own rebellious demeanour towards the bishop. So the name now stands thus – Herba Impia Gorhamensis.[18]

So Hawker contributed a little wit, which is rarely present in these savage religious conflicts, but that was all. The Plymouth conflict, which affected him more closely, became known as the Sellon Controversy.

Priscilla Sellon, the daughter of a naval officer, responded to an appeal from the bishop for help in countering the spiritual privation of the largest conurbation in his diocese, Plymouth, and in particular its port area of Devonport. With his full concurrence she established 'the Church of England Sisterhood of Mercy of Devonport and Plymouth'. This appears to have been an admirably effective organisation, which for example was to provide five recruits for Florence Nightingale's hospital in the Crimea. Initially however it aroused deep suspicion and hostility in Plymouth, where the evangelicals were very much in the ascendancy and Phillpotts had already caused upset by appointing a well known high churchman, George Prynne, to be vicar of one of the principal churches. The ladies were attacked by the 'British Society for the Promotion of the Principles of the Reformation' for engaging in various so-called Romish practices, for example wearing crosses, using beads, and requiring children in their school to bow to the altar. Miss Sellon wrote to Edward Pusey, the leading tractarian who was taking a close interest, 'It is impossible for us to work in quiet; the newspapers attack us; the Plymouth clergy preach against us; the Plymouth low church are mad against us'.[19]

The bishop set up an enquiry, with himself in the chair supported by a general and an admiral, commanders-in-chief respectively of the

Western District and Devonport – remarkable evidence of the ubiquitous nature and indeed power of the established church in the mid-nineteenth century, whether represented by the vicar in his parish or the bishop in his diocese. The enquiry culminated with the bishop's decision, which reads in part:

If there have been some things which these ladies have adopted in this charity that I wish had not been adopted, they are absolutely overpowered by the cloud of virtues and graces in their conduct.

'I know I shall be condemned as a papist', he went on, and then, in response to hisses and laughter,

I entreat you to hiss and hoot as much as you will, unless for your own sakes you cease . . . She [Miss Sellon] has been taunted this day and every day with showing an extreme regard for the Cross . . . She has shown her regard in one way . . . she has followed the precepts and example of our Blessed Lord by taking up her cross and bearing it in such a way as, I trust, no one will forget.[20]

This glimpse of the bishop militant indicates why Hawker held him in such high regard, and also suggests that the men had a lot in common.

Hawker's involvement with the Sellon Controversy was relatively indirect. He wrote a poem, entitled 'A Voice from the Place of St Morwenna in the Rocky Land; Uttered to the Sisters of Mercy at the Tamar Mouth'. The poem reflects the title, too ornate and elaborate to be very appealing, though it is an improvement on some of his commentaries in verse on public events. Like his bishop he responds to the criticism that the Sisters paid excessive devotion to the cross in their worship, and revives 'a lovely legend of the first fathers', the Resurrection of the Real Cross. It will be carried by angels as a rallying point on the Day of Judgment:

> How shall men bear, amid their loss,
> That Resurrection of the Cross!
> The sign they mocked, by angels borne,
> The banner of the Eternal Morn!

A VOICE FROM THE PLACE OF ST MORWENNA
IN THE ROCKY LAND

Uttered to the Sisters of Mercy at the Tamar Mouth

Pause, Pilgrim! where our Severn sea
Rolls its stern waters, wild and free,
And mark, above yon chancel-side,
The Cross! whereon Lord Jesu died!
What memories meet – what visions blend,
On that dear Death-bed of a Friend!

The Priest of Baldiu traced the sign
With mystic lore and rule and line –
Rodolph, the Lord of Clinton, gave
That wall that looks along the wave,
And stately Cross to breathe in stone
Mount Calvary's deed to days unknown.

And be there men, dull, hard, and stern,
Who from that sight can coldly turn?
And, like some loathsome shape, would hide
The last couch of the Crucified?
The latest thing His fingers held
When Heaven was won, and Satan Quelled!

Forgive them, tender Lord and true!
Alas! they heed not what they do;
Heaven's light in them is dim and cold,
They know not what Thy saints behold:
They see not as Thine angels see:
Dark Plym! I wail for them and thee!

O City! where my birth-place stands,
How art thou fallen amid the lands!
Thy daughters bold – thy sons unblest –
A withered Salem of the West!

Hark! from yon hill what tones arise –
"Thy peace is hidden from thine eyes!"

Nay! there be forty – twenty – ten
All women true, and trusty men –
A faithful band, like angels given
To plead the Patriarch's prayer with Heaven;
And one, a thrilling Lady, stands,
Whose voice might rescue sentenced lands!

Daughter! my spirit turns to thee:
Here, by the lonely Severn sea,
I, too, have borne, years fierce and long,
All hatred, and rebuke, and wrong:
And now thy truth shall soothe the sigh –
The life I live – the death I die;

For, lo! the Day – the Thrones are near –
And hark! 'mid sounds of hope and fear,
They call, from countries far and wide,
The wood whereon Messias died!
They bear it forth to bless or ban –
The signal of the Son of Man!

How shall men bear, amid their loss,
That Resurrection of the Cross!
The sign they mocked, by angels borne,
The banner of the Eternal Morn!
Once more beside its Lord to stand,
The Trophy Tree of Holy Land!

Up! Prophet-Lady, stern and calm,
Seek not a tent beneath the Palm,
Like Isha Lapidoth the wise:-
As Jael, Heber's wife – arise –
Up! spare not! wield thy noble name!
The Lord hath sold thee foes and fame!

In a note at the end he adds, 'I recommend the slanderers of God's servants, before they again presume to revile the imaged death-bed of the Lord, to read, carefully and thoroughly, the works of Gretser, published in Latin, in seventeen folio volumes, at Ratisbon, 1734-41'. The serious-minded Dr Lee may have permitted himself a smile when he described that as a 'paragraph of sound and excellent advice'.[22] Certainly the bishop's opponents would be kept out of mischief for some time, and Hawker was in good pugnacious form.

Yet in that same poem he equates the persecution of the Lady Superior with his own avowed suffering:

> Daughter! my spirit turns to thee:
> Here, by the lonely Severn sea,
> I, too, have borne, years fierce and long,
> All hatred, and rebuke, and wrong . . .

A year earlier he had written to a young relative, 'I have no thing, no one, to live for. No single reason why, if I were asked by an angel, I should wish to remain. I loathe life, and I yearn for death as some men do for wealth or rank. I would kiss the hand of any man who gave me to drink some deadly thing. O may God bless you, my dear boy, and make you unlike me!'[23] Thus the vicar, forgetting his beloved and companionable wife, cheered a young man on his way.

So his state of mind vacillated, almost violently, because at much the same time he wrote one of his most cheerful, positive, and indeed best poems, 'Be Of Good Cheer!' Within the brief and concentrated form of a sonnet, actually with fifteen rather than the statutory fourteen lines but such details never greatly worried him, he describes with marvellous simplicity the dilemma of the Christian evangelist and its solution. First comes the enthusiastic start, followed by failure, whether as part of a large missionary enterprise or alone. The great reappraisal follows, and a call for a new vision. Then he brilliantly places the volta, the break in a traditional sonnet to set the theme in a new direction: after all these fine and futile efforts, the answer is to wait, mending your nets like the first disciples, wait patiently but most hopefully for Jesus to come. It is pleasant and appropriate to end a chapter on Hawker's most hopeful decade with a poem which looks calmly forward.

* * * * *

'BE OF GOOD CHEER!'

Come, stand upon the deck, and fish for men!
    Let down and haul, it is Saint Andrew's Day;
    Take we the allotted side, and watch for prey!
We toil all night for nought! – we cast again:
    They who are fain a multitude to hold,
    Break their smooth gear, and not a fish enfold!
The meek and patient catch not: tell me then
    What is our vision? – what the crafty toil
    Whereby to win the draught and share the spoil?
It was on such a day – the where and when –
    Empty the basket – desolate and bare
    The ship of Galilee – yet, faithful there,
The brethren watch'd the deep with patient ken –
    Simon and Andrew sate, and calm on board
    Mended their nets - and waited for the Lord!

7

Into the 1850s, Visitors, Friends and Opinions

Hawker's 'picturesque though uneventful life'[1] seems to have become quieter still during the period between, roughly, 1846 and 1863. He published no further volumes of poetry, though some individual poems appeared in leaflet form, until at the age of sixty he suddenly produced his greatest work, 'The Quest of the Sangraal'. Up to this point his total output had been seven slim volumes, starting with *Tendrils* in 1821. There followed *Records of the Western Shore* in 1832, with a *Second Series* in 1836; *Ecclesia* (1840); *Reeds Shaken with the Wind* (1843) with *Second Cluster* (1844); and *Echoes from Old Cornwall* in 1846. It is not impressive, especially when one has to add that much of the content was repeated in successive volumes. His Newdigate Prize poem, 'Pompeii', drags its slow length through most of them.

Meanwhile a biographer need not despair. There are still plenty of letters, entries in Thought Books and so on, to give an idea of what was going on in his life; and one event which gave him enormous pleasure provides a start. This was a visit from Alfred Tennyson.

Tennyson came to Cornwall several times. He wanted to research his version of the Arthur legends, 'Idylls of the King', and to visualise the stories in what he took to be their setting. Also he delighted in the place for itself, liking its people and, above all, gaining inspiration from the sea. On that first trip, in the summer of 1848, he kept a private journal, in which he wrote of 'sea purple and green like a peacock's neck', 'glorious ranks of waves and billows', 'the long green swell heaving on the black cliff '.[2] He slipped naturally into poetry. In another sense too he slipped naturally. It is strange that this supreme master of precise and limpid descriptive language was also large, clumsy, short-sighted and, especially in Cornwall, accident-prone. On a later visit, in 1860, he visited Slaughterbridge, the legendary site of Arthur's last battle, and expressed a wish to sit on a stone on the river bank where the king is supposed to have paused to rest. He did not stay

141

there long. Caroline Fox, the highly entertaining Cornish diarist, met him shortly afterwards and recorded, 'The River Camel he well believes in, particularly as he slipped his foot and fell in the other day, but found no Excalibur'[3]. An equally characteristic mishap twelve years earlier had brought Tennyson and Hawker together. Tennyson planned to travel to Bude: 'I hear that there are larger waves there than on any other part of the British coast, and must go thither and be alone with God'[4]. On arriving at his hotel he cried, "Where is the sea? Show me the sea!", charged off in the direction pointed out to him, fell off a high wall and crashed onto the beach, damaging his knee. Hawker's brother-in-law, Dr John Dinham, was called in to treat him, and took his patient to meet the local poet.

Hawker's own account of the occasion, faithfully transcribed by Byles, is predictably dramatic. The surprising lack of formal intro-ductions was probably due to Tennyson's obsessive desire to travel incognito: it seems that even Dinham did not know who he was.

I found my guest at his entrance a tall swarthy Spanish-looking man, with an eye like a sword. He sate down and we conversed. I at once found myself with no common mind. All poetry in particular he seemed to use like household words . . . We then talked about Cornwall and King Arthur, my themes, and I quoted Tennyson's fine acct. of the resto-ration of Excalibur to the Lake. Just then he said, "How can you live here thus alone? You don't seem to have any fit companions around you." My answer was another verse, from 'Locksley Hall' –

I to herd with narrow foreheads vacant of our glorious gains,
Like a beast with lower pleasures, like a beast with lower pains!

"Why that man," said he, "seems to be your favourite author." "Not mine only but England's," answered I. . . . he said, "Do you know my name?" – I said, "No, I have not even a guess". – "Do you wish to know it?" – "I don't much care – 'that which we call a rose' etc." – "Well then," said he, "my name is *Tennyson*!!" – "What!" said I, "*the* Tennyson?" – "What do you mean by *the* Tennyson? I am Alfred Tennyson who wrote 'Locksley Hall', which you seem to know by heart."[5]

Tennyson's account of the meeting, in his 'Journal of Cornwall Tour', is more terse. 'Took a gig to Reverend Hawker at Morwenstow, passing Coombe valley – fine view over sea, coldest manner of Vicar till I told my name, then all heartiness. Walked on cliff with him, told of shipwreck.' Hawker supplies more detail.

We talked of the sea, which he and I equally adore. But as he told me strange to say Wordsworth cannot bear its face. My solution was, that nursed among the still waters with a mind as calm and equable as his lakes the scenery of the rough places might be too boisterous for the meek man's soul. He agreed. . . . I questioned him about his mode of composition in this so wandering life. He said he usually made about ten lines every day, multitudes of which were never written down and so were lost for ever. I strongly chode with him for this. By and bye we went back to the house to dine. He said his chief reliance for bodily force was on wine, and I should conceive he yielded to the conqueror of Ariadne ever and anon.

They parted firm friends: "This", said Tennyson, "has indeed been a day to be remembered"; and Hawker, with his enthusiasm for unusual clothing, recorded his guest's appearance.

The Bard is a handsome well-formed man and tall, more like a Spaniard than an Englishman - black, long, elflocks all round his face, mid which his eyes not only shine but glare. His garments loose and full, as bard beseems, and over all a large dark Spanish cloak.

The two men kept in touch intermittently, but sadly there was no repetition of the visit. Still, Hawker felt more cheerful. Earlier in the year he had written that grim letter to a young relative quoted at the end of the last chapter, 'I would kiss the hand of any man who gave me to drink some deadly thing'. One looks in vain for consistency, whether of temperament, or opinion, or treatment of his fellows. Now he rounded off his account, '. . . it is to me a great memorial day in this my solitary place to have heard the voice and seen the form of Alfred Tennyson'.

In 1856 a more humble visitor received a friendly welcome, which was not in his case to last. The story of Hawker's dealings with John Blight tells quite a lot about our man, added to which Blight himself deserves to be remembered.

'We have also had a visit,' he wrote in August 1856, 'from a Mr Blight, son of a schoolmaster in Penzance, an artist, and a most deserving young man'[6]. Blight was indeed young, twenty-one to Hawker's fifty-three, and the vicar treated him in a patronising and almost boorish way: hardly justified given that Blight had already published his first book, *Ancient Crosses and other Antiquities of West Cornwall*, containing numerous very skilled engravings and a scholarly introduction. He came to see Hawker to seek his advice on publishing a second volume, about the crosses of East Cornwall, and as his biographer John Michell remarks in *A Short Life at the Land's End*, 'He probably got much more than he bargained for'.[7] He first received a favour. 'I did for him what I have hitherto steadfastly refused to all, and that is, I stood to him for a sketch of myself in cassock and hat, and this, if he can engrave it satisfactorily, he intends to publish.'[6]

Hawker is also depicted, with one of his dogs, Berg, standing beside 'the Well of St John on Morwenstow Glebe' in the book, *Ancient Crosses of East Cornwall*, which was published in 1858. But above and beyond that, he moved in forcefully to play a major part in its production. He contributed, in prose and verse, a good deal of the commentary on the engravings, insisting that each piece should include his monograph. He also took the opportunity to gratify Sir Thomas Acland, writing to Blight, 'Now mark I have an engraving from a sketch made by Sir T. Acland of a demolished pierhead at Bude that I wish to go in your work with names if he will assent. I think it would make your sale ... Pray throw yourself totally into Sir T. D. Acland's sketch of the pierhead'.[7]

Blight obliged, and the engraving appeared, quite incongruously, among the ancient crosses. But the poor young man spelt the name wrong, 'Ackland', and was duly rebuked by Hawker, 'I must request *immediate* attention to my wishes ... Be careful to remember there is great disrespect in misspelling the names of People of Rank'.[7]

Blight does appear to have been something of a victim-figure. He described himself: 'I am as sensitive as a dove, my bashfulness is sometimes taken for stupidity, and my retiring manners for impudence'.[8] But Hawker did not simply bully him and muscle in on his book. They seem to have had a pleasant relationship as well, though there was no doubt who considered himself in charge. Hawker wanted an engraving done of a particular 'carvure' in Morwenstow church. Blight questioned the existence of the word. Back came the reply, 'If no such word, it is time there should be. I invent it'.[9] More significantly, Hawker used his influence to obtain a much better subscribers' list for the second volume than Blight, alone and known only in Penzance, had managed for the first. He went on to seek, and obtain, permission for the book to be dedicated to the Prince of Wales as Duke of Cornwall. Here indeed was a triumph. He wrote a six-stanza poem, appropriately embellished with exclamation marks but otherwise not notable, to accompany the dedication, and noted, "My letter to the Palace . . . has been fraught with success, and young Blight's fortunate start in life is made".[10] John Michell captures this happy moment.

At the age of twenty-two Blight was near the height of his power as artist and engraver. His depiction of architectural and sculptural detail was always meticulous; with maturing confidence he went on to illustrate the ancient monuments of Cornwall, not merely as archaeological relics, but in relation to local life and landscape, as shrines of the 'genius loci'. Secluded in ferny hollows or high on the windswept moors, the ancient stone crosses, chapels and holy wells memorialise the piety of their founders, and reproach, in their condition of picturesque decay, the iconoclasm of the present. This was Hawker's vision, and from the time of their first meeting in 1856 it became Blight's also. The Vicar of Morwenstow enchanted the sensitive young artist with his mysticism, personality and reputation.[11]

The two men did indeed produce a memorably attractive book, and Blight concluded his introduction with a touch of the charm that he clearly possessed: 'The legends and poetical illustrations which enrich these pages are the kind contributions of a literary friend; and they scarcely require the initial letters of his name to point out the native hand whose numbers have often awakened the "Echoes of Old Cornwall" '.[12]

His next move was to propose the publication of his two volumes, dealing respectively with the crosses of West and East Cornwall, as one book under the title *The Ancient Crosses of Cornwall*: a sensible enough idea, but at this point things began to go wrong, and we see Hawker, sadly, at his pettiest. Blight visualised that the West Cornwall volume, the first, should come first in the joint volume, preceded by the royal dedication. This strictly of course applied only to the East Cornwall volume, which, complete with the 'kind contributions of a literary friend', was to come second.

Hawker was appalled: 'I can hardly find words enough to express my horror at your proposal. It would be a direct fraud, and on Royalty. It would be a trick which would end in your total ruin as an author.'[13]

Undeniably he had a case, albeit a less dramatic one. The dedication had been sought and granted only for the second volume. But as he elaborates, any sympathy drains away. Hawker was worried that the Prince, seeing the dedication attached to the first volume, the inferior one lacking any contribution from Hawker, would 'in light manner and idle mood of a young and occupied man' glance through it and be duly unimpressed. Consequently 'he closes the book and orders it to its shelf and perhaps never opens either again'. In other words the royal eye would never fall upon the work of Robert Stephen Hawker. He adds that 'I do not covet even a shadow of personal recognition'[14], but the damage is done. Hawker's motive in obtaining the dedication for his young protegé becomes all too clear, quite apart from the miscalculation that one senses he is making, of the reading tastes (if any) of the future Edward VII.

Blight obediently placed the East Cornwall volume, complete with dedication, first in the joint volume, and the storm passed. The rest of his life had a tragic inevitability about it. For a few years he flourished, without further assistance from Hawker though the two men remained occasionally in touch. He produced several more books of engravings with lucid commentaries, including A Week at The Land's End in 1861, and worked closely with the famous book collector, Shakespearian scholar and overwhelming personality James Halliwell. At Halliwell's behest he set about sketching every building in the area of Stratford-upon-Avon which Shakespeare would have known. This was of course a strenuous task, and involved spending time far from home, not just in Stratford but in Wales and London, in a very different society from anything Penzance could provide. All too soon, we find him joining that pathetic collection of young men - his almost exact Cornish contemporary, the sculptor Neville Northy

Burnard, is another who comes to mind – who have been unable to cope with such abrupt changes of social setting. In his case the story is even more than usually poignant, because his artistic brilliance never seems to have brought him any financial reward, and he was disastrously unbusinesslike and altogether incapable of coping with the practicalities of life. Early in 1869, at the age of thirty-three, he wrote to Halliwell, 'I have a notion, of which I cannot get rid, that my brain is all wrong'[15], and two years later he was committed to the County Lunatic Asylum where he died, completely forgotten, forty years later. There is no evidence that Hawker gave him a thought after 1870, when he states in a letter that in an address to the Penzance Society Blight 'mentions all the publications of the past and current years, but *omits mine.*[16]

Certainly Hawker does not come well out of the story. One senses the common circumstance of an older man enjoying the company of his junior while he is subservient, respectful, simultaneously perhaps engagingly cheeky; then turning resentful as he climbs the ladder on his own and begins to assert himself.

Meanwhile, despite all his claims of remoteness from the world 'among these rocks', the Vicar of Morwenstow continued to be in touch with events in the world beyond the Tamar. It need hardly be added that he expressed his opinions on them with vigour, despite a story which Byles tells:

One day a tourist asked him – "Mr Hawker, what are your views and opinions?" The vicar took him to a window in the passage facing the sea, and said – "There is Hennacliff, the highest cliff on this coast, on the right; the church on the left; the Atlantic Ocean in the middle. These are my views. My opinions I keep to myself." [17]

The Crimean War worried him a great deal. He deplored the fact that England should be allied with Turkey and hence with Islam. He had already expressed dismay, in a poem called 'The Nun of Carmel's Lament at the Conquest of St Jean d'Acre', at the capture of Acre from the Egyptians by an Anglo-Turkish force in 1840. He saw it as our national duty to defeat 'the crescent', not to be its ally.

THE NUN OF CARMEL'S LAMENT

At the Conquest of St Jean D'Acre
November 2nd, 1840

Weepest thou! weepest thou! with victory won,
Dark-eyed daughter of the Syrian sun!
Where Carmel, a conqueror, cleaves the sky,
With the turban'd palm for his crest on high.

Tears! where the crescent moon is bright,
And the red, red cross hath prevail'd in fight,
And swarthy Misraim's doom is done,
And Syria is safe, and Acco won!

I weep not the home of my Syrian birth,
Nor the victor's foot on my fathers' earth,
Nor the rushing rivers of Gentile gore,
That darken the floods upon Jewry's shore.

But I grieve that the sweet and the holy Sign
With the Moslem banner should wave and shine;
I blush for the battle that blends in fame
Mohammed's and Isa Ben Mariam's name.

Woe worth the war where the gain is loss!
Shame to the Crescent beside the Cross!
Trouble and dread to the pledge that gave
A Christian arm to a Pagan glaive!

I dream of the hearts that are lowly laid,
The warriors that wielded the beamy blade,
And waved to the winds yon blessèd sign,
In war for their God and his tarnished shrine.

I think on the days that are quench'd and gone,
When the souls of England came sternly on,
To sweep from the lands the accursèd horde
That mock'd at the Cross and blasphemed its Lord.

And I see where the Turkish cohorts ride –
The armies of Christ – they are side by side!
And I hear, in the city's funeral knell,
Old England's shout and the Islam yell.

Tears then, and grief, for the Syrian sun,
With victory gained and with Acco won.
Oh! pride will be shame and triumph loss
Till the Crescent shiver beneath the Cross!

❋ ❋ ❋ ❋ ❋

With the outbreak of war he wrote in a Thought Book, 'What is all the Crimean neglect of duty done, but Protestantism carried into a practical climax? Is it not the gigantic sneer of that religious negation that all our works are filthy rags?'[18] He had apparently lost faith in the capacity of England to perform any duty at all. 'England', he wrote in a letter, 'will never win a victory by sea or land. England will fail, and be dishonoured in this war.' He provided reasons.

In former days and later times down to the boasted Waterloo success, this was to a certain extent a Godfearing land. No hand had then been laid on God's Tenth or Tithe – No law had made poverty a guilt and interfered with Christian alms – No efforts had been made to rob the roofs and walls of God of repair by rate – But now all these crimes have been committed, not here and there by men or bodies of men, but by the gathered nation – by assembled voice of law and by collective hand and deed. When victories of old were won, such as are recorded by the prophet Daniel and others, they were never gained by the human army alone but by the Angel expressly sent from on high. The Angel of England is withheld by the Angel's God – and therefore, said I, and so still I say, England will not prevail – no, neither in war nor in council of peace – no more.[19]

These prophecies of doom from Morwenstow failed to rock governments, and as Byles writes, 'There is a parochial character about the Vicar's comments on public affairs which will nowadays provoke a smile'.[20] He also contributed to the public debate a strange poem called 'Baal Zephon', defined in a footnote as 'The God of the North', the domain of demons in his cosmology. He described the poem as containing 'my own solution of the War'.[21] It cannot actually have been much help. The theme, so far as it can be clarified, is that the forces of evil allied with those of Islam are triumphing in the Crimea and it is time for the Lord to rise and defeat them, simultaneously to 'bid the traitor Russ thy banished Name declare' (a reference to the so-called Filioque Controversy, again explained in a footnote, 'The phrase, "And the Son", in the Nicene Creed, is abjured by the Greek Church, with the doctrine which those words contain'). 'Baal Zephon' is a bombastic unrewarding piece of work, casting light only on its author's concern about the war and his country's role in it.

His attitude to the other major conflict of the mid-century, the American Civil War, was less intense, and would not be widely popular today. He found slavery quite acceptable, on two grounds. First, 'the Second Person of the Godhead adopts as his own appellative a hundred times the name of Slave, altho' the Puritan translators corrupted that word into Servant, a word, as significant of one hired for wages, unknown to that age and generation'.[22] Secondly, the dark-skinned races were the sons of Ham:

BAAL ZEPHON

Was it the shout of storms that rent the sky?
    The rush of many a whirlwind from its lair?
Or be the fierce Maozzim loose on high? –
    The old Gods of the North: the Demons of the Air!

Those Tartar hills! billowy with writhing men;
    That yelling Euxine! throttled with her dead:
The quivering air, as thick with ghosts as when
    The severed souls of Syrian armies fled!

Ah fatal field! Ah doomed and deadly sea!
    Where be the hosts of God? – that ancient band;
Michael the Prince! and Uriel! – where are ye,
    That once did valiantly for English land?

Shun ye the flaunting Crescent's baleful sign,
    The circumcisèd hordes of vile Mahound?
Or is the Red-Cross banner loath to shine
    Where Scythian fiends beset the shuddering ground?

Lords of the vassal air, the lightning-tongue,
    The harnessed fires, with footsteps like the storm!
Where is your vaunt, and what your strength among
    Those riders of the cloud, with battle warm?

Sound the stern signal! summon sea and shore;
    Clothe many a steed with thunder for the war! –
An angel, standing at a cottage door
    To guard a peasant's child, is mightier far!

Oh for the Sigil! or the chanted spell!
    The pentacle that Demons know and dread! –
So should Maozzim flee, with baffled yell,
    And the lulled Euxine smooth its billowy bed.

152

Arise O Lord! stretch forth Thy red right hand!
Smite the strong Dragon and his Scythian lair!
God visible! among the nations stand
And bid the traitor Russ thy banished Name declare!

✻ ✻ ✻ ✻ ✻

God made the race only to serve. Dark Christian still dark . . . Ham
is on the road to the palace of a great king. What matters it to him
if he be a loaden slave by the way, a vassal of burthen in the mixed
multitudes of that caravan? A vase of clay holds wine, a leather bag
may be filled with gold.[23]

Hardly the acme of enlightenment, but more charitable than many
of his contemporaries on both sides of the Atlantic; and it has to be
added that he took a rather jaundiced view of Americans overall:

Certain it is that there is something naturally narrow and meagre in the
American mind. There is not, it is said, one original book among their
publications. Nor a single master mind as an orator, or a poet (Longfellow
is tuneful but mediocre) or statesman or divine.[24]

This, when Lincoln was President, was neither fair nor well-
informed, but before offence is taken at such deplorable prejudices,
they can be expressed at a more good-humoured level, with Hawker
at his most engaging. A visitor to Morwenstow was overtaken by
Hawker on horseback, and asked if he was going to call at the vicarage.
He replied that he was not.

"You know the command," he loudly said, "Be not forgetful to entertain
strangers! I shall expect you there!" Slap went the spurs . . . I have the
kindest remembrances of the hospitality of the dining room: the mut-
ton well hanged, the wine good, the fruit ripe and rich; but before the
cheese was brought forth and cut my kind entertainer said: "Which
hunk will you have sir? This is cheddar, this is American. My wife says it
is good: I have never tasted it. I hate everything American.[25]

He also deplored the dangerous influence of the United States on English society, 'the English servant of the nineteenth century is tinged strongly with Americanism and would fain make every house a republic'.[26]

He was distressed by the Indian Mutiny of 1857, grieving at least as much over the treatment of the mutineers as the massacres set in motion by Nana Sahib and his ilk. But it was an event of a different kind in that same year which caused him the most profound concern. A comet appeared, and he hastened to assure Mrs Watson that it was likely to herald the end of the world.

Here is an opportunity, if the comet may be left to follow its course for a moment, to say a word about this lady Mrs Watson. She and Hawker never set eyes on one another, but they corresponded, regularly and vigorously, between 1855 and 1870. She had provided a generous contribution from her home in Budleigh Salterton to his appeal for the repair of the church roof. Unfortunately only his letters to her have been preserved, but the pattern plainly was that she put difficult questions to him, about anything from the future of the universe to the day's news, and he eagerly and confidently replied. He seemed to suspect that they were never to meet, for he told her tales about Morwenstow and the life of its vicar which would have been unlikely to stand up to direct scrutiny. Above all, he loaded her with his copious sorrows, and there must have been some reciprocity, so they would have been a great help to one another. He writes in 1869:

I feel deeply grieved for you amid all my own distress and I pray for you earnestly every day. I do not think such a correspondence as ours ever occurred before. Such a tissue of sorrows and anxieties on both sides and on mine such a strange history of unusual events.[27]

He had written to her about the comet in 1857:

What a thought it is to think that the prediction of St Peter, that this earth and all upon it will be burned up, may be fulfilled in our very sight, and that this comet may be the messenger of wrath to execute the doom. How will men behave as the avenging thing draws slowly on – what will the multitudes in cities shout one to another as they gather in their streets? And what shall we country people do, as night reveals the seething fiery sky? As I said yesterday in church, we shall die in armies assembled in the fields, as they do in war; instead of one by one. Troops together will pass away.[28]

In the event all was well, to the relief no doubt of his congregation; and when another comet was seen four years later, his attitude to it was very different, cavalier rather than apocalyptic. One of the servants at the vicarage spotted the comet and told Hawker, who reported its appearance to his friend Dean Cowie of St Paul's. It was totally unexpected in astronomical circles, his was only the second letter to bring the news to London, and he reported gleefully to Mrs Watson:

. . . as I wrote to Cowie, 'What about the vaunted science of the nineteenth century, when a servant in a Cornish vicarage comes to announce to her master the arrival of a comet which ought to have been calculated in every observatory in England, and foretold to a single night years and months before?' Whereas this sudden stranger of the sky takes the world by surprise.[29]

Although this second phenomenon was not apparently to be alarmed at, it did cause Hawker to write a poem, 'The Comet of 1861'. It begins with an epigraph, from St Luke: 'Fearful sights and great signs shall there be from heaven',[30] and then lets loose a salvo of questions.

> Whence art thou, sudden comet of the sun?
> In what far depths of God thine orient place?
> Whence hath thy world of light such radiance won
> To gleam and curve along the cone of space?

With a confidence that one can only marvel at, and in defiance of 'the vaunted science of the nineteenth century', he defines space in a footnote: 'Space is that measured part of God's presence which is inhabited by the planets and the sun. The boundary of space is the outline of a cone, and the pathway of every planet is one of the sections of that figured form.'

This overweening assumption that he had, by God's grace, all the answers, will need more careful consideration. For the moment, the

THE COMET OF 1861

Whence art thou, sudden comet of the sun?
  In what far depths of God thine orient place?
Whence hath thy world of light such radiance won
  To gleam and curve along the cone of space?

Why comest thou, weird wanderer of the air?
  What is thine oracle for shuddering eyes?
Wilt thou some myth of crownless kings declare,
  Scathed by thy fatal banner of the skies?

Or dost thou glide, a seething orb of doom,
  Bristling with penal fires, and thick with souls –
The severed ghosts that throng thy peopled womb,
  Whom Azrael, warder of the dead, controls?

Throne of some lost archangel, dost thou glare,
  After long battle, on that conquering height?
Vaunt of a victory that is still despair,
  A trophied horror on the arch of night?

But lo! another dream: thou starry god,
  Art thou the mystic seedsman of the sky?
To shed new worlds along thy radiant road,
  That flow in floods of billowy hair on high?

Roll on! yet not almighty: in thy wrath
  Thou bendest like a vassal to his king;
Thou darest not o'erstep thy graven path,
  Nor yet one wanton smile of brightness fling.

Slave of a Mighty Master! be thy brow
  A parable of night, in radiance poured:
Amid thy haughtiest courses, what art thou?
  A lamp to lead some pathway of the Lord!

poem deserves attention. After that lovely example of sound echoing
sense in the fourth line, he goes on to devote three verses to picturing
the comet as a bearer of evil, prophesying the downfall of kings;
operating as a kind of mobile hell carrying damned souls round the
skies; or providing a throne for a lost archangel who can never return
to heaven. In the fifth verse he visualises a creator, not simply a bearer,
of good, bringing new worlds to birth on its course. After these
exciting possibilities, products of an unusual imagination to say the
least, he calms the scene down, as it were with the wave of a wand.
This comet is the 'Slave of a mighty master', performing God's will
though, he hints with relative modesty, it is not for us to know what
that will is.

> Amid thy haughtiest courses, what art thou?
> A lamp to lead some pathway of the Lord!

Here is a favourite, and very effective, technique of Hawker the
poet. In 'The Storm' he describes the frustrated frenzy of the sea and
in the final verse achieves a peacefulness.

> Thy way, O God, is in the sea,
> Thy paths, where awful waters be;
> Thy spirit thrills the conscious stone:
> O Lord, they footsteps are not known!

We have seen that the same effect can be found in the brilliant
sonnet 'Be of Good Cheer'. After reciting various vigorous forms of
evangelising, in the context of fishing for men, and having found
them all wanting, he returns his reader to the shore of Lake Galilee.

> . . .yet faithful there,
> The brethren watch'd the deep with patient ken –
> Simon and Andrew sate, and calm on board
> *Mended their nets* – and waited for the Lord!

So, in 'The Comet of 1861' as elsewhere, he displays his artist's
vivid imagination with a craftsman's skill, to achieve an effect
developed a hundred years later by T. S. Eliot, the peace of God:

I said to my soul, be still, and wait without hope
For hope would be hope for the wrong thing; wait without love
For love would be love of the wrong thing; there is yet faith
But the faith and the love and the hope are all in the waiting.[31]

To Hawker's distress, despite its evident quality, 'The Comet of 1861' failed to find a publisher. He writes towards the end of the same year:

There seems to be no shadow of sympathy between the men of my generation and myself. If I print anything in prose or verse no one cares even to read it . . .Only regard my lines on the Comet. They were tabooed by *The Times*, no literary journal would admit them, the Editor of *The Oriental Budget* rejected them because his paper 'only admitted *literary* compositions'.[32]

The judgment of that editor does indeed seem perverse, and one can feel sympathy for Hawker's grievance. However, as a candid friend or 'neighbourly authority' might have pointed out if only one had existed, he had himself defined the problem, 'no shadow of sympathy between the men of my generation and myself'.

At a time of intense scientific inquiry, anxious but still persistent theological speculation, overall broadening of knowledge, was anyone likely to listen with respect to a man who deliberately denounced and turned his back on such change, and whose concepts, however graphic, might have predated Milton's? Thoughtful people in 1861 would have been reasonably certain that the comet was not, for instance, a throne for a lost archangel. They might have been nervous about expressing doubt that it was 'A lamp to lead some pathway of the Lord'. But the fact still has to be faced. Hawker's views, in this case of celestial phenomena, were hopelessly anachronistic. They would have had nothing to offer to a reading public in search of truth, and were more likely to appear ridiculous.

A comparison with Tennyson's 'Locksley Hall', written twenty years earlier, is apposite. Hawker, as has been seen, particularly admired the poem. We may sneer at Tennyson's mistake about trains, which he supposed ran in grooves; but his powers of prophecy, along with his eagerness to embrace the future, will wipe the smile off our faces.

For I dipt into the future, far as human eye could see,
Saw the vision of the world, and all the wonder that would be;

Saw the heavens fill with commerce, argosies of magic sails,
Pilots of the purple twilight, dropping down with costly bales;

Heard the heavens fill with shouting, and there rained a ghastly dew
From the nations' airy navies grappling in the central blue;

Far along the world-wide whisper of the south-wind rushing warm,
With the standards of the peoples plunging through the thunder-storm;

Till the war-drum throbbed no longer, and the battle-flags were furled
In the parliament of man, the federation of the world.[33]

There are familiar scenes here, even if the vision is not totally
fulfilled yet; and at least Tennyson was trying, and was visualising an
exciting and hopeful future, whereas Hawker sought comfort in the
past and despaired of the future. His validity as a significant poet
does not have to be impaired, even if as an artist he pales a little in
this instance alongside Tennyson. Anachronism need not dictate
literary judgment, certainly not a hundred and forty years later.

Comparisons are easier to make between Hawker and poets of
the mid-seventeenth century, for example George Herbert and Milton,
than with his contemporaries. As a ballad-writer in particular, he was
closer to more immediate precursors such as Thomas Moore and
Walter Scott. But there is also a case for setting him much further
back before his time. Another correspondent whom he never met,
the Rev. William West, described him as a man 'whom I always
think of as our English Dante, born out of due time, some six hundred
years behind the "progress of the age" '.[34] Piers Brendon remarks
that 'it is no exaggeration to say that he was nearer in spirit to the
Middle Ages than to the present day', and goes on:

Yet Hawker was only an extreme symptom of an endemic condition of
nineteenth century country society. Living, as they did, before the com-
munications explosion, the cultural isolation of rural Victorians was
palpable and overwhelming. It determined the whole tenor of their
existence in a way which is almost impossible for us to understand
without a great imaginative leap backward in time.[35]

Hawker wrote himself in 1862, 'Did you ever hear that for every 100 miles you live from London, you must reckon yourself a century back from your own date? We therefore, who are 250 miles off, are now in the year 1610 in all that relates to agriculture and civilisation.'

He qualifies particularly as 'our English Dante' in his concept of the site and nature of Purgatory, or, as he preferred to call it, Hades. Whereas he was generally prepared to share even his most bizarre ideas with friends and correspondents, he kept these views to his private Thought Books, probably because of his obligation as a priest in the Church of England to adhere in public to the Thirty-nine Articles, the twenty-second of which reads, 'The Romish doctrine concerning Purgatory ... is a fond thing vainly invented, and grounded upon no warranty of Scripture, but rather repugnant to the word of God'. His first published account of Purgatory/Hades took the form of a poem, 'Aurora', written in 1870. By then, it seems, he was less concerned to protect his credentials as an Anglican. Meanwhile, he wrote in his 1856 Thought Book:

The earth is hollow throughout, vaulted and arched and its roof is ribbed with branching rocks which are the roots of the mountains and hills. There within the world of the globe is one wide vast deep multitudinous realm sunless and starless but with a soft calm silent mild ethereal thrilling firmament of breath which is alive, and which itself is life and light and air. (Inhabited by myriads of conscious and visible shapes.)

Part of this underworld, the north, was reserved for those souls who were in the power of demons and for whom there was no hope. He makes two notes, both under the heading 'Hades', in 1844 and 1847:

Joyless sunless loveless where hope and memory are extinguished and one long vague remorse replaceth time and eternity.
The realm of the tortured shadows. An endless chasm. An airy sea without a shore.

However, as becomes relatively clear in due course in 'Aurora', there is also the south, 'that calm and glad domain', where hope of redemption can exist:

AURORA

Sunfall, and yet no night! fire floods the earth!
    A molten rainbow flakes the northern sky!
The Polar gates unclose! and, gleaming forth,
    Troop the wild flames that glide and glare on high,
    Tinged in their vaulted home with that deep ruddy dye!

Whence flash these mystic signals? what the scene
    Where the red rivers find their founts of flame?
Far, far away, where icy bulwarks lean
    Along the deep, in seas without a name:
    Where the vast porch of Hades rears its giant frame!

The underworld of souls! severed in twain:
    One, the fell North, perplexed and thick with gloom;
And one, the South, that calm and glad domain,
    Where asphodel and lotus lightly bloom
    'Neath God's own Starry Cross, the shield of peaceful doom.

No quest of man shall touch - no daring keel
    Cleave the dark waters to their awful bourne;
None shall the living sepulchre reveal
    Where separate souls must throng, and pause; and yearn
    For their far dust, the signal, and their glad return.

Ay! ever and anon the gates roll wide,
    When whole battalions yield their sudden breath;
And ghosts in armies gather as they glide,
    Still fierce and vengeful, from the field of death.
    Lo! lightnings lead their hosts, and meteors glare beneath.

* * * * *

Where separate souls must throng, and pause; and yearn
For their far dust, the signal, and their glad return.

In 1851 he proffers the possibility that Sir John Franklin and his crew, who had recently perished in an attempt to find the North-West Passage, had managed to obtain admission. Under that same heading 'Hades' he writes:

Compare the ancient dream it is the vaulted womb of our orb, was the place of sojourn for separate souls. Its gates, the poles, guarded with those walls of thick ribbed frost. What if *Franklin* pierced the boundary and he and his men glided on their decks amid the ghosts! Suddenly! They saw 1851 a calm unfrozen sea, vital with tides and inhabited by birds and fish.

In 1864 he speculates about the climate of Hades.

Descend into the earth, every 45 ft. one degree fahrenheit hotter. Thin crust warmer clime, thick reverse, therefore the poles thinner in crust from the revolving of the orb. Warm hence Aurora, from the poles. Hence a likelihood that the poles have warmth from within without sun heat and may be inhabited by a race wild wonderful and strange.

Wild wonderful and strange indeed, and he decided, after 'an unusually brilliant display of the Aurora Borealis on November 10, 1870',[37] that these beliefs must be released from his Thought Books and broadcast to the world, through the medium of a poem. 'In my "Aurora" it is my great wish', he writes, 'to instruct, to teach my own countrymen what they ought to know'. He adds by way of elucidation:

I adopted a theory of the time of Origen, that the scene of the Intermediate State is the hollow centre of the earth, and that the Northern Lights are flashed from the opening of the gates at the poles.[38]

That direct expression of a didactic purpose is positively alarming. What was good enough for Origen, he seems to say, is good enough for the 1870s. He is now ignoring about sixteen hundred years of scientific advance. Not surprisingly, 'Aurora' met the same fate at the hands of the public as 'The Comet of 1861'. It seems a shame, for the poem is richly colourful and attractive, a delight to read. If there were any people in 1870 who could accept 'that the Northern Lights are flashed from the opening of the gates at the poles', Hawker's deployment of his descriptive powers could well have been not simply convincing but overwhelming. Again however, facts have to be faced. There are unlikely to have been any such people, and yet he saw it as his mission to teach his countrymen what they ought to know.

Overall, as was clear from his reactions to the Crimean War, he despaired of his country and his countrymen. To quote another example:

. . . I predict the utter and speedy extinction of England as a great power. Her three hundred years of dissent, the largest allotted time for any heresy to endure, is now well nigh turned out . . . Why should England stand? What angel could arrive with duties to perform for that large blaspheming smithery, once a great nation, now a forge for railways – a kind of station![39]

He was instinctively repelled by the burgeoning of industry and the spread of railways. It also appears that he was equating heresy and dissent, and tracing both back to the Reformation, another indication of sympathy with Rome. But what concerned him more, as became apparent earlier, was a supposed weakening of the nation's moral fibre, for which he held John Wesley responsible. He had earlier described Methodism in a Thought Book as 'salvation made easy, or every man his own redeemer', and in 1862 he wrote:

Go whither you will – to the condemned cell – the college or the church, and the sole question to the sinner is, 'How do you *feel?* What do you *think?* What is your own judgment in your own case?' There is not one other doctrine in the land.[40]

Viewing the state of the nation as he did from afar, he saw its inevitable downfall as being due first, then, to dissent. The second corrupting force was greed. 'The sin of England has been greed of gold – lust for gain. In pursuit of this the nation has said "tush" to the Most High.'[41] Biblical authority was sought, found and embellished.

In all that is called material success England prospers – in wealth and arts and arms – but that is of the earth and earthly. Demons may be the author of that. For did not the Great Enemy say to our Lord himself when he showed him all the kingdoms of the earth, 'all these,' said he, 'will I give thee for *they are mine* and to whomsoever I will I give them'. There is not in the Bible a more fearful text. To think that earthly success, earthly grandeur may be the direct gift of the Demon.[42]

In the course of his condemnation of contemporary society, he offered Mrs Watson in 1869 a remarkable picture of Morwenstow on the Day of Judgment. One figure, recently deceased, emerges among his predecessors.

I sometimes fancy the ground in my own churchyard unclosing and the bodies of the dead standing up from their graves while the earth falls from their shoulders crumbling down . . . If one of the arisen dead in the churchyard were to turn to another and say 'Hast thou any money?' what a shout of derision would ensue![43]

The lady must have had to learn to be ready for anything.

These views were expressed only to correspondents, though they may first have been tried out on Morwenstow and Welcombe congregations. They would have made no more public impact than his interpretations of comets or the Aurora Borealis, and since they cannot be described as uniformly fair and reasonable, that is probably just as well. He was prepared to expound on anything, with the confidence – he would have said, with the authority – that came with the sureness of his faith. A nephew wrote to him and he replied.

You ask me to 'put in one of my nut-shells' the pith and marrow of the controversy, which at this time pervades the English mind, as to the claims of science and faith. Let me try: The material universe – so the sages allege – is a vast assemblage of atoms or molecules . . .

He provides a brisk exposition of the physics of the universe, inevitably directing it to a well known obstacle. 'But still, a thoughtful mind will venture to demand, whence do these atoms derive their existence? and from what, and from whom, do they inherit the propensities wherewithal they are imbued?'

We are back on his home ground – though it must be added that he handled the physics with aplomb. 'We must lift the veil', he writes, 'we must pass into the border-land between the two worlds, and there enquire at the oracles of revelation touching the unseen and spiritual powers which thrill through the mighty sacrament of the visible creation'. These powers, predictably, are angels, 'in aspect as "young men in white garments", who inhabit the void place between the worlds and their maker, and their God'.

These are they that each with a delegated office fulfil what their 'King Invisible' decrees; not with the dull, inert mechanism of fixed and natural law, but with the unslumbering energy and the rational obedience of spiritual life. They mould the atom; they wield the force; and, as Newton rightly guessed, they rule the world of matter beneath the silent omnipotence of God.[44]

Even the total sceptic, sharing none of Hawker's beliefs, even indeed the mocker of his eccentric views, must surely murmur here 'not bad'. The clarity, the sympathy aligned with dogmatism, can perhaps set in proportion Hawker's opinions on public affairs and celestial phenomena.

Meanwhile, it is time to return to a chronological biography, re-establishing ourselves at the end of the 1850s, and moving towards the most intense emotional crisis of his life from which derived his greatest poetry.

8

1863-4, Charlotte's Death
and 'The Quest of the Sangraal'

Y ou are a woman and I am a man', Hawker wrote to Mrs Watson in September 1863, 'and it is God's wish and gracious law that your sex shall have power to control your own sorrows in order to soothe ours'.[1] This assertion of divine purpose, noteworthy even by his standards, followed upon the death at the age of eighty of his wife Charlotte, which left him in a state of uninhibited grief. He craved for comfort, and it seems very likely that he sought it not simply from ministering females, but from opium. Byles, the loyal son-in-law, brought himself to admit:

> He took opium, at first as a medicine, afterwards from habit, and there can be little doubt that this explained a great deal in his character and mental attitude. Under its influence, perhaps, much of his finest work in poetry was written; but it had its inevitable reaction, in irritability, and moods of profound depression.[2]

Piers Brendon devotes a chapter to speculation on the effect of the drug on Hawker's behaviour, and particularly on his composition of 'The Quest of the Sangraal'. It is all interesting, but at this most significant period of his life the facts are eloquent enough. Charlotte died on February 2nd, 1863 and Hawker was shattered; he was however stimulated into working at his poetry as never before, and by the end of the same year published the first of four projected 'chants' of 'The Quest'. Within the next year his domestic life was transformed as he married again. A further year on, in December 1865, the first of his three children was born. His life has not hitherto been incessantly eventful. Now the pace changes.

Charlotte, it will be remembered, was twenty years older than her husband; and although one suspects that this discrepancy condemned him to a lack of sexual fulfilment which was a factor in his reiterated fits of depression, there is no doubt that they were devoted to one another. There are frequent allusions in his letters to the help she gave him with his parish work, and to the closeness of their lives together. He idolised her, writing again to Mrs Watson:

On close remembrance of the 40 years I cannot discover a single instance of selfishness or of wrongful feeling in all her whole life. It has soothed me exceedingly to find how all in my parish loved my poor dear unassuming wife. She made no pretences of any kind, was never demonstrative even to those she loved best, but then every word was true and sincere, every thought high-principled and just and kind.[3]

Towards the end of her life her eyesight failed her, and a less generous-minded but perhaps more human view of her is provided by a visitor:

. . . an even more eccentric old lady, also considerably older than himself who amused us much by making bad shots, owing to her very defective sight, at the teapot with the kettle and flooding the tray instead. She amused us too by her resolutely expressed determination never to enter a railway train and thus be indebted to a settle for her locomotion.[4]

Before she died she became completely blind, and he nursed her himself, also reading novels aloud to her, which, according to Brendon, 'left no trace on his preoccupied mind, so that he could afterwards remember nothing of plot or characters'.[5] After the event he made no attempt to control his expressions of grief, breaking down in public and sparing his correspondents nothing. There seems to have been no touch of the stoic in Robert Stephen Hawker: as he acknowledged with engaging frankness to Mrs Watson, 'I do not think I am a selfish man but my nature is to lean and not to sustain others as I ought'.[6] The last word on this desperately unhappy period of his life can be left with Bishop Phillpotts, whose wife died later in that same year 1863. Hawker wrote a letter of condolence. The bishop's reply expressed gratitude but also a degree of rebuke, reading in part:

I wish your sympathy were not the reopening of your own sorrows. But the indulgence of these sorrows is I feel an enjoyment. Be moderate in that indulgence.[7]

Hawker regarded 'The Quest of the Sangraal' as an offering to the memory of his beloved wife. A letter to Mrs Watson, written in

November 1863, makes clear that this was the source of his sudden rush of poetic energy, and also provides a version of the story on which the poem is based. For both reasons it merits quoting almost in full.

The Sangraal, as I think I have said before, was the chalice in which Our Lord celebrated his last passover of the Jews and his first eucharist as the Lord of the Church. It was preserved by Joseph of Arimathea, so runs the legend, and brought by him to Glastonbury, where his staff took root and became the celebrated Christmas Thorn. It was taken away when the land became sinful, and the search for it was proclaimed at Dundagel by King Arthur to the Knights of the Round Table. The Sangraal has always been regarded as the type of the gospel, and the loss and recovery are emblems of the failure of our light and its restoration.

   But I must tell you the source of this theme for me. Nine and thirty years agone on the 4th of Novr 1824 [actually November 6th, 1823] I was married, and we went from Stratton where my father was vicar, to Dundagel in lodgings for a month – close to the castle of King Arthur and amid the legends of his life and deeds. There we used to roam about and read all that could be found about those old-world histories, and often was this legend of the Sangraal talked of as a fine subject for verse. Often I have said 'If I could but throw myself back to King Arthur's time and write what he would have said and thought it would make a good Cornish book' . . . Thus I have told you but to nobody else the reason of my choice, and whereas, as you know, the custom is to select some great person as a patron and to dedicate your work to him or her, I shall not do so – but in the place of the dedication shall stand this – 'To: a vacant chair: and an added stone: I chant these solitary sounds'.

   It is to me so striking and so strange that after nine and thirty years of travel thro' life I come back to the same old scene, circling like some hunted animal to die where my life was born . . . [8]

To work back through this revealing document: the moving dedication did indeed stand, though his second wife Pauline, sending to a friend a copy of the book some years after Hawker's death, reported, 'Where a page has been cut out it was done by Mr Hawker's own hand; it was a dedication to his first wife which he always cut out latterly'.[9] This rather drastic action was taken no doubt out of deference to Pauline's feelings.

   Another Arthurian poem follows.

168

THE DOOM-WELL OF ST MADRON

"Plunge thy right hand in St. Madron's spring,
If true to its troth be the palm you bring:
But if a false sigil thy fingers bear,
Lay them the rather on the burning share."

Loud laughed King Arthur whenas he heard
That solemn friar his boding word:
And blithely he sware as a king he may
"We tryst for St. Madron's at break of day."

"Now horse and hattock, both but and ben,"
Was the cry at Lauds, with Dundagel men;
And forth they pricked upon Routorr side,
As goodly a raid as a king could ride.

Proud Gwennivar rode like a queen of the land,
With page and with squire at her bridle hand;
And the twice six knights of the stony ring,
They girded and guarded their Cornish king.

Then they halted their steeds at St. Madron's cell:
And they stood by the monk of the cloistered well;
"Now off with your gauntlets," King Arthur he cried,
"And glory or shame for our Tamar side."

'Twere sooth to sing how Sir Gauvain smiled,
When he grasped the waters so soft and mild;
How Sir Lancelot dashed the glistening spray
O'er the rugged beard of the rough Sir Kay.

Sir Bevis he touched and he found no fear:
'Twas a *bénitée* stoup to Sir Belvidere,
How the fountain flashed o'er King Arthur's Queen
Say, Cornish dames, for ye guess the scene.

"Now rede me my riddle, Sir Mordred, I pray,
My kinsman, mine ancient, my *bien-aimé*;
Now rede me my riddle, and rede it aright,
Art thou traitorous knave or my trusty knight?"

He plunged his right arm in the judgment well,
It bubbled and boiled like a cauldron of hell:
He drew and he lifted his quivering limb,
Ha! Sir Judas, how Madron had sodden him!

Now let Uter Pendragon do what he can,
Still the Tamar river will run as it ran:
Let King or let Kaiser be fond or be fell,
Ye may harowe their troth in St Madron's well.

* * * * *

His explanation of 'the source of this theme', his early interest in the Arthur legends so vividly shared with Charlotte, can perhaps counterbalance any theorising about the contribution of opium; though it should be added that one specialist in the subject writes of the poem's long last verse, 'The horrific intensity of the vision might owe something to opium-dreams'.[10] His enthusiasm for the theme emerges several times in his earlier career, for instance in 'The Doom-Well of St Madron', a fine energetic ballad published in 1855. Arthur invites Guinevere and certain knights to plunge their right hands into the well to test their loyalty: the water will react. All do well, then Sir Mordred's turn comes.

This is a young hearty Arthur, whereas in 'The Quest', conforming with his creator, he is world-weary and sad.

Tennyson's visit of 1848 would also have stirred Hawker; and in any case, Arthur is central to Cornish folklore, Hawker's enthusiasm for 'those old-world histories' is patent, the two could not fail to converge. As will become apparent, he bound himself very close to the legendary king, creating him indeed as his 'alter ego'. Furthermore, not only is this a Cornish Arthur, but the setting is as Hawker describes it, 'monumental Morwenstow throughout. I have touched on every Cornish feature in existence, our rock altars, barrows - moors etc'.[11] He expressed a similar view a few weeks earlier, along with a gloomy prognosis.

The more I think about it the more assured I am that my chant will contain more 'meat' than anything printed for 100 years, but that it will not be appreciated until centuries after I am dead. I have given the record and the rationale of Keltic Cornwall, the rock, barrow, moor, mountain, all there, with the spirit of our fathers rehearsing their intent.[12]

It is time to look at the text of this incomplete masterpiece, on the far side of the illustrations.

✳ ✳ ✳ ✳ ✳

R.S.H. at Oxford

R.S.H. at his vicarage door

R.S.H. from a drawing by the Earl of Carlisle

R.S.H. August 1875, a week before his death, in surplice,
stole and biretta

Morwenstow Vicarage

A House A Glebe A Pound a Day,
A pleasant Place to watch and pray;
Be true to Church, Be kind to Poor,
O Minister, for ever more.

The inscription above the vicarage door

R.S.H. with his dog Berg at St John's Well, drawn by J.T. Blight

A ship wrecked off the coast near Bude

Pauline Hawker, née Kuczynski

'Hawker's Hut' on the cliff

Heavy seas at Morwenstow

Morwenstow Church and churchyard

The interior of Morwenstow Church

R.S.H. characteristically dressed, aged sixty

THE QUEST OF THE SANGRAAL

To a Vacant Chair: and an Added Stone:
I Chant These Solitary Sounds

Ho! for the Sangraal! vanish'd Vase of Heaven!
That held, like Christ's own heart, an hin of blood!
Ho! for the Sangraal! . . .
                How the merry shout
Of reckless riders on their rushing steeds,
Smote the loose echo from the drowsy rock
Of grim Dundagel, thron'd along the sea!

"Unclean! unclean! ten cubits and a span,
Keep from the wholesome touch of human-kind:
Stand at the gate, and beat the leper's bell,
But stretch not forth the hand for holy thing, –   10
Unclean, as Egypt at the ebb of Nile!"
Thus said the monk, a lean and gnarlèd man;

His couch was on the rock, by that wild stream
That floods, in cataract, Saint Nectan's Kieve:
One of the choir, whose life is Orison.
They had their lodges in the wilderness,
Or built them cells beside the shadowy sea,
And there they dwelt with angels, like a dream:
So they unroll'd the volume of the Book,
And fill'd the fields of the Evangelist   20
With antique thoughts, that breath'd of Paradise.

Uprose they for the Quest – the bounding men
Of the siege perilous, and the granite ring –
They gathered at the rock, yon ruddy tor;
The stony depth where lurked the demon-god,
Till Christ, the mighty Master, drave him forth.

There stood the knights, stately, and stern, and tall;
Tristan, and Perceval, Sir Galahad,
And he, the sad Sir Lancelot of the lay:
Ah me! that logan of the rocky hills,   30
Pillar'd in storm, calm in the rush of war,
Shook, at the light touch of his lady's hand!

See! where they move, a battle-shouldering kind!
Massive in mould, but graceful: thorough men:
Built in the mystic measure of the Cross: –
Their lifted arms the transome: and their bulk,
The Tree, where Jesu stately stood to die –
Thence came their mastery in the field of war: –
Ha! one might drive battalions – one, alone!

See! now, they pause; for in their midst, the King,   40
Arthur, the Son of Uter, and the Night,
Helm'd with Pendragon, with the crested Crown,
And belted with the sheath'd Excalibur,
That gnash'd his iron teeth, and yearn'd for war!
Stern was that look (high natures seldom smile)
And in those pulses beat a thousand kings.
A glance! and they were husht: a lifted hand!
And his eye ruled them like a throne of light.
Then, with a voice that rang along the moor,
Like the Archangel's trumpet for the dead,   50
He spake – while Tamar sounded to the sea.

"Comrades in arms! Mates of The Table Round!
Fair Sirs, my fellows in the bannered ring,
Ours is a lofty tryst! this day we meet,
Not under shield, with scarf and knightly gage,
To quench our thirst of love in ladies' eyes:
We shall not mount to-day that goodly throne,
The conscious steed, with thunder in his loins,
To launch along the field the arrowy spear:

Nay, but a holier theme, a mightier Quest –   60
'Ho! for the Sangraal, vanish'd Vase of God!'

"Ye know that in old days, that yellow Jew,
Accursèd Herod; and the earth-wide judge,
Pilate the Roman – doomster for all lands,
Or else the Judgment had not been for all, –
Bound Jesu-Master to the world's tall tree,
Slowly to die. . . .
                    Ha! Sirs, had we been there,
They durst not have assayed their felon deed,
Excalibur had cleft them to the spine!

Slowly He died, a world in every pang,   70
Until the hard centurion's cruel spear
Smote His high heart: and from that severed side,
Rush'd the red stream that quencht the wrath of Heaven!

"Then came Sir Joseph, hight of Arimathèe,
Bearing that awful Vase, the Sangraal!
The Vessel of the Pasch, Shere Thursday night,
The selfsame Cup, wherein the faithful Wine
Heard God, and was obedient unto Blood.
Therewith he knelt and gathered blessèd drops
From his dear Master's Side that sadly fell,   80
The ruddy dews from the great tree of life:
Sweet Lord! what treasures! like the priceless gems
Hid in the tawny casket of a king, –
A ransom for an army, one by one!
That wealth he cherisht long: his very soul
Around his ark: bent as before a shrine!

"He dwelt in Orient Syria: God's own land:
The ladder foot of heaven – where shadowy shapes
In white apparel glided up and down.
His home was like a garner, full of corn,   90

And wine and oil; a granary of God!
Young men, that no one knew, went in and out,
With a far look in their eternal eyes!
All things were strange and rare: the Sangraal,
As though it clung to some ethereal chain,
Brought down high Heaven to earth at Arimathèe.

"He lived long centuries and prophesied.
A girded pilgrim ever and anon,
Cross-staff in hand, and, folded at his side
The mystic marvel of the feast of blood!   100
Once, in old time, he stood in this dear land,
Enthrall'd – for lo! a sign! his grounded staff
Took root, and branch'd, and bloom'd, like Aaron's rod:
Thence came the shrine, the cell; therefore he dwelt,
The vassal of the Vase, at Avalon!

"This could not last, for evil days came on,
And evil men: the garbage of their sin
Tainted this land, and all things holy fled.
The Sangraal was not: on a summer eve,
The silence of the sky brake up in sound!   110
The tree of Joseph glowed with ruddy light:
A harmless fire, curved like a molten vase,
Around the bush, and from the midst, a voice:
Thus hewn by Merlin on a runic stone: –
𝔎irioth : el : 𝔃annah : aulohee : pedah :

"Then said the shuddering seer – he heard and knew
The unutterable words that glide in Heaven,
Without a breath or tongue, from soul to soul –

"'The land is lonely now: Anathema!
The link that bound it to the silent grasp   120
 Of thrilling worlds is gathered up and gone:
The glory is departed; and the disk

So full of radiance from the touch of God!
This orb is darkened to the distant watch
Of Saturn and his reapers, when they pause,
Amid their sheaves, to count the nightly stars.

"'All gone! but not for ever: on a day
There shall arise a king from Keltic loins,
Of mystic birth and name, tender and true;
His vassals shall be noble, to a man: 130
Knights strong in battle till the war is won:
Then while the land is husht on Tamar side,
So that the warder upon Carradon
Shall hear at once the river and the sea –
That king shall call a Quest: a kindling cry:
'Ho! for the Sangraal! vanish'd Vase of God!'

"'Yea! and it shall be won! A chosen knight,
The ninth from Joseph in the line of blood,
Clean as a maid from guile and fleshly sin –
He with the shield of Sarras; and the lance,   140
Ruddy and moisten'd with a freshening stain,
As from a sever'd wound of yesterday –
He shall achieve the Graal: he alone!'

"Thus wrote Bard Merlin on the Runic hide
Of a slain deer: rolled in an aumry chest.

"And now, fair Sirs, your voices: who will gird
His belt for travel in the perilous ways?
This thing must be fulfilled: – in vain our land
Of noble name, high deed, and famous men;
Vain the proud homage of our thrall, the sea,   150
If we be shorn of God. Ah! loathsome shame!
To hurl in battle for the pride of arms:
To ride in native tournay, foreign war:
To count the stars; to ponder pictured runes,

And grasp great knowledge, as the demons do,
If we be shorn of God: – we must assay
The myth and meaning of this marvellous bowl:
It shall be sought and found: –"

                              Thus said the King.

Then rose a storm of voices; like the sea,
When Ocean, bounding, shouts with all his waves.   160
High-hearted men! the purpose and the theme,
Smote the fine chord that thrills the warrior's soul
With touch and impulse for a deed of fame.

Then spake Sir Gauvain, counsellor of the King,
A man of Pentecost for words that burn: –

"Sirs! we are soldiers of the rock and ring:
Our Table Round is earth's most honoured stone;
Thereon two worlds of life and glory blend,
The boss upon the shield of many a land,
The midway link with light beyond the stars!   170
This is our fount of fame! Let us arise,
And cleave the earth like rivers; like the streams
That win from Paradise their immortal name:
To the four winds of God, casting the lot.
So shall we share the regions, and unfold
The shrouded mystery of those fields of air.

"Eastward! the source and spring of life and light!
Thence came, and thither went, the rush of worlds,
When the great cone of space was sown with stars.
There rolled the gateway of the double dawn,   180
When the mere God shone down, a breathing man.
There, up from Bethany, the Syrian Twelve
Watched their dear Master darken into day.
Thence, too, will gleam the Cross, the arisen wood:
Ah, shuddering sign, one day, of terrible doom!

Therefore the Orient is the home of God.
"The West! a Galilee: the shore of men;
The symbol and the scene of populous life:
Full Japhet journeyed thither, Noe's son,
The prophecy of increase in his loins.   190
Westward Lord Jesu looked His latest love,
His yearning Cross along the peopled sea,
The innumerable nations in His soul.
Thus came that type and token of our kind,
The realm and region of the set of sun,
The wide, wide West; the imaged zone of man.

"The North! the lair of demons, where they coil,
And bound, and glide, and travel to and fro:
Their gulph, the underworld, this hollow orb,
Where vaulted columns curve beneath the hills,   200
And shoulder us on their arches: there they throng;
The portal of their pit, the polar gate,
Their fiery dungeon mocked with northern snow:
There, doom and demon haunt a native land,
Where dreamy thunder mutters in the cloud,
Storm broods, and battle breathes, and baleful fires
Shed a fierce horror o'er the shuddering North.

"But thou! O South Wind, breathe thy fragrant sigh!
We follow on thy perfume, breath of heaven!
Myriads, in girded albs, for ever young,   210
Their stately semblance of embodied air,
Troop round the footstool of the Southern Cross,
That pentacle of stars: the very sign
That led the Wise Men towards the Awful Child,
Then came and stood to rule the peaceful sea.
So, too, Lord Jesu from His mighty tomb
Cast the dear shadow of his red right hand,
To soothe the happy South – the angels' home.

"Then let us search the regions, one by one,
And pluck this Sangraal from its cloudy cave."   220

So Merlin brought the arrows: graven lots,
Shrouded from sight within a quiver'd sheath,
For choice and guidance in the perilous path,
That so the travellers might divide the lands.
They met at Lauds, in good Saint Nectan's cell,
For fast, and vigil, and their knightly vow:
Then knelt, and prayed, and all received their God.

"Now for the silvery arrows! Grasp and hold!"

Sir Lancelot drew the North: that fell domain,
Where fleshly man must brook the airy fiend –   230
His battle-foe, the demon – ghastly War!
Ho! stout Saint Michael shield them, knight and knave!

The South fell softly to Sir Perceval's hand:
Some shadowy angel breathed a silent sign,
That so that blameless man, that courteous knight,
Might mount and mingle with the happy host
Of God's white army in their native land.
Yea! they shall woo and soothe him, like the dove.

But hark! the greeting – "Tristan for the West!"
Among the multitudes, his watchful way,   240
The billowy hordes beside the seething sea;
But will the glory gleam in loathsome lands?
Will the lost pearl shine out among the swine?
Woe, father Adam, to thy loins and thee!

Sir Galahad holds the Orient arrow's name:
His chosen hand unbars the gate of day;
There glows that heart, fill'd with his mother's blood,
That rules in every pulse, the world of man;
Link of the awful Three, with many a star.

O! blessèd East! 'mid visions such as thine,   250
' Twere well to grasp the Sangraal, and die.

Now feast and festival in Arthur's hall:
Hark! stern Dundagel softens into song!
They meet for solemn severance, knight and king,
Where gate and bulwark darken o'er the sea.
Strong men for meat, and warriors at the wine,
They wreak the wrath of hunger on the beeves,
They rend rich morsels from the savoury deer,
And quench the flagon like Brun-guillie dew!
Hear! how the minstrels prophesy in sound,   260
Shout the King's Waes-hael, and Drink-hael the Queen!
Then said Sir Kay, he of the arrowy tongue,
"Joseph and Pharaoh! how they build their bones!
Happier the boar were quick than dead to-day."

The Queen! the Queen! how haughty on the dais!
The sunset tangled in her golden hair:
A dove amid the eagles – Gwennivar!
Aishah! what might is in that glorious eye!

See their tamed lion from Brocelian's glade,
Couched on the granite like a captive king!   270
A word – a gesture – or a mute caress –
How fiercely fond he droops his billowy mane,
And wooes, with tawny lip, his lady's hand!

The dawn is deep; the mountains yearn for day;
The hooting cairn is husht – that fiendish noise,
Yelled from the utterance of the rending rock,
When the fierce dog of Cain barks from the moon.

The bird of judgment chants the doom of night,
The billows laugh a welcome to the day,
And Camlan ripples, seaward, with a smile.   280

"Down with the eastern bridge! the warriors ride,
And thou Sir Herald, blazon as they pass!"
Foremost sad Lancelot, throned upon his steed,
His yellow banner, northward, lapping light:
The crest, a lily, with a broken stem,
The legend, 𝔖tately once and ever fair;
It hath a meaning, seek it not, O King!

A quaint embroidery Sir Perceval wore;
A turbaned Syrian, underneath a palm,
Wrestled for mastery with a stately foe,   290
Robed in a Levite's raiment, white as wool:
His touch o'erwhelmed the Hebrew, and his word,
𝔚hoso is strong with 𝔊od shall conquer man,
Coil'd in rich tracery round the knightly shield.
Did Ysolt's delicate fingers weave the web,
That gleamed in silken radiance o'er her lord?
A molten rainbow, bent, that arch in heaven,
Which leads straightway to Paradise and God;
Beneath, came up a gloved and sigilled hand,
Amid this cunning needlework of words,   300
𝔚hen toil and tears have worn the westering day,
𝔅ehold the smile of fame! so brief; so bright.

A vast archangel floods Sir Galahad's shield:
Mid-breast, and lifted high, an Orient cruse,
Full filled, and running o'er with Numynous light,
As though it held and shed the visible God;
Then shone this utterance as in graven fire,
𝔍 thirst! 𝔒 𝔍esu! let me drink and die!

So forth they fare, King Arthur and his men,
Like stout quaternions of the Maccabee: 310
They halt, and form at craggy Carradon;
Fit scene for haughty hope and stern farewell.
Lo! the rude altar, and the rough-hewn rock,

The grim and ghastly semblance of the fiend,
His haunt and coil within that pillar'd home.
Hark! the wild echo! Did the demon breathe
That yell of vengeance from the conscious stone?

There the brown barrow curves its sullen breast,
Above the bones of some dead Gentile's soul:
All husht - and calm - and cold - until anon   320
Gleams the old dawn - the well-remembered day -
Then may you hear, beneath that hollow cairn,
The clash of arms: the muffled shout of war;
Blent with the rustle of the kindling dead!

They stand - and hush their hearts to hear the King.
Then said he, like a prince of Tamar-land -
Around his soul, Dundagel and the sea -

"Ha! Sirs - ye seek a noble crest to-day,
To win and wear the starry Sangraal,
The link that binds to God a lonely land.   330
Would that my arm went with you, like my heart!
But the true shepherd must not shun the fold;
For in this flock are crouching grievous wolves,
And chief among them all, my own false kin.
Therefore I tarry by the cruel sea,
To hear at eve the treacherous mermaid's song,
And watch the wallowing monsters of the wave, -
'Mid all things fierce, and wild, and strange, alone!

"Ay! all beside can win companionship:
The churl may clip his mate beneath the thatch,   340
While his brown urchins nestle at his knees:
The soldier give and grasp a mutual palm,
Knit to his flesh in sinewy bonds of war:
The knight may seek at eve his castle-gate,
Mount the old stair, and lift the accustom'd latch,

To find, for throbbing brow and weary limb,
That paradise of pillows, one true breast:
But he, the lofty ruler of the land,
Like yonder Tor, first greeted by the dawn,
And wooed the latest by the lingering day,   350
With happy homes and hearths beneath his breast,
Must soar and gleam in solitary snow.
The lonely one is, evermore, the King.
So now farewell, my lieges, fare ye well,
And God's sweet Mother be your benison!
Since by grey Merlin's gloss, this wondrous cup
Is, like the golden vase in Aaron's ark,
A fount of manha for a yearning world,
As full as it can hold of God and heaven
Search the four winds until the balsam breathe,   360
Then grasp, and fold it in your very soul!

"I have no son, no daughter of my loins,
To breathe, 'mid future men, their father's name:
My blood will perish when these veins are dry;
Yet am I fain some deeds of mine should live –
I would not be forgotten in this land:
I yearn that men I know not, men unborn,
Should find, amid these fields, King Arthur's fame!
Here let them say, by proud Dundagel's walls –
'They brought the Sangraal back by his command,   370
They touched these rugged rocks with hues of God:'
So shall my name have worship, and my land.

"Ah! native Cornwall! throned upon the hills,
Thy moorland pathways worn by Angel feet,
Thy streams that march in music to the sea
'Mid Ocean's merry noise, his billowy laugh!
Ah me! a gloom falls heavy on my soul –
The birds that sung to me in youth are dead;
I think, in dreamy vigils of the night,

It may be God is angry with my land,   380
Too much athirst for fame, too fond of blood;
And all for earth, for shadows, and the dream
To glean an echo from the winds of song!

"But now, let hearts be high! the Archangel held
A tournay with the fiend on Abarim,
And good Saint Michael won his dragon-crest!

"Be this our cry! the battle is for God!
If bevies of foul fiends withstand your path,
Nay! if strong angels hold the watch and ward,
Plunge in their midst, and shout, 'A Sangraal!'"   390

He ceased; the warriors bent a knightly knee,
And touched, with kiss and sign, Excalibur;
Then turned, and mounted for their perilous way!

That night Dundagel shuddered into storm –
The deep foundations shook beneath the sea:
Yet there they stood, beneath the murky moon,
 Above the bastion, Merlin and the King.
Thrice waved the sage his staff, and thrice they saw
A peopled vision throng the rocky moor.

First fell a gloom, thick as a thousand nights,   400
A pall that hid whole armies; and beneath
Stormed the wild tide of war; until on high
Gleamed red the dragon, and the Keltic glaive
Smote the loose battle of the roving Dane!
Then yelled a fiercer fight: for brother blood
Rushed mingling, and twin dragons fought the field!
The grisly shadows of his faithful knights
Perplext their lord: and in their midst, behold!
His own stern semblance waved a phantom brand,

Drooped, and went down the war. Then cried the King,   410
"Ho! Arthur to the rescue!" and half drew
Excalibur; but sank, and fell entranced.

A touch aroused the monarch: and there stood
He, of the billowy beard and awful eye,
The ashes of whole ages on his brow –
Merlin the bard, son of a demon-sire!
High, like Ben Amram at the thirsty rock,
He raised his prophet staff: that runic rod,
The stem of Igdrasil – the crutch of Raun –
And wrote strange words along the conscious air.   420

Forth gleamed the east, and yet it was not day!
A white and glowing horse outrode the dawn;
A youthful rider ruled the bounding rein,
And he, in semblance of Sir Galahad shone:
A vase he held on high; one molten gem,
Like massive ruby or the chrysolite:
Thence gushed the light in flakes; and flowing, fell
As though the pavement of the sky brake up,
And stars were shed to sojourn on the hills,
From grey Morwenna's stone to Michael's tor,   430
Until the rocky land was like a heaven.

Then saw they that the mighty Quest was won!
The Sangraal swoon'd along the golden air:
The sea breathed balsam, like Gennesaret:
The streams were touched with supernatural light:
And fonts of Saxon rock, stood, full of God!
Altars arose, each like a kingly throne,
Where the royal chalice, with its lineal blood,
The Glory of the Presence, ruled and reigned.
This lasted long: until the white horse fled,   440
The fierce fangs of the libbard in his loins:
Whole ages glided in that blink of time,

While Merlin and the King, looked, wondering, on.

But see! once more the wizard-wand arise,
To cleave the air with signals, and a scene.

Troops of the demon-north, in yellow garb,
The sickly hue of vile Iscariot's hair,
Mingle with men, in unseen multitudes!
Unscared, they throng the valley and the hill;
The shrines were darkened and the chalice void: 450
That which held God was gone: Maran-atha!
The awful shadows of the Sangraal, fled!
Yet giant-men arose, that seemed as gods,
Such might they gathered from the swarthy kind:
The myths were rendered up: and one by one,
The Fire – the Light – the Air – were tamed and bound
Like votive vassals at their chariot-wheel.
Then learnt they War: yet not that noble wrath,
That brings the generous champion face to face
With equal shield, and with a measured brand,   460
To peril life for life, and do or die;
But the false valour of the lurking fiend
To hurl a distant death from some deep den:
To wing with flame the metal of the mine:
And so they rend God's image, reck not who!

"Ah! haughty England! lady of the wave!"
Thus said pale Merlin to the listening King,
"What is thy glory in the world of stars?
To scorch and slay: to win demoniac fame,
In arts and arms; and then to flash and die!   470
Thou art the diamond of the demon-crown,
Smitten by Michael upon Abarim,
That fell; and glared, an island of the sea.
Ah! native England! wake thine ancient cry;
Ho! for the Sangraal! vanish'd Vase of Heaven,

That held, like Christ's own heart, an hin of blood!"
He ceased; and all around was dreamy night:
There stood Dundagel, throned: and the great sea
Lay, a strong vassal at his master's gate,
And, like a drunken giant, sobb'd in sleep!   480

* * * * *

In the course of looking more closely at 'The Quest of the Sangraal',
we can perhaps make some comparisons with two more famous expressions of the Arthur legends, Sir Thomas Malory's fifteenth century prose work *Le Morte d'Arthur*, and Alfred Tennyson's contemporary *Idylls of the King*. Hawker will not necessarily suffer from these
comparisons. He introduces his poem with a splendid vigour which
he sustains, lines that he was proud to quote frequently in letters of
the time:

> Ho! for the Sangraal! vanished vase of Heaven!
> That held, like Christ's own heart, an hin of blood!
> Ho! for the Sangraal!

Such battle-cries can be more significant for their sound than for
their sense, but in this case some explanation is called for. A 'hin' is
a Hebrew measure of ten pints, so the Sangraal of Hawker, the vase,
the chalice, the cup, was of a substantial size, and there is also a built-
in double meaning: the Holy Grail, the cup from which Jesus and his
disciples drank at the Last Supper, alternatively the Sang Real, the
real blood, the chalice from which Joseph of Arimathea took blood
from Christ's body on the cross. Hawker himself seemed to support
the first interpretation, writing in 1861, 'What is the exact origin

etymon and usage of Sangreal? It is W. Maskell's opinion that some reference was intended to the Real Blood, but I don't think so.'[13] In the poem he manages to retain both (ll. 74-80):

> Then came Sir Joseph, hight of Arimathèe,
> Bearing that awful vase, the Sangraal!
> The Vessel of the Pasch, Shere Thursday night,
> The selfsame cup, wherein the faithful wine
> Heard God, and was obedient unto blood.
> Therewith he knelt and gathered blessed drops
> From his dear master's side that sadly fell . . .

He emphasises the unique holiness of the Sangraal, containing as it does the blood attained by transubstantiation, and the blood of Jesus on the cross. This suggests a new dimension for the doctrine of transubstantiation, incidentally by no means an appropriate concern for an Anglican priest.

Such a degree of complexity, all hinted at if not expressed in the first three lines, does not persist. Hawker goes on to fling open a door to a Cornish gale as he introduces Arthur's knights, 'reckless riders on their rushing steeds'. A commentator in 1903 wrote, in an article celebrating the centenary of Hawker's birth, 'The clatter of the iron hoofs on the granite rocks of Cornwall is here'.[14] The setting is rapidly established, 'monumental Morwenstow throughout', and these knights, these 'bounding men', will soon be doing justice to a banquet (ll. 256-59):

> Strong men for meat, and warriors at the wine,
> They wreak the wrath of hunger on the beeves,
> They rend rich morsels from the savoury deer,
> And quench the flagon like Brun-guillie dew!

A particular knight comments on their eating habits:

> Then said Sir Kay, he of the arrowy tongue,
> 'Joseph and Pharaoh! how they build their bones!
> Happier the boar were quick than dead to-day.'

Hawker replied to an inquirer, 'The four [sic] lines you stumble at I merely meant as a touch of character to identify Sir Kay and to contrast with the general gravity of the poem. Kay was a kind of Thersites of Dundagel – always at hand with a sarcasm and sneer – hence 'arrowy tongue'.[15] Regret can only intensify, that he left three-quarters of the poem unwritten, and provided only this hint of attractively human knights and their sneering observer. They can also be seen as Cornishmen of a golden age, like the Irish gentlemen described by W. B. Yeats, or indeed like his own Sir Beville Grenville in the ballad, 'Sir Beville – The Gate-Song of Stowe' (see Appendix).

Before leaving these bounding knights and their interest in food, it is worth introducing Sir Thomas Malory's treatment of the story. He describes the effect on the knights who were present at Camelot of the vision of the Sangraal:

Than entird into the halle the Holy Grayle coverde with whyght samyte, but there was none that myght se hit nother whom that bare hit. And there was all the halle fulfylled with good odoures, and every knyght had such metis and drynkes as he best loved in thys worlde.[16]

There is something poignant about this passage. Malory wrote *Le Morte d'Arthur* in prison – not, as his name and title might imply, for the political offence of being on the wrong side in the Wars of the Roses, but for the less admirable misdeed of cattle-rustling. In those circumstances there must be a particular unattainable happiness in first smelling and then eating one's favourite food. To the reader not languishing in jail, the reaction may seem inappropriate. Certainly Tennyson in 'The Holy Grail' preferred to omit this element, simply having his knights marvel at the presence of the Grail, invisible as it was to all except Galahad. So Hawker's knights feast, Malory's yearn, Tennyson's live above such considerations. The impression is confirmed, of a more natural setting for Hawker's story, and the presence of real people.

But almost as soon as as they enter the story, Hawker's knights are denounced as 'Unclean!' Like lepers they must keep their distance, for they are sinners, not fit to reach for the Sangraal. So Hawker

introduces 'the monk, a lean and gnarlèd man' and almost instantly
dismisses him, first giving him a memorable verse (ll.13-21):

> His couch was on the rock, by that wild stream
> That floods, in cataract, Saint Nectan's Kieve;
> One of the choir, whose life is Orison.
> They had their lodges in the wilderness,
> Or built them cells beside the shadowy sea,
> And there they dwelt with angels, like a dream:
> So they unroll'd the volume of the Book,
> And fill'd the fields of the Evangelist
> With antique thoughts, that breath'd of Paradise.

Here is a blend of the terrestrial and the spiritual, precisely
appropriate to Hawker's Morwenstow. Saint Nectan's Kieve, or
cauldron, is the setting of one of his early poems, 'The Sisters of
Glen Nectan', and was also incidentally a favourite haunt of Thomas
Hardy when he was wooing Emma Gifford. It is a spectacular waterfall
near Boscastle, above it the cell of Nectan, traditionally Morwenna's
brother, one of the Celtic Saints whose names are commemorated
in a hundred Cornish villages. In this local setting and alongside this
local lore the monk, like the poet, 'dwelt with angels' and delighted
in 'antique thoughts'.

It is already detectable at this early stage that antiquity permeates,
not simply the subject matter, but the verse form of the poem. Hawker
employs blank verse for the first time, but of the kind that marks the
work of Christopher Marlowe and his predecessors, with end-stopt
lines as its main characteristic. There is none of the flexibility that
comes with the caesuras and feminine endings of, most notably,
Shakespeare's last plays. Whether deliberately or not, Hawker uses a
constricted and antiquated verse form harking back to the late Middle
Ages which arguably suits his subject matter well.

So he moves on, to describe the four leading knights, Tristan,
Perceval, Galahad and Lancelot, whose adventures in search of the
Sangraal, it is safe to assume, would have comprised much of the
subject matter of the unwritten Chants. Only Lancelot is particularly
described, in an image which movingly blends the legendary power

and weakness of the man with the massive yet vulnerable 'shuddering stone' among the Cornish rocks (ll. 29-32).

> And he, the sad Sir Lancelot of the lay:
> Ah me! that logan of the rocky hills,
> Pillar'd in storm, calm in the rush of war,
> Shook, at the light touch of his lady's hand!

As Arthur appears among them, it is as though the mist clears and the pattern of the poem becomes apparent. It is due to operate at three levels. First, Arthur is about to entrust to his four knights the supreme spiritual task, finding the Sangraal which has been lost as 'evil days came on, And evil men'. Second, the setting, Arthur's kingdom and his home and the point of departure for the Quest, is an exalted manifestation of Cornwall. Third, though this takes longer to develop, Arthur's soul-searching and expressions of frustration within this setting are also those of the poet.

The king has a story to tell. He describes the crucifixion, exciting his listeners with the notion of mounting a rescue, and tells how Joseph of Arimathea took charge of the Sangraal, eventually bringing it to Glastonbury. His account of the Syrian home of 'Sir Joseph, hight of Arimathèe' provides a specially vivid picture, quoted earlier and worth repeating, of the poet's idea of angels (ll. 87-96):

> He dwelt in Orient Syria: God's own land:
> The ladder foot of heaven – where shadowy shapes
> In white apparel glided up and down.
> His home was like a garner, full of corn,
> And wine and oil; a granary of God!
> Young men, whom no one knew, went in and out,
> With a far look in their eternal eyes!
> All things were strange and rare: the Sangraal,
> As though it clung to some ethereal chain,
> Brought down high Heaven to earth at Arimathèe.

This vision of heaven, Arthur continues, was not due to last. Merlin enters his story and tells how in the sinful locale of England the Sangraal disappeared, as the entire world became dark and reverted to paganism (ll.124-26):

> This orb is darkened to the distant watch
> Of Saturn and his reapers, when they pause,
> Amid their sheaves, to count the nightly stars.

He goes on to prophesy redemption; and significantly, the backward glance to a dark age was mildly expressed compared to the 'anathema' that is to come, the vision of the future that Merlin conjures up after the knights have departed. For the moment, 'There shall arise a king from Keltic loins', specifically a Cornish king (ll. 132-36):

> Then while the land is husht on Tamar side,
> So that the warder upon Caradon
> Shall hear at once the river and the sea –
> That king shall call a Quest: a kindling cry:
> 'Ho! for the Sangraal! vanish'd Vase of God!'

Arthur, taking on the role, calls a Quest, and the response is instant (ll. 159-63):

> Then rose a storm of voices; like the sea,
> When Ocean, bounding, shouts with all his waves.
> High-hearted men! the purpose and the theme,
> Smote the fine chord that thrills the warrior's soul
> With touch and impulse for a deed of fame.

Optimism and energy are paramount; and again Hawker's Arthur diverges from the Arthurs of Malory and Tennyson, providing a simple positive response where they prevaricate at the crucial moment. Malory's king, after the vision in the hall of Camelot, is distressed by his knights' solemn oath to pursue the quest, because an oath once sworn is totally binding and his fellowship will now break up. Tennyson begs them not to pursue unattainable ideals while there is so plainly work to be done at home:

> Yet – for ye know the cries of all my realm
> Pass through this hall – how often O my knights,
> Your places being vacant at my side,
> This chance of noble deeds will come and go
> Unchallenged, while ye follow wandering fires
> Lost in the quagmire![17]

Malory, in his late mediaeval setting, is describing a military society which operates within a set of rules. Tennyson's Arthur might be Gladstone advising against imperial adventures when Ireland still awaited pacification. Hawker's king by contrast initiates the quest, even though, as becomes apparent, he knows that he cannot participate himself. So he speaks for his creator, as one catches a glimpse of the Oxford graduate's boundless aspirations thirty years earlier, and their disappointment.

Gawain now defines the four regions which must be searched, providing an insight into Hawker's concept of cosmology which was touched upon in 'The Comet of 1861'. The east is 'the home of God', the setting for the cross, from which Jesus 'looked his latest love', across to the west, 'the imaged zone of man'. The north is 'the lair of demons', and the south 'the angels' home'. Merlin summons the four knights to St Nectan's cell – again, a local Cornish scene for a moment of universal import, as they draw lots. Inevitably, Lancelot finds that his quest lies to the north; equally inevitably Galahad is allocated the east; Perceval is to go south and Tristan west. The three lines that he wrote of the second chant make clear that it was to be concerned with Lancelot's journey, and presumably the pattern would have continued.

The time for feasting has arrived, as 'They meet for solemn severance, knight and king, Where gate and bulwark darken o'er the sea', and Queen Gwennivar makes a brief appearance accompanied by an affectionate lion. The night passes, and Hawker indulges us with a Cornish morning, celebrating in a single word the River Camel and its tributary the Allen (ll. 279-80) :

> The billows laugh a welcome to the day,
> And Camlan ripples, seaward, with a smile.

After an appropriately colourful heraldic passage depicting the dress and accoutrements of their four leaders, the knights assemble at 'craggy Caradon', the tor on Bodmin Moor which had been the centrepiece of Hawker's early poem, 'A Rapture on the Cornish Hills'. This hill with its unique collection of burial cairns plainly induced a profound respect in the poet; yet whereas in 1832 its supernatural power seems to have been inspired by God, thirty years later, despite the dominant presence of King Arthur, there is an evil force lurking which may again have bearing on the development of the Quest story (ll. 313-17):

> Lo! the rude altar, and the rough-hewn rock,
> The grim and ghastly semblance of the fiend,
> His haunt and coil within that pillar'd home.
> Hark! the wild echo! Did the demon breathe
> That yell of vengeance from the conscious stone?

The Quest, beginning at such a place, is destined to be hard, as another element yet, 'the kindling dead', struggles towards resurrection 'beneath that hollow cairn'. The scene is crowded with, it seems, contrary and conflicting forces, while the king speaks. Yesterday he had inspired the Quest, now he expresses the loneliness which will afflict him when the knights depart. The poignancy of the passage, at this time in Hawker's life, is sharp, as one recalls that only months earlier he had written, 'My brave and true-hearted wife died yesterday'.[18] Now, 'Would that my arm went with you, like my heart!' He, the king, the solitary stranded priest, must stay to guard his flock, despite the nightmarish quality that his kingdom, his parish, his home has acquired (ll. 335-38):

> Therefore I tarry by the cruel sea,
> To hear at eve the treacherous mermaid's song,
> And watch the wallowing monsters of the wave, –
> 'Mid all things fierce, and wild, and strange, alone!

'Ay! all beside can win companionship', peasant and knight return to their loved ones, but 'the lonely one is, evermore,

the king', and this king, this priest, has not even the comfort
of children (ll. 362-66):

> I have no son, no daughter of my loins,
> To breathe, 'mid future men, their father's name:
> My blood will perish when these veins are dry;
> Yet am I fain some deeds of mine should live –
> I would not be forgotten in this land . . .

So the huge hope is pronounced. 'Here let them say, by proud Dundagel's
walls – They brought the Sangraal back by his command. . . .'

He is still uneasy, not simply anxious lest he be forgotten. In a
verse which vividly expresses the conflict between hope and despair,
good and evil, happiness and misery, which dominated Hawker's
life, he tells of a wider anxiety (ll. 373-81):

> Ah! native Cornwall! throned upon the hills,
> Thy moorland pathways worn by angel feet,
> Thy streams that march in music to the sea
> 'Mid Ocean's merry noise, his billowy laugh!
> Ah me! a gloom falls heavy on my soul –
> The birds that sung to me in youth are dead;
> I think, in dreamy vigils of the night,
> It may be God is angry with my land,
> Too much athirst for fame, too fond of blood . . .

He just manages to send off his knights cheerfully, 'But now, let
hearts be high!' They go, and Arthur and Merlin are left alone.

There follows an accumulation of visions, induced by Merlin.
First, Celts fight Danes, and Arthur's own wars are shown and his
death prophesied. As he struggles as in a nightmare to rescue his own
likeness, he faints, and is revived by Merlin so that he can witness the
second vision, the trumphant return of Galahad with the Sangraal.
A heaven on earth is created, and 'This lasted long', to be destroyed
in its turn and replaced, following invasion by swarms of demons, by
a remarkable premonition of modern war. Fire, light and air are
brought under human control in the industrial revolution that
Hawker so deplored. The new species of war is not of the noble kind

which Arthur represented, but an oracular depiction of something recognisable as the First World War finally mixed with contemporary terrorism (ll. 462-65):

> . . . the false valour of the lurking fiend
> To hurl a distant death from some deep den:
> To wing with flame the metal of the mine:
> And, so they rend God's image, reck not who!

Hawker's gift of prophetic vision perhaps after all rivals Tennyson's.

Merlin now speaks himself, appealing to England to lead the fight against this concatenation of evil, and repeats the war-cry that begins the poem (ll. 474-76):

> Ah! native England! wake thine ancient cry;
> Ho! for the Sangraal! vanished vase of heaven,
> That held, like Christ's own heart, an hin of blood!

So the poem appears to end on a note of hope, however indistinct compared to the dramatic depiction of evil power. But actually Hawker has not quite finished. There are four lines left, which have been described as 'the most graphic description of the sea after a storm that any poet of the sea has ever given us'.[19]

> He ceased; and all around was dreamy night:
> There stood Dundagel, throned: and the great sea
> Lay, a strong vassal at his master's gate,
> And, like a drunken giant, sobb'd in sleep!

He has achieved it again, perhaps his most notable poetic skill, the cathartic quiet to end a poem, the 'calm of mind, all passion spent' that concludes the agonisings of Milton's Samson Agonistes. At least three examples have been seen already, in 'The Storm', 'Be of Good Cheer', and 'The Comet of 1861'. It is appropriate that this first and only 'chant', still his greatest poem, should conclude with the most powerful of all these performances.

'The Quest of the Sangraal' is Hawker's masterpiece. It would be hard to argue otherwise, not simply because there is nothing on the same scale in competition, but also because of its manifest concentration of poetic power, contained in the passages quoted and still more forcefully in the poem gathered together as a whole. The earthy human quality of the bounding knights, the primitive vigour of the Celtic saint who denounces them, the authority and single-mindedness of the king and his heavy-hearted anxieties which are so poignantly those of the poet, and the culminating vision of the future followed by the moment of calm, all operating within the bounds of the entire Christian creation which is simultaneously Cornwall, can only leave one exclaiming with his friend R. J. King, 'I *wish* there had been more of it . . . Would that any words of mine could induce you to try'.[20]

Hawker was immensely stimulated by the public interest which 'The Quest' aroused, and nothing pleased him more than Tennyson's comment, 'Hawker has beaten me on my own ground'.[21] The Poet Laureate – as by now he was, following Wordsworth's death in 1850 – had been working on his version of the story of King Arthur for much of his life, and did not actually finish *Idylls of the King* until 1885. The Idyll which lends itself most closely to comparison with Hawker's poem, 'The Holy Grail', was published in 1869. It may seem disproportionate to 'compare and contrast', in the manner beloved of examiners. Hawker's poem is central to his poetic achievement and indeed to his life, Tennyson's is part of a much larger whole. Also as has been seen their approaches to the story differ fundamentally, Hawker's Arthur inspiring the quest while Tennyson's tries in vain to discourage it; and one must also bear in mind that Hawker never wavered in his Christian beliefs, whereas Tennyson was racked with uncertainty. The fact remains that Tennyson rated his poem highly, as he simultaneously defined his aim:

Faith declines, religion in many turns from practical goodness to the quest after the supernatural and marvellous and selfish religious excitement. Few are those for whom the quest is a source of spiritual strength . . . 'The Holy Grail' is one of the most imaginative of all my poems. I have expressed there my strong feeling as to the Reality of the Unseen.[22]

Hallam Tennyson added, 'My father looked on this description of Sir Galahad's quest, and on that of Sir Lancelot, as among the best blank verse he had written'.[23] It will be worthwhile therefore to focus briefly upon passages where the two poets are treating a similar subject, the spectacle of Galahad with the Sangraal, seen by Arthur and Merlin in 'The Quest' ll. 421-43, and by Perceval in 'The Holy Grail'. Tennyson's Perceval and Galahad are crossing a ghastly waste land, and Galahad accompanied by the Grail perseveres to 'the spiritual city' which the flawed Perceval can see but where he cannot follow him. Galahad crosses bridges which burn and disappear behind him, then races on a boat which mounts into the sky, and the Grail, no longer 'Clothed in white samite', descends into the city in a scene of apocalyptic grandeur which derives from chapter 21 of the Book of Revelations. It is all very splendid. His Grail is 'Redder than any rose, a joy to me', while Hawker, likening it to a 'massive ruby', makes more of its 'supernatural light', using imagery which recalls his description of the comet in his earlier poem, and of the Aurora Borealis in one that is yet to be written. Hawker's Galahad's course is more briefly described as he 'ruled the bounding rein' and 'outrode the dawn'; indeed he is more succinct altogether, while Tennyson tends to live up to his reputation half-heartedly defined by T. S. Eliot for 'abundance, variety, and complete competence', notably here abundance. A sharper contrast can be found in their descriptions of the Grail's future, Tennyson stating through Perceval that it will never reappear whereas Hawker's Merlin seems set to summon a fresh quest as 'Whole ages glided in the blink of time' – a line which incidentally Brendon isolated to indicate how 'Hawker encapsulated the opium addict's familiar experience of bewildering temporal elasticity'.[24] Somehow, despite Tennyson's capacity for brilliantly colourful description, one can never think of him as a devourer of opium.

The impression remains that Tennyson is writing a quasi-mediaeval legend, while with Hawker there are no half-measures, he seeks to interpret the future. Apocalyptic overtones can be found in each case, but Tennyson's are descriptive, Hawker's visionary. Tennyson may be striving to express 'my strong feeling as to the Reality of the Unseen', but Hawker's poem is stronger on reality, and altogether events in and around Dundagel are more persuasive than events in and around Camelot. Byles should have the last word, 'The quality of Tennyson's poetry is ethereal beauty, that of Hawker's rugged strength'.

9

Second Marriage and Last Years, 1864-75

The last twelve years of Hawker's life were very different from the rest. For the first time, he was able to enjoy the company of a young woman. Charlotte had been forty-one when they married in 1823, and he twenty, and one cannot help detecting from time to time in his poetry over the forty years of their life together some degree of frustration. To take for instance two of his poems, both already discussed, 'Home Once More!' and 'The Token Stream of Tidna Combe': the first contains a rare, still only indirect, mention of Charlotte, suggesting that they will die together.

> Still, home once more; for in this dell
> The dust of love will fondly dwell;
> And scenes so dear to life shall hide
> The hearts that death could not divide.

'The Token Stream', addressing the river, traces a cheerless prognostication of the remainder of his life: 'Our years began alike, so let them end, We live with many men, we die alone'. There is no recognition of Charlotte's existence. He wrote both these poems in his late thirties, when she was coming up to sixty.

To say, as he in his turn passed sixty, that there was a new spring in the poet's step is a classic understatement.

> There's a face will o'ershadow all faces!
> There's an eye that will brighten a room:
> There's a form that would win mid the Graces:
> The Maid of the Crooks of Coombe!

A favourite haunt of the lady concerned, Miss Kuczynski, was the small river Crooks which flows down the Coombe Valley close to Morwenstow. More solemn, and more sensual, were these lines which he called 'A Thought in the Busy City':

Myriads of faces throng this peopled scene:
Ten thousand hearts are throbbing side by side:
But one sole brow they wear, Pauline, Pauline:
A single sigh they sob, my bride, my bride!

O! that her hand could tingle in my own:
Her thrilling pulses smite my conscious breast:
How would we grasp and glide, we two alone,
The eagle and his mate, to one far nest!

Neither of these poems is published in any edition of Hawker's Poems: they are to be found among Nicholas Ross's papers in the Bodleian Library.[1] One which successive editors did let in, a modest two verses long and all the more substantial for that, is entitled 'Lava'.

I thought the quench'd volcano's tide
Slept well within the mountain side:
That Time's cold touch would still control
The warring Hecla of my soul!

Why did we meet? For me to learn
The ashes of my heart would burn!
That the dark flame at last would rise,
Kindled beneath those flashing eyes!

Hawker has recalled and rewritten a poem written nearly thirty years earlier, in which he expressed himself resigned to a life devoid of 'high hopes' of any kind. 'The Western Shore' received brief attention earlier, and needs now to be quoted again in full, the two poems together providing such a very conscious and calculated record of the effect of Pauline.

Thou lovely land! where, kindling, throng
Scenes that should breathe the soul of song;
Home of high hopes that once were mine
Of loftier verse and nobler line!

'Tis past – the quench'd volcano's tide
Sleeps well within the mountain-side;

Henceforth shall time's cold touch control
The warring Hecla of my soul.

Welcome! wild rock and lonely shore,
Where round my days dark seas shall roar;
And thy gray fane, Morwenna, stand
The beacon of the Eternal Land!

The story behind this transformation has a special charm. Pauline
Kuczynski was the daughter of an exiled Polish nobleman who married
'a Lincolnshire lady, a Newton of the family of Sir Isaac', and died a
few years later. His widow remarried, a well known American book-
dealer called Henry Stevens who lost much of his fortune in the
Civil War. Pauline, having been brought up mainly in London as one
of a wealthy family, found herself obliged at the age of twenty to earn
her own living, and became governess to the children of the Valentine
family. Mr Valentine, a Yorkshire vicar, had bought a house at
Morwenstow as a holiday home and became a great asset to Hawker,
for example helping out with services in the months following
Charlotte's death. Towards the end of the eventful year 1863,
contrasting letters were posted from Morwenstow. Hawker wrote to
J. G. Godwin: 'O how I wish this fatal season, this fearful year were
over. I sometimes think I must give up the battle of life'.[3]

Meanwhile the governess wrote twice to an uncle in London.
'The rector, Mr Hawker, is a clever man but most eccentric, and tip-
top high church.' – 'Mr Hawker our vicar is slightly cracked – but
he's a very clever old soul.' She was mildly perturbed by his strangeness:
'He instills into the youthful mind of Morwenstow the most absurd
superstitions about ghosts and brownies, which he believes actually
exist'.[4] But already by the beginning of 1864, his obvious appeal was
beginning to have its effect.

New Year's Day afternoon and evening I spent with Mr V and the
children at the Vicar's. Mr Hawker took me and the children to *his*
cliff – his glebe land lies on the cliffs chiefly – a little way down one
called Vicarage Cliff he has made out of the hull of one of the
vessels wrecked on Morwenstow a hut. There we sat an hour as snug
as possible, with the most splendid panorama of sky sea and rock

before us and Mr Hawker telling me most interesting accounts of
wrecks off this immediate coast . . . [5]

The magic worked. Before the end of the year Hawker was writing
to Mrs Henry Stevens, Pauline's mother, who was understandably
expressing some reservations about the prospect of her daughter
marrying a man forty years older than she was – though Pauline
herself had stated 'that she would prefer ten years with him to a
lifetime with another man'.[6]

DEAR MADAM,
I have not the happiness to be personally known to you but the theme
of my intrusion will amply justify it. Ever since I knew her, a year and a
day from this date, I have fondly and unswervingly loved your daughter
Pauline. It is true that I have not until lately asked her to become my
wife, but it has been for this simple and sincere reason that I durst not
hope that a young woman with a face and form to win an emperor, a
mind to comprehend the universe, and a taste and judgment congenial
with all that is great and good among men, would condescend to take
me as her husband. But she has consented to make my home as happy
as a Paradise by promising to enter it as my wife. She will tell you all her
hopes and the likelihood of happiness and homage from one so devoted to her future life as I must be. But I could not fold her in my arms
as my wife with perfect tranquillity if I had not the inestimable shield of
a mother's blessing. Give it I entreat you to us and our home to your
own dear daughter Pauline and to one who will become to you.
        Your faithful and affectionate son-in-law,
                                                    R. S. HAWKER[7]

Despite so imposing a plea, Pauline's mother continued to
hesitate, and Hawker wrote to Mrs Watson, his confidante in this
matter as in all others (with the added piquancy now, that she might
have been a little jealous), 'I write in a state of extreme anguish.
Pauline is at her mother's in London utterly overcome.'[8] The only
answer was a direct appeal to Mrs Stevens, and Hawker set out on his
first visit to London. He lost his hat on the way: the story has already
been told in Chapter One. He described his adventures when he was
safely back in Morwenstow:

My own journey by train was to me a very wondrous event. I breakfasted
in this vicarage and I dined the same day in London, having travelled

all the vast distance in the second class carriage of the South Western
Railway Company for £1.17s.0d. This my second experience of railways
has by no means increased my desire to move away from Morwenstow:
on the contrary with all its cares and all its anxieties and terrors there is
no place to me like my own vicarage.[9]

He had not been impressed by London. 'This is a most sorry
wretched place. It costs us ten shillings a day to go about in what
they call cabs.' But such financial concerns did not extend to his
parish. Here there was major cause for celebration. The vicar was
bringing home his new young bride, in time for Christmas. The
letter, to his churchwarden Thomas Cann, went on, 'Let Tom Lang
deck the church as usual with holly and ivy. Let Mary make a large
and very good wedding cake ... Cakes for the children on Christmas
Day.'[10] In no time at all, it seems, he and Pauline were 'as quiet and
matter-of-fact in our vicarage as if we had been married a year'.[11]

Here surely was potential for lasting happiness; and for a time
indeed, all was idyllic. Pauline was made very welcome. Hawker
reported that at a gathering of clergy at Bude,

. . . not only did they all from the archdeacon downwards treat me
with marked and cheerful kindness, but the dean rural [Simcoe] in
a kind and happy speech proposed Mrs Hawker's health which was
drunk with acclamation. Nothing could be in better taste or more
cordial sympathy than their demeanour the whole day – it quite
roused me, for I am proud of my little wife and it did gratify me to
see how they all appreciated her.[12]

The refreshing presence of a young wife in the vicarage affected
even family prayers, when according to Byles 'he would sometimes
read out passages that seemed strangely appropriate to recent domestic
incidents. Mrs Hawker on these occasions could not always retain
her gravity, and the vicar would pause and say, in a tone of reproach,
"Pauline!" Afterwards she would say, "Robert, I'm sure what you
were reading isn't in the Bible". "My dear," would be the reply, "that
is because you don't understand Greek. I read from the Greek
Testament, translating as I go along."'[13] Byles must have heard this
story from his wife Rosalind, the Hawkers' second daughter, who in

her turn must have heard it from her mother: she and her sisters were only small children when their father died.

There were eventually three daughters, Morwenna born in 1865, Rosalind in 1867, and Juliot in 1869. Both parents rejoiced in their young family, and the vicar must have been specially gratified, if not astonished, thus to achieve fatherhood in his sixties. But the clouds were gathering again. From his point of view, his children brought two problems with them. First, his capacity for self-pity was not likely to diminish in old age, and Pauline was not able to minister exclusively to him. He must have hoped that she would do just that. Three little girls would not have been part of his calculations. He complains to his sister Caroline in 1871.

We cannot go out anywhere, my spirits are much too broken, and Pauline is so absorbed with the children that they occupy her total time. We went to the beach at Coombe last week. The children all got sopping wet playing about in the pools and have been laid up all three in coughs and colds ever since . . . She has neither a thought nor a moment for anything but the children and I am utterly shattered.[14]

Secondly, he agonised over money problems. They had always been with him. He wrote to Godwin in 1870, 'All my griefs through life and my terrors have flowed from one sole source the want of L-S-D. I shall die the victim of this great sorrow. Very often my whole future hinges on the temporary acquisition of £5 or £10 and many very narrow escapes have I lately had'.[15] These concerns of course became intensified as he found himself sharing his home with 'three lovely little girls whose faces I cannot look at without a shudder as to their future life'.[16]

It has to be added that Hawker's mismanagement of money constitutes the least attractive side of his many-faceted personality. He was a lavish spender, both on behalf of his parish and parishioners, and on himself, with his extravagant tastes in creature comforts.. An article in the *Cornish Review* in 1957 by J. H. Adams, grandson of John Adams whose friendship he seems to have lost through duplicitous financial dealing, uncovers a rather horrid tale of failure to repay debts and even destruction of promissory notes. 'Hawker was quite feckless where money was concerned,' he writes, 'and was perpetually hard up and reduced to borrowing from anyone whom he could persuade to lend.'[17]

He tried to write his way out of trouble, offering articles to London magazines about life in Cornwall, especially in and around Morwenstow. These were collected and published in 1870 as *Footprints of Former Men in Far Cornwall.* Quotations from them have already appeared extensively in these pages. It is hard to admire *Footprints* overall. He adopted a pseudo-archaic style; and far from having any regard for historical accuracy, he embellished what would in most cases already have been good stories, to such an extent that it becomes hard to separate truth from invention. For example, he contributed to *All the Year Round* an article, 'Daniel Gumb's Rock', about a remarkable man who lived with his family in a cavern close to the Cheesewring on Bodmin Moor in the eighteenth century. There is certainly evidence that Daniel Gumb possessed much knowledge and curiosity about mathematics and astronomy, and he remains an intriguing, rather mysterious figure. Hawker visited the place and claimed to have had a sight of 'a few written fragments of his thoughts and studies', which he quotes at length. By this means he takes possession of Daniel Gumb, making him his own, providing him with the character, which he regarded as appropriate, of a simple and puzzled yet amazingly enlightened peasant. Even Byles, the loyal son-in-law, felt obliged to add a footnote in his 1908 edition of *Footprints*, 'Evidences of thought and style make it almost certain that these ingenious "fragments" are Hawker's own invention'. A similar fabrication is to be found in his account of 'Antony Payne, a Cornish Giant', a renowned Cornish figure who served the Grenville family and who famously, when the great Sir Beville was killed at the battle of Lansdown in the Civil War, picked up his young son John and flung him on his father's horse. The boy led the Cornish Army to victory: a good enough story. Hawker had this uneducated man of action, as he surely was, write an eloquent letter to Lady Grenville beginning, 'Honoured Madam, – Ill news flieth apace . . .'[18] An irritated commentator writes, 'We fear the touching letter from Anthony Payne to Lady Grenville . . . that is so often printed is a mere forgery by the late Rev. R. S. Hawker, who had no shame in such matters'.[19]

Whether or not it can be labelled unethical, it is a profoundly irksome trait (one that he shared with his biographer Sabine Baring-Gould). One is left wishing that he had been content to remain loyal to the attractive rugged style of his letters, and also that he had just taken a little more trouble to research, rather than invent, his history. These semi-fictional efforts do no service to his reputation as a writer; nor indeed to his beloved Cornwall, and the Cornish characters whom he claimed to depict. One has to add in fairness that he did succeed in selling some articles, so helping to feed his family. He did specially well with the magazine *All the Year Round*, and these remarks about its editor suggest that he knew what he was doing to his art: 'It is mortifying to be compelled to submit to the caprice and vulgar taste of an uneducated captious prig like Wills the editor. I ought to have known that if he did not habitually admit the low and mean and reject the great and good his periodical would not be what it is.'[20]

Here is also proof if needed that there was still plenty of fight in him, throughout these demanding last years. But above and beyond his money worries and his frustrating attempts to solve them, he agonised over doctrinal difficulties, while also wrestling with a patent yearning for the Roman Catholic church. Plainly the very last thing he could do was to set his position as Vicar of Morwenstow at risk, 'A house, a glebe, a pound a day'. Presumably he could have made the change during the brief period when he was a childless widower. Now he had a young wife and in due course three small children to support.

Doctrinal problems within the Church of England overshadowed his life during the 1860s. He was disturbed by the Colenso Judgment, when the Privy Council countermanded the dismissal from office of a bishop who had questioned some traditional views of the Bible following sharp questions from Zulus in his South African diocese. Hawker, deploring as he did Colenso and the state's intervention, addressed the matter in broadly similar terms to his earlier denunciations of Methodism:

A man may now preach almost whatever he likes and deny as many tenets as he pleases and although his bishop may disapprove and censure he cannot deprive him of his endowments or revenue or silence his voice.[21]

He was anxious too about the appropriateness of A.C.Tait's appointment in 1869 as Archbishop of Canterbury, on the grounds that he had never been baptised. Evidence either way need not detain us, but given the emphasis that Hawker placed on the sacrament of baptism, given also that Pauline had been confirmed by Tait, here was particular cause for concern. Thirdly, also in 1869, Frederick Temple was appointed Bishop of Exeter following the death of Hawker's patron Henry Phillpotts. Hawker described his new diocesan as 'a very infidel writer', one of the authors of *Essays and Reviews*, 'that is to say, suggestions of doubt and disbelief in the old testament and the new'.[22] Each of these matters in turn shook his confidence in the Church of England, in which he had been ordained and to which he had remained loyal after his fashion for nearly fifty years.

He was simultaneously under pressure from senior Roman Catholics to change his faith, particularly at the time of Charlotte's death and the publication of 'The Quest of the Sangraal'. His habit of sending copies of his poems to Catholic bishops would have invited such attention: one wonders which was cause and which effect. As early as 1861 Dr Thomas Grant, Bishop of Southwark, wrote to acknowledge a copy of the poem on the Comet.

I am all the more pleased to get this letter as I feared from your silence that I had gone too far in asking you to let me say how anxious I was to see you a member of the Holy Church.

I thank you very sincerely, and I humbly cherish the hope that you who look much at the stars will recollect the saying of a peasant who hearing Mrs Shelley exclaim as she looked at the stars "Quanto e bello", replied, "Ah, if the reverse of the medal is so beautiful, fancy the front thereof!" . . . And how shall we meet in Heaven unless we enter as children of the Holy Church and of Her whom you love to invoke as 'Stella matutina'?[23]

Two years later he was commiserating with Hawker on the death of Charlotte.

How earnestly I pray that you may be consoled in your sorrow for the
departed . . . by coming to the one fold under the Chief Pastor, St Peter's
successor. In that fold alone will your love of Mary immaculate and
blessed, and your quest of the treasure that made the Sangraal holy be
satisfied.[24]

Hawker replied by sending him a copy of 'The Quest', and the
pressure was duly kept up as the bishop wrote on Christmas Eve
1863, 'May the Star of Bethlehem guide you to that church in which
alone you can honour St Morwenna and love the Immaculate Mother
of our Infant Saviour'. A further letter six months later strikes a
more urgent note. 'His Eminence' would have been Cardinal
Wiseman.

If his Eminence is in town, he will receive your book with its message
and will welcome both today. I am much obliged to you for your goodness in making me the bearer of both to him.

How happy you could make me were I to be the messenger of the
better tidings to the Heavenly Prince of whose goodness and power you
sing so eloquently! Why not snap your chain, saying 'Benedictus Deus
qui vincula nostra disrupit'.

The debt that alarms you will have to be paid after your death lest
your good name should suffer, why not pay it now that your heart and
soul may be free, and that you may unite with us in finding the treasure
which the Sangraal guarded, and in loving Her for whose sake the
earthly banquet was gladdened by becoming an emblem and promise of
the greater banquet of the . . . [last word illegible].

The bishop adds below his signature, 'Come, *come & tarry not, nox
appropinquat.*' To a hypochondriac like Hawker, a reminder of the
approach of night was likely to make an impact, even if the unworldly
advice on debts would have been less than useful. In that same year,
1864, Hawker was expecting a visit from William Vaughan, Bishop
of Plymouth, who was staying at Bude. It did not materialise, and
the bishop – another recipient of 'The Quest' – wrote to apologise,
remarking:

If I might be allowed to make one remark it would be this. Rest not
satisfied with throwing the charm of poesy onto the Quest of the Sangraal

but seek in the bosom of the Catholic Church the true chalice of Christ's blood and it will fill all the desires of your soul.

It seems that, coincidentally with Hawker's second marriage, the chase was called off; but a significant letter exists dated 1872 from William Brindle, a Catholic priest in Barnstaple, just up the coast from Morwenstow:

I beg to acknowledge with many thanks your kind letter and your contribution in honour of the Blessed Virgin. St Bernard maintained that no one was ever truly devoted to our Blessed Lady and was lost. I hope she may show herself a mother to you and that she will obtain for you an abundant supply of grace.

Since your visit I have often thought of you and of your peculiar situation. I said Mass for you on Friday and again on Saturday and I shall continue to pray for you that you may be enabled to do the will of God.[25]

'Your peculiar situation' indeed, and bearing in mind that in each case Hawker provided the opportunity for this concentrated persuasion, we can surely assume that Pauline was performing his will when he lay on his deathbed and she sent for a Catholic priest: especially when one adds further that the last poem he wrote was entitled 'Psalmus Cantici (Lines written on Manning's Elevation to the Cardinalate, 15th March, 1875)'. It is no masterpiece, and its interest lies in its subject matter: the author seems to anticipate, and welcome, a counter-reformation.

> A prince shall reign from the great Gregory's line,
> A prelate wield Augustine's mighty name;
> They live and breathe again, as though their shrine
> Gave back the buried saints to life and fame.

But this is to anticipate. The catalogue of burdens upon him in the years of his second marriage is unhappily still incomplete. *Nox appropinquat* – as Hawker approached the dreaded age of seventy his health was seriously breaking down. Physically, he remained remarkably strong, reporting to Mrs Watson in June 1865, 'The clergy around all express their wonder how I can go thro' my Sunday work

PSALMUS CANTICI

*(Lines written on Manning's Elevation
to the Cardinalate, 15th March, 1875.)*

Shout! for the Word is breathed: the deed is done!
    Let the Hills Echo to the listening Plains!
The House of God reveals a lineal Son,
    And princely blood shall flow in English Veins.

Kings, stand aloof; and Queens, within your Bowers
    Hide the vain symbols of the Crown and Rod;
"Thrones, Dominations, Princedoms, Virtues, Powers,"
    Droop in deep homage to the Man of God.

Behold the ruddy Coif, the scarlet Vest,
    The sigill'd Glove, red with symbolic Blood,
The placid brow above the thrilling Breast,
    Where throbs the pulse of an Ethereal flood.

Shout, Happy England, for the sceptred Hand,
    The Rod of Aaron and the barren stems,
The throne of Rock amid a quivering Land,
    The Brow to sway a thousand diadems.

A Prince shall reign from the great Gregory's line,
    A Prelate wield Augustine's mighty name;
They live and breathe again, as though their shrine
    Gave back the buried Saints to Life and fame.

Again their names ascend the ancient Throne,
    Sooth'd by the Sign of Edward's sever'd Tree,
They greet the rescued Realm once more their own,
    Queen of the Lands and Lady of the Sea!

- three full services, sometimes four, and such a ride as very few could bear'.[26] He was fortunate in his doctor, who must have possessed exemplary patience, 'Nothing can be kinder than Budd's demeanour to me for many long years'. But he continued with a certain inevitability:

... his chief advice I am not able to follow. It is to keep myself very quiet and to allow nothing to dwell in my mind. He little knows the nature of my terrors and troubles.[27]

By 1870 he was suffering from eczema, and was drinking laudanum which induced insomnia. Pauline, still not thirty, was often seriously ill too, with rheumatic gout. In early 1874, according to her husband, she almost died.

A further anxiety was the broken down state of Morwenstow Church. Hawker had insisted on reroofing it with oak shingles, because that was the material from which Noah's Ark had been constructed, and soon the rain poured in, and the floor was full of holes, a particularly alarming state of affairs as there were coffins immediately below. Plainly he was losing his hold on such elementary matters of upkeep which were his direct responsibility.

One is easily tempted with Hawker to subtract a proportion of the woes he expresses, as he implores the sympathy of his long-suffering correspondents. But in those last years the woes really did pile in. Lack of money, and concern about debts, along with the desperate worry about his young wife and family, would have been enough alone, but one has to add his uncertainties about the state of the Church of England, to which he felt obliged to remain ostensibly loyal for practical if not for doctrinal reasons; the simultaneous pressures upon him, which he appears if anything to have encouraged, to become a Roman Catholic; Pauline's as well as his own poor health; and mounting anxieties about the fabric of the beloved church which loomed over his vicarage. It is a formidable list by any standards.

In 1874 he sought a dramatic solution to the last two at least. He took Pauline to London, partly to seek medical advice for them both, partly by means of preaching to obtain funds for the restoration of his church. It was a gallant foray, but sadly little success was achieved with either aim, and he wrote to Dr F.G. Lee, his future biographer and principal friend among the London clergy, 'I accept the omens', adding, 'I am getting paralysed and stricken down with anxiety about the future'.[28]

Yet all was not gloom and despair. He continued to write pungent and witty letters, scattered among the unhappy ones. He enjoyed adventures in London, alone and with his family.

Conceive my assisting, as the French say, at the opening of Parliament! I saw the Speaker chosen and heard the speeches of the mover and the seconder and of Mr Gladstone. I have also taken the children to the zoo and their remarks were very original. Nothing could induce Juliot to put a piece of biscuit 'up the elephant's nose'.[29]

He must have taken special pleasure in the report in 1874 of an Inspector of Schools, Matthew Arnold's younger brother Edward, 'I cannot help congratulating the vicar, of whose uphill labours to support a school in this remote district I have been witness for so many years . . .'[30] At a more informal level, Byles repeats a story which he would have heard from the family.

One day, when he went over with his wife and her aunt to consult Dr. Budd, they went into a confectioner's shop. There was no one there to serve. The vicar slipped behind the counter, laid aside his hat, and tied an apron that was lying near round his waist. Some customers came into the shop and he gravely served them, while the ladies were overcome with laughter outside.[31]

This is something that a great many people must have longed to do when waiting in an empty shop. It took a Hawker to do it, as it took a Hawker to sit out on the rocks pretending to be a mermaid nearly sixty years earlier. He also persisted in expressing strange theories which delighted him, for instance noticing that the baby Morwenna had inherited from him a lack of ear-lobes, a characteristic shared not only with the Duke of Wellington but also, 'I hope I may say so without impropriety', with Jesus Christ.[32] Above all, he continued through the sixties, right up to his death in 1875, to write some very acceptable poetry: for example 'A Canticle for Christmas, 1874'.

Before attempting to set this poem within a pattern of Hawker's achievement as a poet, it is necessary to face up to an element in it, the repeated use of the term 'awful child'. 'Awful', of course, jars. The modern connotation of 'appalling', 'deplorable', as opposed to the meaning intended by Hawker, 'demanding intense respect', was actually already in use in his time, having entered the language from America. However, the first recorded use of it is dated 1845, by which time he was well settled in Morwenstow, out of touch with the world in general and semantic change in particular. It is impossible when reading the poem to avoid a linguistic hiccup, which is a great pity: a fine poem unfairly spoilt.

Once that little problem is out of the way, the poem recalls at a less complex level 'Aishah Shechinah', celebrating as it does the miracle of God in a baby, and Mary's abiding amazement at the divine nature of the child on her knee, which she can nonetheless embrace and take to her breast:

It is her God! It is her Son!

The earler poem 'Modryb Marya –Aunt Mary' is another that expresses a close personal affection. The three poems happen to be spaced evenly through his career as a poet, written in 1874, 1859 and 1838 respectively. The theme meant much to him, he kept returning to it. One is reminded too of the passages in his Thought Books, when he visualises Jesus and Mary talking in a warm and loving way.

This ability to depict in poetry the simultaneous divinity and humanity of Jesus is I believe unique to Hawker. Something approaching it can be found in, for example, the words quoted earlier of Lancelot Andrewes, 'Verbum infans, the Word without a word, unable to speak a word'. Among the metaphysical poets, Richard Crashaw comes close, first in a poem on the Epiphany.

O little all, in thy embrace,
The world lies warm, and likes his place,
Nor does the full globe fail to be
Kiss'd on both his cheeks by thee.

CANTICLE FOR CHRISTMAS, 1874

Lo! a pure Maiden, meek and mild,
Yearns to embrace an awful Child!
Those limbs, her tenderest touch might win:
Yet thrill they with the God within!

She gazes! and what doth she see?
A gleaming Infant on her knee!
She pauses: can she dare to press
That Glory with a fond caress?

Yet 'tis her flesh: that Form so fair!
Her very blood is bounding there!
The mother's heart the victory won:
It is her God! it is her Son!

Hers the proud gladness mothers know,
Without a thrill, without a throe;
And Mary – Mary undefiled,
Claims for her breast that awful Child.

A conceit peeps out. Hawker keeps it more simple. Several poets
have of course written marvellously about the infant Jesus: Milton's
and Crashaw's nativity odes, written in the mid-seventeenth century,
come to mind. In each case however, they are commemorating
something that is happening on a huge scale, the effect on the entire
creation of the divine birth. They seem some distance from 'Mary,
and Joseph, and the babe lying in a manger'. Milton perhaps
approaches nearest to Hawker's – and St Luke's – intimacy, the
manifest reality of mother and child, in his final verse.

But see the Virgin blest,
Hath laid her babe to rest.
Time is our tedious song should here have ending;
Heaven's youngest teemed star,
Hath fixt her polisht car,
Her sleeping Lord with handmaid lamp attending:
And all about the courtly stable,
Bright-harnest angels sit in order serviceable.

Crashaw, in his equally impressive 'Hymn of the Nativity', is more tentative. He seeks to find a resting place for the child which is both pure and warm. Snow will not serve, 'Your fleece is white, but 'tis too cold'. Perhaps the wings of seraphim might be better, but no, 'Well done, said I: but are you sure, Your down so warm, will pass for pure?' He moves on to something more in touch with physical reality:

No, no, your king's not yet to seek
Where to repose his royal head,
See see, how soon his new-bloom'd cheek
Twixt's mother's breasts is gone to bed.
Sweet choice, said we! no way but so
Not to lie cold, yet sleep in snow.

It is hardly sensible to compare Hawker favourably with Milton and Crashaw, and that is not my intention. They were trying to do different things, or at least to express their understanding of the nativity in different ways. The suggestion simply is that Hawker's way is valid, and is his alone. Throughout his life as a poet, and still at the age of seventy-one, he was celebrating in verse his own special devoted relationship with Jesus and his mother.

Lo! a pure maiden, meek and mild,
Yearns to embrace an awful child!
Those limbs, her tenderest touch might win:
Yet thrill they with the God within!

It happens that Hawker's final days, and the aftermath of his death, comprise an unhappy story; so it seems appropriate to conclude this chapter with a reminder of his capacity for creating and sharing enjoyment. In those last years he also wrote a delightful poem which he called 'A Cornish Folk Song', in which he praises the clever cuckoo, going on for five dashing verses. He may have been ill, in debt, tormented by doctrinal worries, desperately anxious for the future; but he still spread happiness around him.

*   *   *   *   *

A CORNISH FOLK SONG

Now, of all the birds that keep the tree,
    Which is the wittiest fowl?
Oh, the Cuckoo – the Cuckoo's the one! – for he
    Is wiser than the owl!

He dresses his wife in her Sunday's best,
    And they never have rent to pay;
For she folds her feathers in a neighbour's nest,
    And thither she goes to lay!

He winked with his eye, and he buttoned his purse,
    When the breeding time began;
For he'd put his children out to nurse
    In the house of another man!

Then his child, though born in a stranger's bed,
    Is his own true father's son;
For he gobbles the lawful children's bread,
    And he starves them one by one!

So, of all the birds that keep the tree,
    This is the wittiest fowl!
Oh, the Cuckoo – the Cuckoo's the one! – for he
    Is wiser than the owl!

10

Death-Bed Conversion

The end of Robert Stephen Hawker's life came rapidly, the after-math dragged on. In June 1875, having secured the services of a curate, a Mr Comber from Truro, he set off with his family to stay with his brother Claud at Boscastle. However, Claud had just become ill, so they felt obliged to move on again, unable to return to Morwenstow as the Comber family was installed in the vicarage. They found lodgings in Plymouth, Hawker's birthplace, now to be the setting for his death. He sickened steadily during their two month stay there, and on August 15th he died, having suffered what appears to have been a cruelly conclusive stroke.

An event during the night of August 14th, as he lay dying, was the cause of a bitter controversy. Pauline of her own volition summoned a Roman Catholic priest, Canon Mansfield, to her husband's bedside, and he was received into the Church of Rome. He was buried two days later in Plymouth Cemetery. The mourners wore purple, out of respect for his renowned aversion to clerical black. The inscription on his tombstone reads in part 'Robert Stephen Hawker, for 41 years Vicar of Morwenstow in Cornwall . . . who died in Plymouth in the Catholic Faith'.

These are the simple facts. The disputes that arose, as some members of the Church of England expressed perturbation, indignation and even rage, revolve round more complex questions: what were Pauline's motives; and was Hawker in a fit state when Mansfield saw him to understand what was going on, in other words was his secession an act of conscious will? No acceptable answers were forthcoming then, and certainly none will emerge now, well over a hundred years later.

Pauline was not herself a Catholic, despite her Polish maiden name which aroused deep suspicion. Her father had died when she was eight, and she had been brought up by her mother and her American stepfather, in America and England, as an Anglican. She was in no way due to benefit from her husband's secession, rather the contrary. She wrote to a friend:

Robert would never himself have sent for him, because he had no doubt a prevision of all the trouble his avowal would bring upon me after his death, and his great love made him willing to risk the salvation of his soul rather than bring by his own act possible misery on me. That was Robert Hawker's character.

So there is no doubt that it was entirely her decision; but her account goes on:

When I told my husband what I had done, he raised himself instantly, and, seeming for the moment as if all bodily anguish was forgotten, exclaimed, 'Thank God, the Church, and Pauline'.[1]

Of course, the doubter might say, she would wish to justify herself. But there was another witness. Miss Savage, who was with the family party looking after the children, and who was not herself a Catholic either, supports the story:

I saw and stayed with him for some time; he was quite conscious; knew everything and each of us who attended to him. On that Saturday morning I was present when he was told that Canon Mansfield was coming that evening to receive him into the Church. I shall never forget the scene. He looked so peaceful, and was so full of thankfulness.[2]

One could go on to quote at least one contrary view: for instance John Olde, Hawker's manservant, was by no means so sure that he was in possession of his faculties at that stage. But it is hard to see that any purpose would be served. What is worth adding however is that there is plenty of evidence, accumulated in this book and elsewhere, of Hawker's sympathy with the Church of Rome: going back, according to Nicholas Ross, to 1845. One recalls particularly his correspondence with Catholic bishops, and his poems addressed to Cardinals Wiseman and Manning. Simultaneously he was distressed, as again we have seen, by changes that he saw occurring in the Church of England, due in his view to bring about a disastrous reduction in that authority of the priesthood which was so central to his beliefs.

The notion that, whether or not inadvertently, Hawker did something dreadful on August 14th, 1875, was still finding champions more than fifty years later. In 1927 a successor of Hawker as Vicar of Morwenstow, H. Hugh Breton, produced a booklet which included a chapter headed '46 Stories about Hawker'. These are predictable, mildly amusing, mainly apocryphal, until he comes to the 46th which reads, simply and crudely, 'The abominable scandal of Hawker becoming a pervert to Rome'. So the controversy dragged on; but it was of course at its fiercest in the months and years immediately following his death.

Sabine Baring-Gould fanned the flame. He published his so-called memoir, *The Vicar of Morwenstow*, in 1876, less than a year after Hawker died. He was in a great hurry for two reasons. First, he had an eye for a good story, reckoned that Hawker's life could be made into one, and wanted to be first in the field, knowing that Dr Lee was also at work. He in fact had nothing to fear from Lee, whose biography, largely concerned as it is with his interpretation of Hawker's churchmanship, adds little to our knowledge or understanding of the man and is very heavy going, whereas Baring-Gould's positively sparkles with entertainment. Secondly, as an Anglican priest himself he wanted to have his say about the deathbed conversion, the secession. Piers Brendon sums up admirably the quality of his contribution to Hawker's story:

From the first sentence, which gets both the place and date of Hawker's birth wrong, via colourful inventions like the story of his wife's riding pillion up to Oxford, to the confident but erroneous remarks about Hawker's deathbed conversion, Baring-Gould's book is a work of fiction.[3]

Baring-Gould casts Pauline in the role of villain. The first edition of his book – as we shall see there were two within the year – includes a disquisition on the history of Roman Catholicism in Poland: the name of Kuczynski proved useful. He goes on to hint heavily that Pauline on that fateful evening kept out of the way people who might have protested at her action in summoning Canon Mansfield, and then, having written that 'It is far from my intention to enter into controversy over the last sad transaction in the life of him whose memoir I have written', he adds:

Much allowance must be made for the love of a devoted wife, caring above all things for the welfare of a husband's soul, and believing that she was acting so as to best ensure its future felicity, and reunion with herself, when it should please God to call her. Not one ungenerous, or unkind word would I speak to wound a widow's sacred feelings . . . [4]

The speciousness of these tender remarks can be judged from his subsequent treatment of the Hawker family. He did in fact produce a revised edition of *The Vicar of Morwenstow* in that same year 1876, but that followed protests from the Adams family. They insisted on the deletion of a story about them, thinly disguised under the name of Andrews, which included an accusation that a son of the family, whom Hawker had helped to obtain a place at Oxford, had repaid the vicar's kindness by stealing some lines from an unpublished poem to absorb into his entry for the Newdigate Prize. This fabrication, as they claimed it was, had in their judgment been designed to divert interest in an allegation that the vicar owed the family money. Quite possibly he did: his financial affairs, undeniably, sometimes shaded into the murky.

Pauline was needed, to contribute some dignity to an increasingly ridiculous scene. She wrote a letter to *The Athenaeum* in April 1876, part of which reads:

Even when Mr Baring-Gould's book was published, I still kept silence, notwithstanding that it is full of mis-statements, and written by one whose personal knowledge of Mr Hawker was scarcely that of a mere acquaintance. I may say also that he wrote the Memoir without the least reference to myself, or the slightest regard to any feeling or wish that I might have, or how much additional sorrow it might cause me.

There was much vigorous writing in *The Athenaeum* during 1876: two reviews, one of each edition, of *The Vicar of Morwenstow*, and indignant rejoinders from its author. The reviewer was William

Maskell, a close friend of Robert Stephen Hawker. He did not spare his adversary, concluding his second review, 'Mr Baring-Gould's Memoir of Robert Stephen Hawker when first printed was a discredit, and in its "revised" shape is a disgrace, to English biographical literature'.[5]

Not only did Baring-Gould ignore Pauline's grief: over twenty years later, when a new edition of his book was due to be published in 1899, he treated with equal apparent scorn a plea from her daughter Rosalind Byles.

Would you not be willing to insert a fair, true, and, as far as is possible at this distance of time, full account of my father's last years and of my mother's conduct at the time of the latter? The book as it stood always gave my mother the greatest possible pain, and she suffered more than you can credit from the effects of all it contained respecting her.[6]

In 1916 Baring-Gould declined an opportunity to inspect a letter by Hawker 'as I have lost interest in the subject'. He had done his worst: caused considerable unhappiness to the family, and damaged Hawker's reputation by writing 'a gossiping book'[7], disseminating anecdotage about him which was more often than not apocryphal and sometimes quite untrue. At the same time, paradoxically, one must maintain a grudging gratitude to him for keeping Hawker's name alive. *The Vicar of Morwenstow* has run to at least twelve editions, and is still popular. Certainly more people have read it than are acquainted with Hawker's own work, poetry or prose. The problem is that the man portrayed is a travesty of the actual man Robert Stephen Hawker.

Admirers of Sabine Baring-Gould would wish to add that I in my turn have produced a travesty of their man. Perversely enough, I admire him myself. He was a remarkably gifted individual. He was skilled, confident and influential in so many different roles, whether as hymn-writer, poet, priest, theologian, archaeologist, historian, novelist: one of that company of late Victorian polymaths whom one can only respect and marvel at. The pity of it is that he was also remarkably insensitive; one is tempted to say, cruel.

The circumstances of the death of Robert Stephen Hawker, and its aftermath, were untidy, doubtful, bitter and altogether most regrettable. But as one looks back over the seventy-two years of his life, there is so much to admire and be thankful for, and those final events can be placed firmly in proportion. Priest, eccentric, mystic, poet, Cornishman, his name surely deserves to be remembered and celebrated. Hitherto, for reasons that must be clear, he is remembered principally as an eccentric. Even now, newspapers seeking for an unusual subject to entertain their readers occasionally home in on him. 'Clifftop Oddball' was the heading of a recent article. Piers Brendon did not help by giving his book the sub-title *Portrait of a Victorian Eccentric.*

My own interest, as may have been apparent, is first and foremost in the poet, though I have tried to do justice as well to the priest, the mystic and the Cornishman, and have not been able to resist pausing from time to time to smile at the eccentric. I believe that he has been grievously underrated as a poet. In the thirty years following his death, three different editions of his collected poems were published; over the past hundred years, no more than modest selections. Only 'The Song of the Western Men' is still widely known. Yet as I have endeavoured to show, twenty or more of his poems are immensely rewarding to read, and parts of his crowning achievement, 'The Quest of the Sangraal', can be ranked with the finest poetry ever written. It is fitting therefore that this attempt to offer a fresh view of an intensely engaging, profoundly Christian, strangely magnetic man should conclude with his warm-blooded Arthur's plea to posterity.

> Yet am I fain some deeds of mine should live –
> I would not be forgotten in this land:
> I yearn that men I know not, men unborn,
> Should find, amid these fields, King Arthur's fame!
> Here let them say, by proud Dundagel's walls –
> 'They brought the Sangraal back by his command,
> They touched these rugged rocks with hues of God':
> So shall my name have worship, and my land.

Appendix

THE WRECK

Adieu! Adieu! my own dear shore,
    The Isles, where angry spirits dwell;
De Rosa views thy coast no more –
    Ye winds! is this his last farewell?

Adieu! tall Chili's mountains bold,
    Parana's sands and rich Peru:
To deep Potosi's mines of gold;
    To Empelada's shores adieu!

The setting sun sinks fast and deep
    Beneath thy hot and waveless seas:
"Oh! for full sails this calm to sweep!
    The Petrel's wing to cleave the breeze!"

Hush! Mariner, that heedless word:
    The clouds – the winds – that voice obey:
Lo! at thy wish the fatal bird
    Skims o'er the wave at break of day!

Unseen the forms that fill the sky,
    To watch the seaman's reckless hour:
Thy sin hath brought the Avenger nigh:
    The spirit of the storm hath power.

"Nine awful days – nine hopeless nights
    Have seen us tossed from strand to strand:
Pilot, are these Morena's heights?
    Pilot, is this my native land?"

De Rosa, no! not these thine hills,
    Nor they Morena's mountains blue:
No groves of cork, no shining rills,
    Nor vine nor olive meet thy view.

Thou seest dark Cornwall's rifted shore,
   Old Arthur's stern and rugged keep:
There, where proud billows dash and roar,
   His haughty turret guards the deep.

And mark yon bird of sable wing,
   Talons and beak all red with blood:
The spirit of the long-lost king
   Pass'd in that shape from Camlan's flood!

And still, when loudliest howls the storm,
   And darkliest lowers his native sky,
The king's fierce soul is in that form:
   The warrior's spirit threatens nigh!

"Pilot! they say when tempests rave
   Dark Cornwall's sons will haunt the main,
Watch the wild wreck, yet not to save:
   Oh! for Paranas sands again!"

Is it the mermaid, cold and pale,
   That glides within yon cloister'd cave?
Hark! 'tis her wild and broken wail
   Above the shipwrecked seaman's grave!

Away! away! before the wind!
   Fury and wrath are on the blast:
Tintagel's keep, far, far behind:
   Tremoutha's bay is won and past.

Away! away! what shall avail
   In the fierce hands of such a sea?
She bends – she quivers to the gale –
   And Bude's dark rocks are on the lee!

Her race is run – deep in that sand
   She yields her to the conquering wave –
And Cornwall's sons – they line the strand –
   Rush they for plunder? No! to save!

High honour to his heart and name!
    Who stood that day with sheltering form,
To gives these shores a gentler fame,
    To soothe the anguish of the storm!

Thenceforth, when voice and bowl went round,
    De Rosa's pledge was true and loud –
"To every man on Cornish ground!"
    And every Cornish heart was proud.

And still when breathes the seaman's vow,
    This thought will mingle with his fear –
Would that we saw one absent brow!
    Would that the I'ans voice were here!

     ❋ ❋ ❋ ❋ ❋

POMPEII

How fair the scene! the sunny smiles of day
Flash o'er the wave in glad Sorrento's bay;
Far, far along mild Sarno's glancing stream,
The fruits and flowers of golden summer beam,
And cheer, with bright'ning hues, the lonely gloom,
That shrouds yon silent City of the Tomb!
Yes, sad Pompeii! Time's deep shadows fall
On every ruin'd arch and broken wall;
But Nature smiles as in thy happiest hour,
And decks thy lowly rest with many a flower.
Around, above, in blended beauty shine
The graceful poplar and the clasping vine;
Still the young violet, in her chalice blue,
Bears to the lip of Morn her votive dew;
Still the green laurel springs to life the while,
Beneath her own Apollo's golden smile;
And o'er thy fallen beauties beams on high
The glory of the heavens – Italia's sky!

How fair the scene! e'en now to Fancy's gaze
Return the shadowy forms of other days:
Those halls, of old with mirth and music rife,
Those echoing streets that teem'd with joyous life,
The stately towers that look'd along the plain,
And the light barks that swept yon silvery main.
And see! they meet beneath the chestnut shades,
Pompeii's joyous sons and graceful maids,
Weave the light dance – the rosy chaplet twine,
Or snatch the cluster from the weary vine;
Nor think that Death can haunt so fair a scene
The Heavens' deep blue, the Earth's unsullied green.

Devoted City! could not aught avail
When the dark omen told thy fearful tale?
The giant phantom dimly seen to glide,
And the loud voice that shook the mountain-side,
With warning tones that bade thy children roam,
to seek in happier climes a calmer home?
In vain! they will not break the fatal rest
That woos them to the mountain's treacherous breast:
Fond memory blends with every mossy stone
Some early joy, some tale of pleasure flown;
And they must die where those around will weep,
And sleep for ever where their fathers sleep.
Yes! they must die: behold! yon gathering gloom
Brings on the fearful silence of the tomb;
Along Campania's sky yon murky cloud
Spreads its dark form – a City's funeral shroud.

How brightly rose Pompeii's latest day!
the sun, unclouded, held his golden way;
Vineyards, in autumn's purple glories drest,
Slept in soft beauty on the mountain's breast;
The gale that wanton'd round his crested brow,
Shook living fragrance from the blossom'd bough;
And many a laughing mead and silvery stream
Drank the deep lustre of the noonday beam:
Then echoing Music rang, and Mirth grew loud
In the glad voices of the festal crowd;

The opening Theatre's wide gates invite,
The choral dance is there, the solemn rite –
There breathes the immortal Muse her spell around,
And swelling thousands flood the fated ground.

See! where arise before th'enraptur'd throng,
The fabled scenes, the shadowy forms of Song!
Gods, that with heroes leave their starry bowers,
Their fragrant hair entwin'd with radiant flowers,
Haunt the dim grove, beside the fountain dwell –
Strike the deep lyre, or sound the wreathèd shell –
With forms of heavenly mould, but hearts that glow
With human passion, melt with human woe:
Breathless they gaze, while white-robed priests advance,
And graceful virgins lead the sacred dance;
They listen, mute, while mingling tones prolong
The lofty accent, and the pealing song,
Echo th'unbending Titan's haughty groan,.
Or in the Colchian's woes forgot their own!

Why feels each throbbing heart that shuddering chill?
The Music falters, and the Dance is still –
"Is it pale twilight stealing o'er the plain?
Or starless eve that holds unwonted reign?"
Hark to the thrilling answer! Who shall tell
When thick and fast th'unsparing tempest fell,
And stern Vesuvius pour'd along the vale
His molten cataracts, and his burning hail?
Oh! who shall paint, in that o'erwhelming hour,
Death's varying forms, and Horror's withering power?
Earthquake! wild Earthquake! rends that heaving plain,
Cleaves the firm rock, and swells the beetling main:
Here, yawns the ready grave, and, raging, leap
Earth's secret fountains from their troubled sleep;
There, from the quivering mountain bursts on high
The pillar'd flame that wars along the sky!
On, on they press, and maddening seek in vain
Some soothing refuge from the fiery rain –
Their home? it can but yield a living tomb!
Round the lov'd hearth is brooding deepest gloom.

Yon sea? its angry surges scorching rave,
And death-fires gleam upon the ruddy wave!
Oh! for one breath of that reviving gale,
That swept at dewy morn along the vale!
For one sad glance of their beloved sky,
To soothe, though vain, their parting agony!
Yon mother bows in vain her shuddering form,
Her babe to shield from that relentless storm:
Cold are those limbs her clasping arms constrain,
Even the soft shelter of her breast is vain!
Gaze on that form! 'tis Beauty's softest maid,
The rose's rival in her native shade –
For her had Pleasure reared her fairest bowers,
And Song and Dance had sped the laughing hours:
See! o'er her brow the kindling ashes glow,
And the red shower o'erwhelms her breast of snow;
She seeks that loved one - never false till then –
She calls on him – who answers not again:
Loose o'er her bosom flames her golden hair,
And every thrilling accent breathes despair!
Even the stern priest, who saw with raptur'd view
The deathless forms of Heaven's ethereal blue,
Who drank, with glowing ear, the mystic tone,
That clothes his lips with wonders not their own,
Beheld the immortal marble frown in vain,
And fires triumphant grasp the sacred fane,
Forsook at last the unavailing shrine,
And cursed his faithless gods – no more divine!

Morn came in beauty still – and shone as fair,
Though cold the hearts that hail'd its radiance there,
And Evening, crown'd with many a starry gem,
Sent down her softest smile –though not for them!
Where gleam'd afar Pompeii's graceful towers,
Where hill and vale were cloth'd with vintage bowers,
O'er a dark waste the smouldering ashes spread,
A pall above the dying and the dead.

Still the dim city slept in safest shade,
Though the wild waves another Queen obeyed,

And sad Italia, on her angry shore,
Beheld the North its ruthless myriads pour;
And nature scattered all her treasures round,
And graced with fairest hues the blighted ground.
There oft, at glowing noon, the village maid
Sought the deep shelter of the vineyard shade;
Beheld the olive bud – the wild-flower wave,
Nor knew her step was on a people's grave!
But see! once more beneath the smiles of day,
The dreary mist of ages melts away!
Again Pompeii, 'mid the brightening gloom,
Comes forth in beauty from her lonely tomb.
Lovely in ruin – graceful in decay,
The silent City rears her walls of grey:
The clasping ivy hangs her faithful shade,
As if to hide the wreck that time had made;
The shattered column on the lonely ground
Is glittering still, with fresh acanthus crowned;
And where her Parian rival moulders near,
The drooping lily pours her softest tear!
How sadly sweet with pensive step to roam
Amid the ruin'd wall, the tottering dome!
The path just worn by human feet is here,
Their echoes almost reach the listening ear;
The marble halls with rich mosaic drest;
The portal wide that woos the lingering guest;
Altars, with fresh and living chaplets crown'd,
From those wild flowers that spring fantastic round;
The unfinished painting, and the pallet nigh,
Whose added hues must fairer charms supply –
These mingle here, until th'unconscious feet
Roam on, intent some gathering crowd to meet;
And cheated Fancy, in her dreamy mood,
Will half forget that it is solitude!

Yes, all is solitude! fear not to tread,
Through gates unwatch'd, the City of the Dead!
Explore with pausing step th'unpeopled path,
View the proud hall – survey the stately bath,
Where swelling roofs their noblest shelter raise;

Enter! no voice shall check th'intruder's gaze!
See! the dread legion's peaceful home is here,
The signs of martial life are scattered near.
Yon helm, unclasp'd to ease some Warrior's brow,
The sword his weary arm resign'd but now,
Th'unfinish'd sentence traced along the wall,
Broke by the hoarse Centurion's startling call:
Hark! did their sounding tramp re-echo round?
Or breath'd the hollow gale that fancied sound?
Behold! where 'mid yon fane, so long divine,
Sad Isis mourns her desolated shrine!
Will none the mellow reed's soft music breathe?
Or twine from yonder flowers the victim's wreath?
None to yon altar lead with suppliant strain
The milk-white monarch of the herd again?
All, all is mute! save sadly answering nigh
The night-bird's shriek, the shrill cicada's cry.
Yet may you trace along the furrow'd street,
The chariot's track - the print of frequent feet;
The gate unclosed, as if by recent hand;
The hearth, where yet the guardian Lares stand;
Still on the walls the words of welcome shine,
And ready vases proffer joyous wine:
But where the hum of men? the sounds of life?
The Temple's pageant, and the Forum's strife?
The forms and voices, such as should belong
To that bright clime, the land of Love and Song?
How sadly echoing to the stranger's tread,
These walls respond, like voices from the dead!
And sadder traces – darker scenes are there,
Tales of the Tomb, and records of Despair;
In Death's chill grasp unconscious arms enfold
The fatal burden of their cherished gold.
Here, wasted relics, as in mockery, dwell
Beside some treasure loved in life too well;
There, faithful hearts have moulder'd side by side,
And hands are claspt that Death could not divide!
None, none shall tell that hour of fearful strife,
When Death must share the consciousness of Life;
When sullen Famine, slow Despair consume
The living tenants of the massive tomb;

Long could they hear, above th'incumbent plain,
The music of the breeze awake again,
The waves' deep echo on the distant shore,
And murmuring streams, that they should see no more!
Away! dread scene! and o'er the harrowing view
Let Night's dim shadows fling their darkest hue!

But there, if still beneath some nameless stone,
By waving weeds and ivy-wreaths o'ergrown,
Lurk the grey spoils of Poet or of Sage,
Tully's deep lore, or Livy's pictured page.
If sweet Menander, where his relics fade,
Mourn the dark refuge of Oblivion's shade;
Oh! may their treasures burst the darkling mine;
Glow in the living voice, the breathing line;
Their vestal fire our midnight lamp illume,
And kindle Learning's torch from sad Pompeii's tomb!

* * * * *

TETCOTT, 1831

*In which year Sir William Molesworth Caused the Old House
to be Taken Down, and a New One Built.*

Shade of the Hunter old! if aught could roam
From the dim cloisters of that shadowy home,
Where the far spirits of each severed clime,
The sad and placid, coil and bide their time,
If love survive, or memory endear,
Shade of the Hunter old! thou would'st be here!

Oh, for the Squire that shook at break of morn,
Dew from the trees with echo of his horn!
The gathering scene, where Arscott's lightest word
Went like a trumpet to the hearts that heard!
The dogs that knew the meaning of his voice,
From the grim fox-hound to my lady's choice.
The steed that waited till his hand carest,
And old Black John that gave and bare the jest.

The good old Squire! once more along the glen,
Oh, for the scenes of old! the former men!
That hill's far echoes sped the starting cry,
Within yon vale the worn prey rushed to die.
Yes! in these fields, beneath his stately form,
Dashed the wild steed with footsteps like the storm.

'Tis past; that ivy, last of all her race,
Yields the grey dwelling from her sad embrace.
The walls! the walls! that felt his father's breath,
Th'accustomed room he loved so well in death,
Are lowly laid – and in their place will stand
A roof unknown – a stranger in the land.

* ❈ * ❈ *

GENOVEVA

Part the First

MORNING

Now hearken, lords and ladies gay,
　And ye shall understand
The wonders of a legend-lay
　From the old German land!
She, of my song, in Eden's bowers,
　A sainted lady lies;
And wears a chaplet of the flowers
　That grow in Paradise.

Her father gloried in her birth,
　That daughter of his fame;
The sweetest sound he knew on earth
　Was Genoveva's name.
She dwelt, a fair and holy child,
　Beside her mother's knee:
She grew, a maiden meek and mild,
　And pure as pure could be.

And so it was, that when the maid
　Fulfilled her childhood's vow,
Saint Hildorf's lifted hands were laid
　Upon no lovelier brow.
And said they, as along the aisle
　The lords and ladies poured,
"How will she gladden with her smile
　The castle of her lord!"

Right soon a stately champion came
　For that bright damsel's hand;
The sound of County Siegfried's fame
　Was sung in many a land.
He came, he knelt, he woo'd, he won,
　As warriors win the bride;
Duke Pfalz hath hailed him as his son,
　At Genoveva's side.

Then might you hear the matin-bell,
 With echoes low and sweet,
Where at Saint Hildorf's sacred cell
 The youth and maiden meet.
And hark! they plight the mystic vow,
 The troth that time shall try,
When years have worn the beamy brow,
 And quenched the laughing eye.

Now turn we to the castle gate,
 Wreathed with the peaceful vine,
Where County Siegfried holds his state,
 Beside the Rhine! the Rhine!
They bring white blossoms from the bowers,
 The rose-leaves hide the ground;
Ah! gentle dame, beneath the flowers
 The coiling worm is found!

Yet day by day went bounding on,
 Nor would the warrior roam:
The brightness of his lady shone
 Throughout Lord Siegfried's home.
She was the garland of his days,
 His blessing and his fame:
His happy hearth hath won the praise
 Of Genoveva's name.

But hark! that stern and sudden sound,
 Along the castle wall:
It shook the echo from the ground,
 That startling trumpet-call.
"To arms! To horse! The Moor!
    The Moor!
 His pagan banners fly:
The Spaniard and the Frank implore
 Thy German chivalry."

Then might you see, at break of day,
 The stately Siegfried stand:
Harnessed, and in his old array,
 His good sword in his hand.
"And fare-thee-well!" the soldier said,

"My lady bright and dear:"
He spake, and bent his haughty head,
 To hide a warrior's tear.

"Farewell! and thou my castellain,
 My liege-man true and tried,
Shield, till thy lord shall turn again,
 My lady and my bride.
And ye, good Saints, with unseen eyes,
 Watch her in solemn care;
An angel well might leave the skies
 At Genoveva's prayer."

Part the Second

EVENING

Ah! woe is me! and well-a-day!
 What scenes of sorrow rise;
And hark! the music of my lay
 Must breathe the breath of sighs.
That guardian – he of trusty fame,
 He seeks a deed abhorred;
He woos to sorrow and to shame,
 The lady of his lord.

But she, fair Genoveva, stands,
 A pure and peerless bride;
Her angel lifts his sheltering hands,
 For ever at her side.
She kneels, she breathes some simple verse,
 Taught by her mother's care;
And the good Saints in Heaven rehearse
 The gentle lady's prayer.

Yet Strife and anguish lasted long,
 Till he – that fiendish man,
The anger of his sin was strong,
 And thus his fury ran:-
"Bind ye this foul and wanton dame,
 False to my master's bed;
Hide in the earth both sin and shame,
 Her blood be on her head."

They took the stern command he gave,
　Two vassals fierce and rude;
They bare her to a nameless grave,
　Far in a distant wood.
There knelt she down and meekly prayed,
　In language soft and mild:
"I bear beneath my breast," she said,
　"Your lord, Count Siegfried's child.

Then let me tarry but awhile,
　Far, far, from earthly eye,
That I may see my infant smile,
　And lay me down and die.
Nay, spare me, in sweet Mary's name,
　Who stood by Jesu's cross;
He from a mother's bosom came,
　That He might die for us."

They melted at the voice they heard,
　They left her lonely there!
The holy angels helped her word –
　There is such force in prayer.
Then wandered she, where that wild wood
　A tangled pathway gave,
Till, lo! in secret solitude,
　A deep and mossy cave.

A source of quiet waters shone
　Along a shadowy glade;
And branches, fair to look upon,
　A dreamy shelter gave.
Her eyes are closed, but not to sleep;
　She bends, but not to pray;
Thrilled with the throes that mothers weep,
　The lonely lady lay.

She sees – what is it nestling near?
　A soft, fair form is nigh:
She hears – sweet Lord, what doth she hear?
　A low and infant cry.
It is her son! her son! the child,
　The first-born of her vow:

See, in his face his father smiled,
　He bears Lord Siegfried's brow.
Good angels! 'twas a sight to see
　That cavern dark and wild;
The nameless stream – the silent tree,
　The mother and her child.
And hark! he weeps - that voice of tears
　Proclaims a child of earth;
O, what shall soothe for holier years
　The sorrow of his birth!

There was no font, no sacred shrine,
　No servant of the Lord;
The waters of the mystic sign
　A mother's hand hath poured.
She breathed on him a word of woes,
　His life in tears begun;
The name a Hebrew mother chose,
　Ben-oni – Sorrow's son.

But ah! what miseries betide
　A mother and her pains!
Her child must die, for famine dried
　The fountain of her veins.
She saw the anguish of his face,
　She heard his bitter cry,
And went forth from that woeful place,
　She could not see him die.

Yet still, again, her feet must turn
　Back to that cavern wild:
Yea! even in death, she fain would yearn
　Once more upon her child.
What doth she see? A fair young doe
　A mother's task hath done,
Bent at his side: her milk must flow
　To soothe the lady's son.

She wept – she wept, she could no less,
　Tears sweet and grateful ran;
The mute thing of the wilderness
　Hath softer heart than man.

She came, that wild deer of the herd,
  Moved by some strange control,
There was a mystic touch that stirred
  The yearnings of her soul.

And there they dwelt, the gentle three –
  In peace, if not in joy,
Until he stood beside her knee,
  A fair and thoughtful boy.
The doe, the lady, and the youth,
  Seven long and weary years,
Their calm and patient life; in sooth
  It was a sight for tears.

She fed him with the forest fruits
  That summer branches gave;
She gathered wild and wholesome roots,
  To cheer their wintry cave:
They drank from that fair fountain's bed
  Whose faithful waters run
Bright as when first his name they shed,
  Ben-oni – Sorrow's son.

And she hath framed, with chosen boughs,
  A simple cross of wood;
And taught the lad his childhood's vows,
  To Jesu, mild and good.
He learned the legend of the Cross,
  How Mary's blessèd Son
Came down from heaven to die for us,
  And peace and pardon won.

He heard that shadowy angels roam
  Along the woodland dell,
To lead the blessèd to a home
  Where saints and martyrs dwell.
So, when the lady wept and prayed,
  He soothed her secret sighs:
"Sweet mother, let us die," he said,
  "And rest in Paradise."

"Alas! my son, my tender son,
  What wilt thou do," she sighed,

"When I thy mother shall be gone? –
  Thou hast no friend beside.
There is thy Sire of Heavenly birth,
  His love is strong and sure:
But he, thy father of the earth,
  He spurns thee from his door."

"Nay, tell me, mother dear," he said,
  "I pray thee tell to me,
Are they not, all men, gone and dead,
  Except thy son and thee?"
"Ah! no, there be, my gentle child,
  Whole multitudes afar;
Yet is it happier in this wild,
  Than where their dwellings are.

They cast me out to woe and shame,
  Here in this den to hide:
They blighted Genoveva's name,
  Lord Siegfried's chosen bride.
But soon the weary will have rest,
  I breathe with failing breath;
There is within thy mother's breast,
  The bitterness of death."

"Then, mother kind, in thy dark grave,
  Alone, thou shalt not lie:
Before our Cross, here in this grave,
  Together let us die.
Yea, let me look on no man's face,
  Since such stern hearts there be:
But here, in this our lonely place,
  Here will I die with thee."

"Ah! noble heart! thy words are sooth,
  I breathe their sound again:
Better to pass away in youth,
  Than live with bearded men."
And thou! the Lady of his birth,
  Farewell! a calm farewell!
Thou wert not meant for this vile earth,
  But with the saints to dwell.

Part the Third

ANOTHER DAY

Mark ye, how spear and helmet glare,
  And red-cross banners shine,
While thrilling trumpets cleave the air
  Along the Rhine! the Rhine!
Count Siegfried from the wars is come,
  And gathering vassals wait
To welcome the stern warrior home
  To his own castle gate.

But where is she, his joy, his pride,
  The garland of his fame?
Away! away! her image hide,
  He cannot brook her name.
Yet soon the whispered words are breathed,
  And faithful lips declare
How a vile serpent's folds were wreathed
  Around their lady fair.

They tell his vassal's treacherous crime,
  The bow his malice bent,
Till Genoveva, in her prime,
  Had perished, innocent.
Alas! what torrent tears must roll
  In fierce and angry shower!
O! what shall soothe Count Siegfried's soul
  In that o'erwhelming hour?

He hides him in some vaulted room,
  Far from the light of day;
He will not look on beauty's bloom,
  Nor hear the minstrel's lay.
They try him with the trumpet sound
  On many an echoing morn;
They tempt him forth with hawk and
                    hound,
  And breathe the hunter's horn.

They loose the gazehound from the chain,
  They bring both steed and spear,
Lord Siegrried's hand must rule the rein,
  And rouse the ruddy deer.
On! through the wild, the war-horse bounds
  Beneath his stately form,
He charges 'mid those rushing hounds
  With footsteps like the storm.

"Down! Donner, down! hold, Hubert, hold!"
  What is yon sight of fear?
A strange wild youth, a maiden bold
  That guard yon panting deer!"
A fleecy skin was folded round
  Her breast, with woman's pride,
And some dead fawn the youth hath found,
  He wears its dappled hide.

"Who? whence are ye?" the warrior said,
  "That haunt this secret cave?
Ha! is it so? and do the dead
  Come from their hollow grave?"
"I live, I breathe the breath of life,
  No evil have I done;
I am thy true, thy chosen wife,
  And this is Siegfried's son!"

He stood, as severed souls may stand
  At first, when forth they fare,
And shadowy forms – a stranger-band –
  Will greet them in the air.
He bounds, he binds her to his heart,
  His own, his rescued bride:
No more! O! never more to part,
  E'en death shall not divide.

See now, they move along the wild,
  With solemn feet and slow,
The warrior and his graceful child,
  The lady and the doe.
They stand before the castle-gate,
  Rich with the clustering vine,
Again shall Siegfried hold his state,
  Beside the Rhine! the Rhine!

They come, they haste from many a land,
   For fast the tidings spread,
And there doth Genoveva stand,
   Bright as the arisen dead.
Her mother weeps, by God's dear grace,
   Glad tears are in her eye;
Duke Pfalz has seen his daughter's face,
   And now – now let him die.

Yea, from his calm and distant cell
   The sainted Hildorf came,
His spirit bowed beneath the spell
   Of Genoveva's name.
He came, he sought that solemn cave,
   The lady's patient home,
He measured it with aisle and nave,
   He shaped a shadowy dome.

He knelt in votive solitude,
   He fixed both saint and sign,
And bade them build, in that lone wood,
   A fair and stately shrine.
There might you read for many an age,
   In the rich window's ray,
Traced, as along some pictured page,
   The legend of my lay.

The image of their youth was there,
   The bridegroom and he bride;
The porch, where Genoveva fair
   Knelt at her Siegfried's side.
There, through the storied glass, the scene
   In molten beauty falls,
When she, with mild and matron mien,
   Shone in her husband's halls.

There was the cave, the wood, the stream,
   In radiance soft and warm,
And evermore the noon-day beam
   Came through some angel's form.
The youth was shown in that wild dress,
   His mother's cross he bare;
Saint John in the old wilderness
   was not more strangely fair.

But where they breathe their holiest vows,
   And eastern sunbeams fall,
A simple cross, of woodland boughs,
   Stands by the chancel wall.
It is the lady's lonely sign,
   By mournful fingers made,
That self-same symbol decks the shrine
   That soothed the cavern's shade.

Behind yon altar, reared on high,
   A lady breathes in stone;
A sculptured deer is crouching nigh,
   An infant weeps alone.
A word is there, but not of woe,
   One voice, a prayer to claim,
Beneath the lady and the doe
   Is Genoveva's name.

Thus lived, thus loved she, and she died,
   But old, and full of days;
Ask ye how time and truth have tried
   The legend of her praise?
She of my song, in Eden's bowers
   A sainted lady lies,
And wears a garland of the flowers
   That grow in Paradise.

✻ ❈ ✻ ❈ ✻

SIR BEVILLE – THE GATE-SONG OF STOWE

Arise! and away! for the King and the land;
    Farewell to the couch and the pillow:
With spear in the rest, and with rein in the hand,
    Let us rush on the foe like a billow.

Call the hind from the plough, and the herd from the
      fold,
    Bid the wassailer cease from his revel:
And ride for old Stowe, where the banner's unrolled,
    For the cause of King Charles and Sir Beville.

Trevanion is up, and Godolphin is nigh,
    And Harris of Hayne's o'er the river;
From Lundy to Looe, "One and all!" is the cry,
    And the King and Sir Beville for ever!

Ay! by Tre, Pol, and Pen, ye may know Cornish men,
    'Mid the names and the nobles of Devon;
But if truth to the King be a signal, why then
    Ye can find out the Granville in heaven.

Ride! ride! with red spur, there is death in delay,
    'Tis a race for dear life with the devil;
If dark Cromwell prevail, and the King must give way,
    This earth is no place for Sir Beville.

So at Stamford he fought, and at Lansdown he fell,
    But vain were the visions he cherished:
For the great Cornish heart, that the King loved so well,
    In the grave of the Granville it perished.

References

Certain books to which reference is frequently made are listed in shortened forms as:

Baring-Gould: S. Baring-Gould, *The Vicar of Morwenstow, A Life of Robert Stephen Hawker, MA* (London: Henry S. King, 1876)

Brendon: Piers Brendon, *Hawker of Morwenstow, Portrait of a Victorian Eccentric* (London: Cape, 1975)

Byles: C.E. Byles, *The Life and Letters of R.S. Hawker (sometime Vicar of Morwenstow)* (London: John Lane, The Bodley Head, 1908) *Footsteps*: R.S. Hawker, *Foorsteps of Former Men in Far Cornwall* (London: John Lane, The Bodley Head, 1908)

Lee: The Rev. Dr Frederick George Lee, *Memorials of the Late Rev. Robert Stephen Hawker, MA* (London: Chatto & Windus, 1876)

Michell: John Michell, *A Short Life at the Land's End, J.T.Blight F.S.A., Artist, Penzance* (Bath, printed privately for subscribers, 1977)

West: The Rev. William West

INTRODUCTION
1. *Footprints*, p.46

CHAPTER 1. EARLY DAYS, 1803-1829
1. *Dictionary of National Biography*, article on Dr Robert Hawker, DD, 1753-1827
2. Byles, p.99
3. Letter to Mrs Watson, 1867, quoted by Brendon, pp.38-9
4. S. Baring-Gould, *The Vicar of Morwenstow, A Life of Robert Stephen Hawker, MA*, 1st edn (London: Henry S. King, 1876)
5. Arthur Bell, *Tudor Foundation, A Sketch of the History of Richard Pate's Foundation in Cheltenham* (Chalfont St Giles: Richard Sadler, 1974) p.99
6. J. Ashcroft Noble, *The Sonnet in England*, quoted by Byles, p.10
7. Christopher Harris, article in *John Bull*, 15 April 1876, quoted by Byles, p.16
8. Margaret Jeune Gifford, *The Diary of an Oxford Lady 1843-1862* (Oxford: The Shakespeare Head Press, 1932), typed extract at The Old Vicarage, Morwenstow
9. Baring-Gould, p.17
10. Letter to Mrs Watson, 22 November 1863: Byles, p.412
11. *Footprints*, p.181
12. Letter, 1861: Byles, p. 19
13. Macaulay, *History of England* (Longman's 1899 edn), vol.1, pp.509-10

14. Letter, 2 February 1862: Byles, p.24
15. Letter, 1856: Byles, p.17
16. Letter to J.G. Godwin, 8 September 1863: Byles, p.429.
17. Letter to Godwin, 14 October 1867: Byles, p.559
18. Letter to Godwin, 1862: Byles, p.39

CHAPTER 2. NORTH TAMERTON TO MORWENSTOW, 1830-35
1. *Footprints*, pp.79-89
2. Sarah Dopp, *Cornish Elements in the Poetry and Prose of Robert Stephen Hawker*, unpublished thesis presented to the Faculty of the Graduate College of the University of Vermont, March 1982: chapter 3
3. Letter to the Editor of *Blackwood's Magazine*, January 1858: Byles, p.62
4. Extracts from longer passages quoted by Byles, p.129-132
5. *Footprints*, p.7
6. H. Miles Brown, *The Church in Cornwall* (Truro: Oscar Blackford, 1964), p.16
7. *Footprints*, pp.32-36
8. Byles, p.44
9. Letter to R.A. Mountjoy, 27 July 1868: Byles, p.575
10. Written in Hawker's own copy of *Cornish Ballads and Other Poems*
11. Quoted by Byles, p.134
12. The Rev. W. Haslam, *From Death into Life* (London: Morgan and Scott, 1897), p.30

13. Byles, p.163
14. Byles, p.83

CHAPTER 3. DISSENTERS, AND POETRY, INTO THE 1840s

1   Byles, p.77
2. Poems for the Parson, Robert Stephen Hawker, 1803-1875 (Bude: J.Gunner, 1975)
3. Elie Halevy, A History of the English People in the Nineteenth Century, vol.4 (London: Benn, 1951), p.387
4. Footprints, p.47
5. Letter to Godwin, 3 December 1863: Byles, p.461
6. Nicholas Orme, Unity and Variety, a History of the Church in Devon and Cornwall (Exeter: University of Exeter Press, 1991), p.135
7. John Wesley, Journal, quoted in the Guide to the Church of St Denys, North Tamerton
8. Report to the Bishop of Exeter by the Rev. Thomas Vivian, 1747: quoted by John Probert, The Worship and Devotion of Cornish Methodism (privately printed, 1978), p.8
9. Quoted by Brendon, p.80
10. John Wesley, Journal, 1739
11. John Wesley, Journal, 1778
12. John Wesley, Journal, 1789
13. R.S. Hawker, Stones Broken from the Rocks, Extracts from the Manuscript Note-books, ed. C.E. Byles (Oxford: Blackwell, 1922), p.102
14. Quoted by Brendon, p.172
15. Baring-Gould, p.174
16. Article by Francis Gribble, 'Robert Stephen Hawker', in The Treasury, vol. II, 1904, p.222
17. Byles, p.120
18. Byles, p.150
19. Letter to Sir Thomas Acland, 26 September 1865 (Bodleian Library)
20. Letter to Mrs Watson, 23 August 1863: Byles, p.425
21. William Gregory Harris, Letter to a local newspaper, 1875: quoted at greater length by Byles, p.156
22. The Devonport Independent, April 1866
23. Quoted by W. Gregory Harris (nephew of Hawker's church-

warden), 'Hawker and the Quest of the Sangraal', in The Methodist Recorder, 14 September 1899
24. Byles, p.132
25. The Royal Cornwall Gazette, 27 December 1878
26. John Drinkwater, Introduction to Twenty Poems by Robert Stephen Hawker (New York: Duffield, 1925), p.15
27. Dept of Western MS, Bodleian Library, undated
28. Lord Byron, Childe Harold's Pilgrimage, canto 4, stanza 178
29. John Betjeman, 'Greenaway', in Collected Poems (London: John Murray, 1958), pp. 184-185

CHAPTER 4. THE CHURCHMAN AND THE MYSTIC

1. Thought Book 1845
2. Letter to West, 27 December 1852: Byles, p.228
3. Margaret F. Burrows, Robert Stephen Hawker, A Study of his Thought and Poetry (Oxford: Blackwell, 1926), p.156
4. The Rev. J.F. Chanter, quoted by Byles, pp.618-9
5. Thought Book, quoted by Byles, p.137
6. Letter to Dr F.G. Lee, 12 July 1854: Byles, p.232
7. Letter to the Rev. W.D. Anderson, 3 May 1852: Byles, p.220
8. Letter to Godwin 21 September 1874: quoted by Lee, p.147
9. Letter to Mrs Watson, 31 March 1861: Byles, pp.336-7
10. Thought Book 1845
11. Thought Book, quoted in Stones Broken from the Rocks, p.35
12. Letter to Godwin, 5 November 1863: Byles, p.440
13. Quoted by Byles, p.100 (dated 1856)
14. Letter to William Maskell, 1856: Byles, p.100
15. Letter to West, 27 December 1852: Byles, p.227
16. Thought Book, quoted in Stones Broken from the Rocks, p.16
17. Thought Book, 1858
18. Letter to Godwin, 16 November 1863: Byles, p.443
19. Lee, p.85
20. Letter to Sir Thomas Acland, 29

October 1856: Nicholas Ross typescript, Bodleian Library

21. Typed copy of a letter, unattributed, at The Old Vicarage, Morwenstow

22. Lancelot Andrewes, 'Sermon of the Nativity', 1612

23. *Betjeman's Cornwall* (London: Murray, 1984), p.52: quoted from John Betjeman, 'First and Last Loves', 1952

24 George Herbert, 'The Church Floore'

25 Isaiah 6.5

26 Matthew 13.11

27 Byles, p.55

28 G.B. Tennyson, *Victorian Devotional Poetry, The Tractarian Mode* (Cambridge, Mass.: Harvard University Press, 1981), p.45

29 G.B. Tennyson, p.156

30 *Footprints*, pp.18-19

31 G.B. Tennyson, p.178

CHAPTER 5. A SHIP ASHORE SIR

1. Byles, p.198

2. *Footprints*, p.53

3. Quoted by Byles, p.160 (dated 22 September 1842.)

4. Byles, p.163

5. Quoted by Byles, p.162 (dated 22 September 1842.)

6. *Footprints*, p.61

7. Quoted by Brendon, pp.129-30

8. Letter to Godwin, 23 October 1862: Byles, pp.396-97

9. Letter to Godwin, December 1863: Byles, pp.459-4 62

10. C.F. Crofton, *Bencoolen to Capricorno*, quoted by Byles, p.397

11. Letter to Mountjoy, 5 February 1866: Byles, p.532

CHAPTER 6. THE EIGHTEEN-FORTIES: POETRY AND CONFLICTS

1. R.S. Hawker, *Cornish Ballads & Other Poems* (London: John Lane, 1904), p.128

2. Letter to Godwin, 18 February 1862: Byles, p.384

3. Letter to Sir Thomas Acland, 19 October 1855: Byles, pp.243-44

4. Quoted by Byles, p.168

5. Quoted (in full) by Byles, p.169

6. Byles, p.170

7. Copy in the Dept of Western MS, Bodleian Library

8. Quoted (in full) by Byles, p.171

9. Quoted by Byles, p.112

10. R.S. Hawker, *Rural Synods* (London: Edwards & Hughes, 1849) pp.22-3

11. Letter to John Walter, Editor of The Times, 27 November 1844: quoted (in full) by Byles, pp.174-77

12. Quoted (in full) by Byles, p.177 (dated 18 December 1844)

13. 'The Field of Rephidim: A Visitation Sermon in the Diocese of Exeter - Written by the Vicar of Morwenstow, in Cornwall; Delivered in the Church of St Mary Magdalene, Launceston, June 27, 1845, by T.N. Harper, BA., Curate of Stratton' (London: Edwards & Hughes, 1845), pp.7-8

14. 'Visitation Sermon', pp.10-11

15. 'Visitation Sermon', pp.11-12

16. Quoted by Nicholas Orme, *Unity and Variety: A History of the Church in Devon and Cornwall* (Exeter: Exeter University Press, 1991) p.111

17. G.C. B. Davies, *Henry Phillpotts, Bishop of Exeter, 1778-1869* (London: SPCK, 1954), p.95

18. Quoted by Byles, p.205

19. Davies (see above), pp.299-300

20. Davies, pp.293-4

21. Lee, p.83

22. Letter to 'My Dear William', 13 February 1848: Byles, p.188

CHAPTER 7. INTO THE 1850s, VISITORS, FRIENDS AND OPINIONS

1. Cecil Woolf, 'Some Uncollected Authors XXXIX, Hawker of Morwenstow, 1803-1875', Bibliography with Introduction, in successive numbers of *The Book Collector*, Spring and Summer 1965, p.62

2. *The Letters of Alfred Lord Tennyson*, ed. by Cecil Y. Lang and Edgar F. Shannon Jr, 3 vols (Oxford, the Clarendon Press, 1982) I, p.289

3. *The Letters of Alfred Lord Tennyson*, II, p.267

4. *The Letters of Alfred Lord Tennyson*, I, p.288

5. This quotation and those that follow are taken from the account by Byles, chapter XII, 'Tennyson at Morwenstow'
6. Letter 6 August 1856, quoted by Byles, p.263
7. Michell, p.21
8. Michell, p.19
9. Quoted by Byles, p.265
10. Letter 21 December 1857, quoted by Byles, p.264
11. Michell, pp.22-3
12. J.T. Blight, *Ancient Crosses, and Other Antiquities in the East of Cornwall* 2nd edn (London: Simpkin, Marshall, 1872), p.v.
13. Michell, p.25
14. Michell, p.26
15. Michell, p.57
16. Michell, p.58
17. Byles, p.92
18. Thought Book 1855
19. Letter to Mrs Watson, 24 March 1856: Byles, p.281
20. Byles, p.280
21. Letter to the Editor of *Willis's*, March 1855: Byles, p.253
22. Letter to Godwin, 5 May 1865: Byles, p.517
23. Thought Book 1856
24. Letter to Mrs Watson, 12 January 1862: Byles, p.354
25. Quoted by Brendon, p.149
26. Quoted by Brendon, p.164
27. Letter to Mrs Watson, 24 October 1869: Byles, p.583
28. Letter to Mrs Watson, 8 June 1857: Byles, pp.296-7
29. Letter to Mrs Watson, 7 July 1861: Byles, p.342
30. Luke 21.11
31. T.S. Eliot, 'East Coker', in *Four Quartets* (London: Faber & Faber, 1945), p. 19
32. Letter to West, 7 November 1861: Byles, p.277
33. Alfred Tennyson, 'Locksley Hall'
34. Quoted by Brendon, p.154
35. Brendon, p.30
36. Letter to Mrs Watson, 6 July 1862: Byles, p.361
37. Footnote to 'Aurora' added by Byles
38. Quoted by Byles, p.591
39. Letter to the Rev. W.D. Anderson, 15 February 1855: Byles, p.240
40. Letter to Godwin, 5 April 1862: Byles, p.387
41. Letter to Mrs Watson, 24 September 1857: Byles, p.302
42. Letter to Godwin, 13 November 1863: Byles, pp.441-42
43. Letter to Mrs Watson, 4 March 1866: Byles, pp.535-56
44. Letter, undated, quoted at length by Byles, pp.122-24

CHAPTER 8. CHARLOTTE'S DEATH AND 'THE QUEST OF THE SANGRAAL'
1 Letter to Mrs Watson, 27 September 1863: Byles, p.432
2 Byles, p.102
3 Letter to Mrs Watson, 22 February 1863: Byles, p.407
4 Typewritten note, unattributed, at The Old Vicarage, Morwenstow
5 Brendon, p.197
6 Letter to Mrs Watson, 30 August 1863: Byles, p.427
7 Letter from Dr Phillpotts to RSH, 29 October 1863: Byles, pp.438-39
8 Letter to Mrs Watson, 22 November 1863: Byles, pp.412-13
9. Letter from Pauline Hawker to Mr Fleming, 7 November 1892: Bodleian Library
10. Sheila Smith, 'Ho! "For the Sangraal": Opium and Robert Stephen Hawker's Arthurian Legend', from *Beyond the Pleasure Dome, Writing and Addiction from the Romantics*, ed. by Sue Vice (Sheffield: Sheffield Academic Press, 1994) p.119
11. Letter to Godwin, 25 November 1863: Byles, p.446
12. Letter to Godwin, 5 November 1863: Byles, pp.439-40
13. Letter to West, 1861: Byles, p.413
14. Article by Francis Gribble, 'Robert Stephen Hawker', in The Treasury, vol. II, 1904, p.225
15. Letter to Godwin, 2 January 1864: Byles, p.455
16. *The Works of Sir Thomas Malory*, ed. by Eugene Vinaver (Oxford: Oxford University Press, 1964) p.634
17. *The Poems of Tennyson*, ed. by

Christopher Ricks (London: Longman, Annotated English Poets, 1969) p.1671

18. Letter to Godwin, 3 February 1863: Byles, p.404
19. Article by Francis Gribble, p.224
20. Letter from R.J. King to RSH, December 1863: Byles, p.451
21. Quoted by Byles, p.418
22. Quoted by Christopher Ricks in his introduction to 'The Holy Grail', in *Poems of Tennyson*, p.1661
23. Ricks, p.1661
24. Brendon, p.208

CHAPTER 9. SECOND MARRIAGE AND LAST YEARS, 1864-75

1. Bodleian MS Eng. Poet. d.191; e.114
2. Letter to John Somers James, 6 January 1865: Byles, p.506
3. Letter to Godwin, 20 December 1863: Byles, p.450
4. Letters from Pauline Kuczynski to her uncle, dated December 1863, quoted by Byles p.444
5. Letter dated 4 January 1864: Byles, p.444-5
6. Byles, p.498
7. Letter to Mrs Henry Stevens, 17 November 1864: Byles, p.499
8. Letter to Mrs Watson, 11 December 1864: Byles, p.503
9. Quoted by Byles, p.505
10. Letter to Thomas Cann, 18 December 1864: Byles, p.505
11. Letter to Mrs Watson: Byles, p.505
12. Letter to Godwin, 17 June 1865: Byles, p.521
13. Byles, p.605
14. Letter to Caroline Kingdon, 27 September 1871: Nicholas Ross Papers, Bodleian Library
15. Letter to Godwin, 2 March 1870: Byles, p.587
16. Nicholas Ross Papers, Bodleian Library
17. J.H. Adams, 'New Light on R.S. Hawker', in *The Cornish Review*, Autumn 1957, p.33
18. Both articles were reprinted in *Footprints*
19. J.G. Daniel, *A Compendium of the History and Geography of Cornwall* (Truro: Netherton & Worth, 1906) p.71
20. Quoted by Brendon, p.181
21. Letter to Mrs Watson, 26 March 1865: Byles, p.512
22. Letter, dated 1861, quoted by Byles, p.19
23. Letter to RSH from Dr Grant, 29 July 1861: Byles, pp.379-80
24. Letter to RSH from Dr Grant, 9 November 1863: Byles, pp.442-43
25. This and the three preceding quotations are from letters at The Old Vicarage, Morwenstow
26. Letter to Mrs Watson, 25 June 1865: Byles, p.522
27. Letter to Mrs Watson, 13 August 1865: Byles, p.524
28. Letter to Lee, April 1874: Byles, p.616
29. Letter to William Maskell, 19 March 1874: Byles, p.610
30. The Rev. E.P. Arnold, entry in the report book of Morwenstow Parish School, 9 July 1874: Byles, p.619
31. Byles, p.605
32. Letter to Mrs Watson, 3 December 1865: Byles, p.530

CHAPTER 10. DEATH-BED CONVERSION

1. Quoted by Byles, p.636
2. Quoted by Byles, p.637
3. Brendon, p.26
4. Baring-Gould, p.269
5. *The Athenaeum*, 17 June 1876: Review of *The Vicar of Morwenstow* by Sabine Baring-Gould, New and Revised Edition
6. Quoted by Harold Kirk-Smith, *Now the Day is Over, the Life and Times of Sabine Baring-Gould 1834-1924* (Boston: Richard Kay, 1997), p.112
7. Baring-Gould, p.73
8. *The Mail on Sunday*, 2 March 1997

Bibliography

EDITIONS OF R.S.H.'s WORKS

Note. Hawker frequently published individual poems and prose passages in leaflet form, and these are listed in detail by C.E.Woolf in 'The Book Collector' Spring 1965 (pp.62-71) and Summer 1965 (pp.202-211) under the title 'Some Uncollected Authors XXXIX, Hawker of Morwenstow 1803-1875'.

C.E. Byles in his *Life and Letters* (1905: see below) also provides a substantial Bibliography.

Poetry

The Rev. R.S. Hawker, Vicar of Morwenstow, *The Cornish Ballads and Other Poems* (Oxford: James Parker, 1869).

Robert Stephen Hawker, Vicar of Morwenstow, Cornwall, *The Poetical Works*, ed. by J.G. Godwin (London: C. Kegan Paul, 1879).

Robert Stephen Hawker, M.A., sometime Vicar of Morwenstow, Cornwall, *The Poetical Works*, ed. by Alfred Wallis (London: John Lane, The Bodley Head, 1899).

R.S. Hawker, Vicar of Morwenstow, *Cornish Ballads and Other Poems*, ed. by C.E. Byles (London: John Lane, The Bodley Head, 1904, 1908).

Twenty Poems by Robert Stephen Hawker (Little Nineteenth Century Classics), intro. by John Drinkwater (New York: Duffield & Co, 1925).

Robert Stephen Hawker, *Selected Poems*, ed. with intro. by Cecil Woolf (London: Cecil Woolf Publishers, 1975).

Hawker's Cornish Ballads, ed. by Piers Brendon (St Germans: Elephant Press, 1975).

Prose

'The Field of Rephidim: A Visitation Sermon in the Diocese of Exeter Written by the Vicar of Morwenstow . . .' (London: Edwards & Hughes, 1845).

R.S. Hawker, *Rural Synods* (London: Edwards & Hughes, 1849).

R.S. Hawker, Vicar of Morwenstow, *Footprints of Former Men in Far Cornwall* (London: John Russell Smith, 1870); ed. by C.E. Byles (London: John Lane, The Bodley Head, 1903, 1908).

Rev. R.S. Hawker, Vicar of Morwenstow, *The Prose Works* (Edinburgh: Wm Blackwood, 1893).

Robert Stephen Hawker, Vicar of Morwenstow 1834-1875, *Stones Broken from the Rocks, Extracts from the Manuscript Note-Books* ed. by C.E. Byles (Oxford: Basil Blackwell, 1922).

R.S. Hawker, Thought Books 1844-1858, Bodleian Library.

BIOGRAPHIES AND CRITICAL WORKS

Sabine Baring-Gould, *The Vicar of Morwenstow, A Life of Robert Stephen Hawker*, M.A. (London: Henry S. King, 1876; new and revised edition, 1876).

The Rev. Dr Frederick George Lee, *Memorials of the Late Rev. Robert Stephen Hawker*, M.A. (London: Chatto and Windus, 1876).

C.E. Byles, *The Life and Letters of R.S.Hawker (sometime Vicar of Morwenstow)* (London: John Lane, The Bodley Head, 1905).

Margaret F. Burrows, *Robert Stephen Hawker, a Study of his Thought and Poetry* (Oxford: Basil Blackwell, 1926).

Piers Brendon, *Hawker of Morwenstow, Portrait of a Victorian Eccentric* (London: Jonathan Cape, 1975).

Sarah L. Dopp, 'Cornish Elements in the Poetry and Prose of Robert Stephen Hawker' (unpublished master's thesis, Graduate College of Vermont, 1982).

OTHER WORKS

J.H. Adams, 'New Light on R.S.Hawker', article in *The Cornish Review*, Autumn 1957.

J.T. Blight, *Ancient Crosses and Other Antiquities in the East of Cornwall, West of Cornwall* (London: Simpkin Marshall, 1858).

H. Miles Brown, *The Catholic Revival in Cornish Anglicanism, a Study of the Tractarians in Cornwall 1833-1906* (privately printed, St Winnow, 1980).

H. Miles Brown, *The Church in Cornwall* (Truro: Oscar Blandford, 1964).

A.O.J. Cockshut, *Anglican Attitudes, a Study of Victorian Religious Controversies* (London: Collins, 1959).

G.C.B. Davies, *Henry Phillpotts, Bishop of Exeter, 1778-1869* (London: SPCK, 1954).

Francis Gribble, 'Robert Stephen Hawker', article in *The Treasury*, vol.II, 1904.

W.Gregory Harris, 'Hawker and The Quest of the Sangraal', article in *Old Cornwall*, vol.II no. 3, Summer 1932.

The Rev. W. Haslam, *From Death into Life* (London: Morgan and Scott, 1897).

David Hopkinson, *Edward Penrose Arnold, a Victorian Family Portrait* (Penzance: Alison Hodge, 1981).

Margaret Jeune Gifford, *The Diary of an Oxford Lady 1843-1862* (Oxford: The Shakespeare Head Press, 1932).

John Michell, *A Short Life at The Land's End: J.T. Blight, F.S.A., Artist Penzance* (Bath: privately printed, 1977).

Edward Norman, *The English Catholic Church in the Nineteenth Century* (Oxford: Clarendon Press, 1984).

Nicholas Orme (ed.), *Unity and Variety: A History of the Church in Devon and Cornwall* (Exeter: University of Exeter Press, 1991).

Margaret J.C. Reid, *The Arthurian Legend* (London: Oliver and Boyd, 1938).

Joan Rendell, *The Hawker Country* (Bodmin: Bossiney Books, 1980).

A.L. Rowse, *The Little Land of Cornwall* (Truro: Dyllansaw Truran, 1986).

Arthur L. Salmon, *Literary Rambles in the West of England* (London: Chapman & Hall, 1906).

Sheila Smith, 'Ho! for the Sangraal! Opium and Robert Stephen Hawker's Arthurian Legend', from *Beyond the Pleasure Dome, Writing and Addiction from the Romantics*, ed. by Sue Vice (Sheffield: Sheffield Academic Press, 1994).

Mary Tagert, *The Story of Morwenstow* (London: John Lane, 1929).

Nigel Tangye, *Voyaging into Cornwall's Past* (London: William Kimber, 1978).

G.B. Tennyson, *Victorian Devotional Poetry, The Tractarian Mode* (Cambridge, Mass: Harvard University Press, 1981).

E.W.F. Tomlin, *The Church of St Morwenna and St John the Baptist, Morwenstow, a Guide and History* (1990 2nd edn).

Index